Davis, Jim, 1945 July 28
Garfield worldwide /
2007.
33305245151141
mi   06/05/19

Garfield worldwide

BY JIM DAVIS

Ballantine Books • New York

2007 Ballantine Books Trade Paperback Edition

Copyright © 1988, 2007 by PAWS, Inc. All rights reserved.
"GARFIELD" and the GARFIELD characters are registered and unregistered trademarks of PAWS, Inc.

Published in the United States by Ballantine Books, an imprint of The Random House Publishing Group,
a division of Random House, Inc., New York.

BALLANTINE and colophon are registered trademarks of Random House, Inc.

Originally published in slightly different form in the United States by Ballantine Books, an imprint of
The Random House Publishing Group, a division of Random House, Inc., in 1988.

ISBN 978-0-345-91754-6
Printed in China

www.ballantinebooks.com

9 8 7 6 5 4

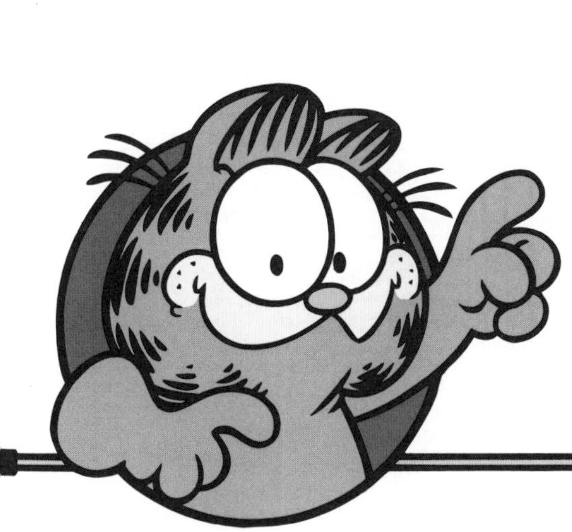

ATTENTION, CONSUMERS!

NOT THE REAL GARFIELD

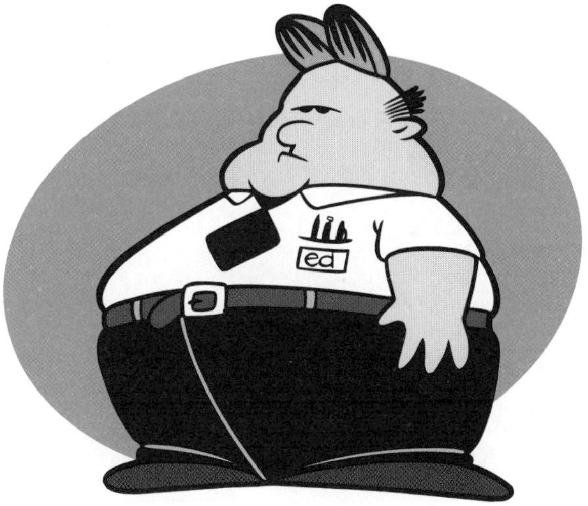

NOT THE REAL GARFIELD

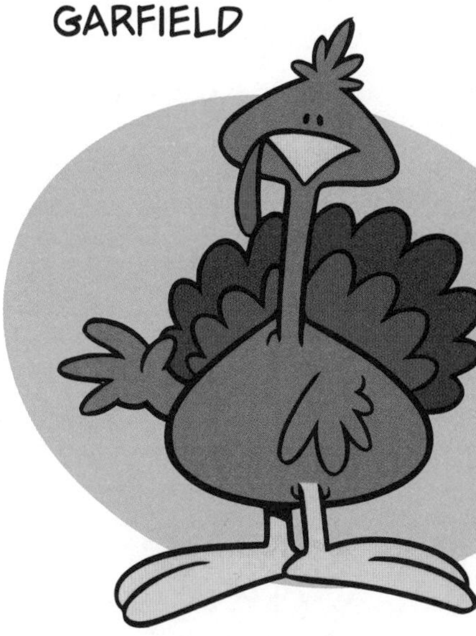

NOT THE REAL GARFIELD

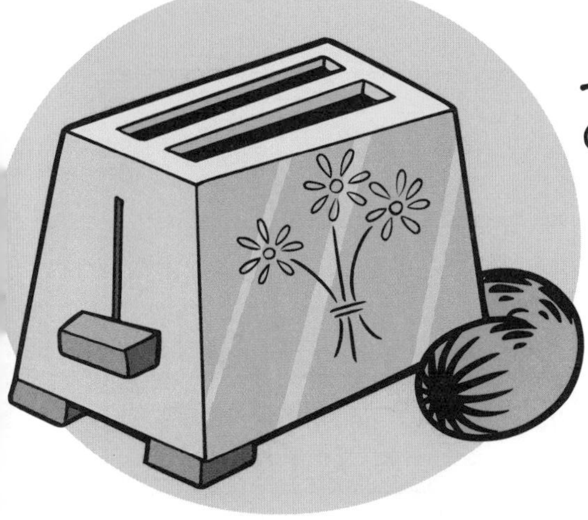

DEMAND THE GENUINE ARTICLE!

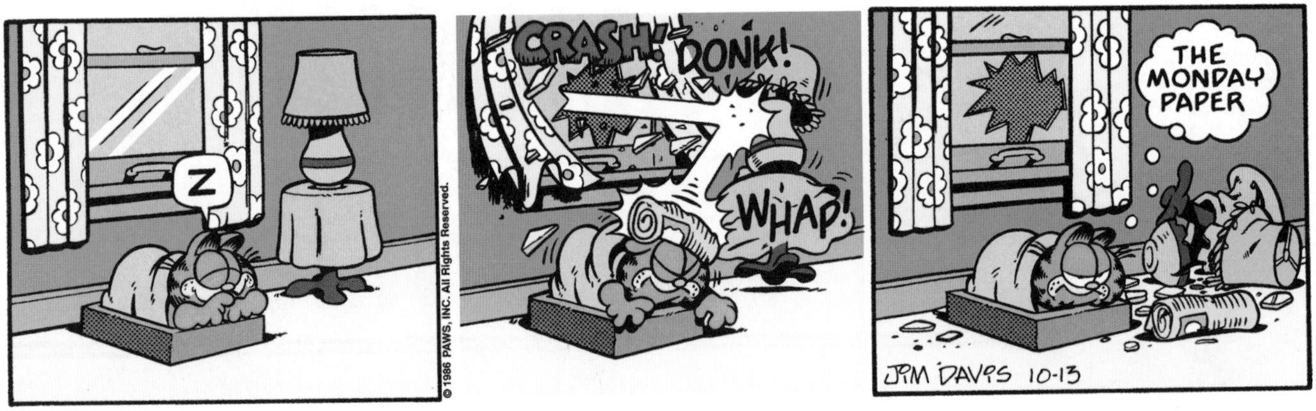
Z
CRASH! DONK!
WHAP!
THE MONDAY PAPER
JIM DAVIS 10-13
© 1986 PAWS, INC. All Rights Reserved.

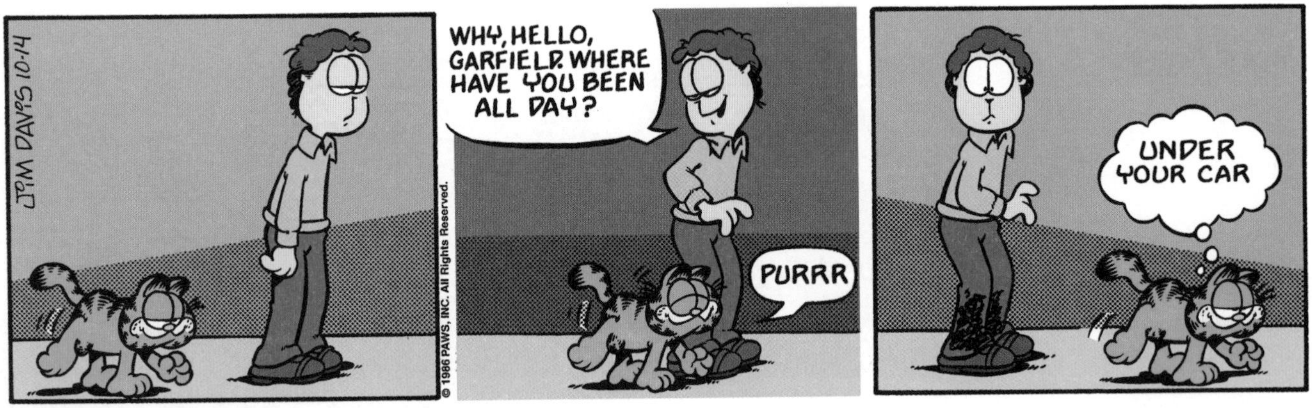
JIM DAVIS 10-14
WHY, HELLO, GARFIELD. WHERE HAVE YOU BEEN ALL DAY?
PURRR
UNDER YOUR CAR
© 1986 PAWS, INC. All Rights Reserved.

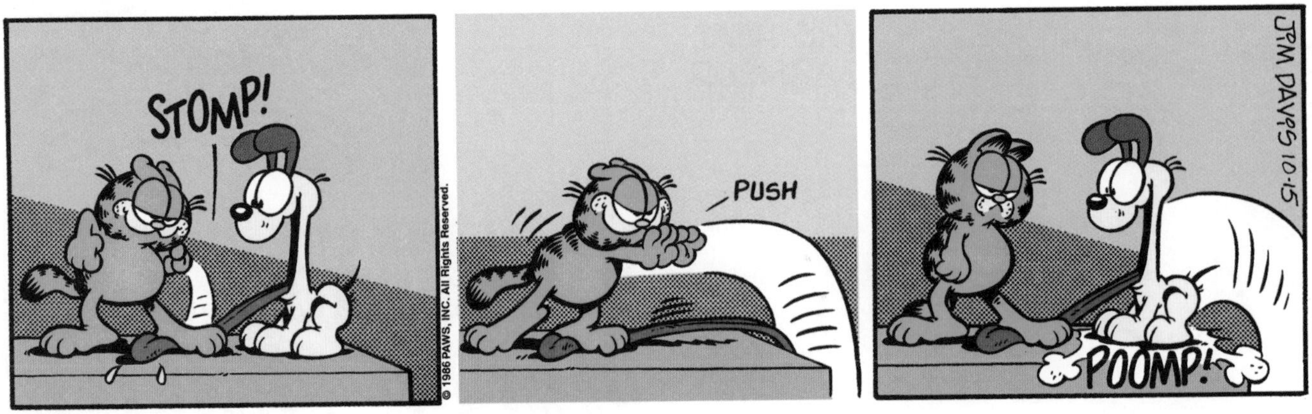
STOMP!
PUSH
POOMP!
JIM DAVIS 10-15
© 1986 PAWS, INC. All Rights Reserved.

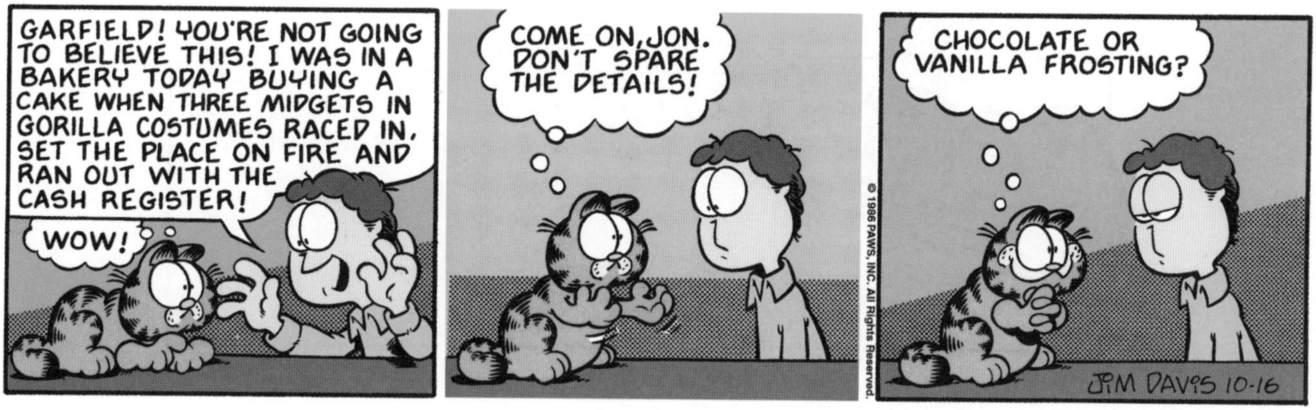
GARFIELD! YOU'RE NOT GOING TO BELIEVE THIS! I WAS IN A BAKERY TODAY BUYING A CAKE WHEN THREE MIDGETS IN GORILLA COSTUMES RACED IN, SET THE PLACE ON FIRE AND RAN OUT WITH THE CASH REGISTER!
WOW!
COME ON, JON. DON'T SPARE THE DETAILS!
© 1986 PAWS, INC. All Rights Reserved.
CHOCOLATE OR VANILLA FROSTING?
JIM DAVIS 10-16

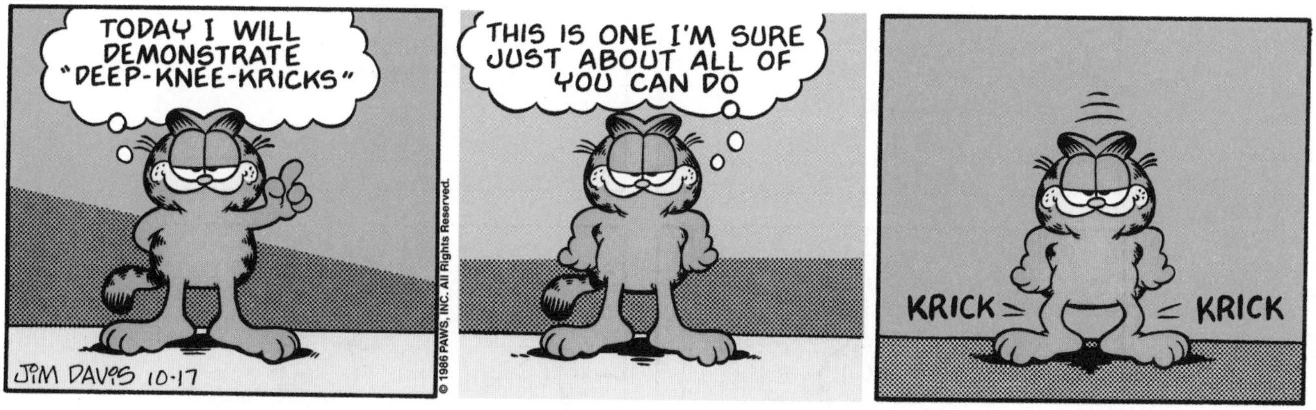
TODAY I WILL DEMONSTRATE "DEEP-KNEE-KRICKS"
JIM DAVIS 10-17
© 1986 PAWS, INC. All Rights Reserved.
THIS IS ONE I'M SURE JUST ABOUT ALL OF YOU CAN DO
KRICK
KRICK

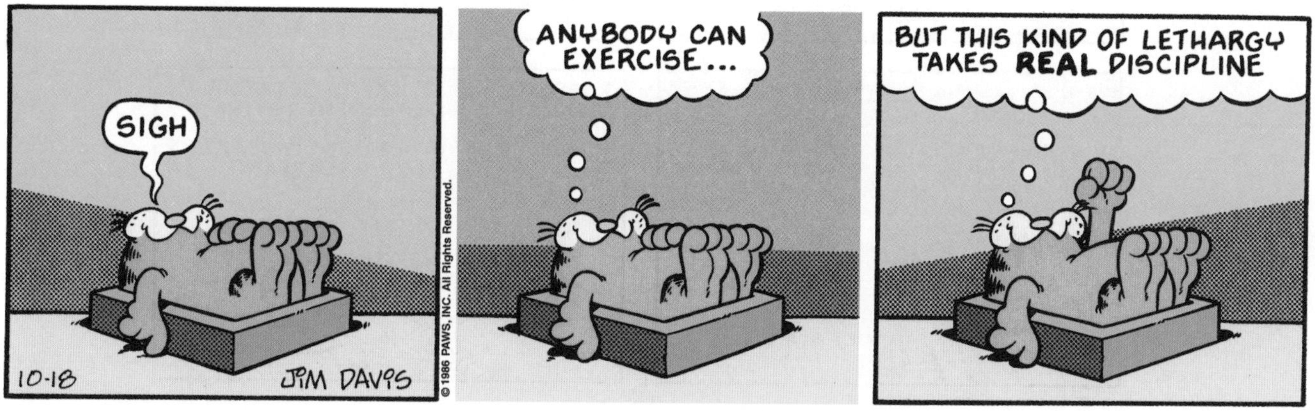
SIGH
10-18
JIM DAVIS
© 1986 PAWS, INC. All Rights Reserved.
ANYBODY CAN EXERCISE...
BUT THIS KIND OF LETHARGY TAKES **REAL** DISCIPLINE

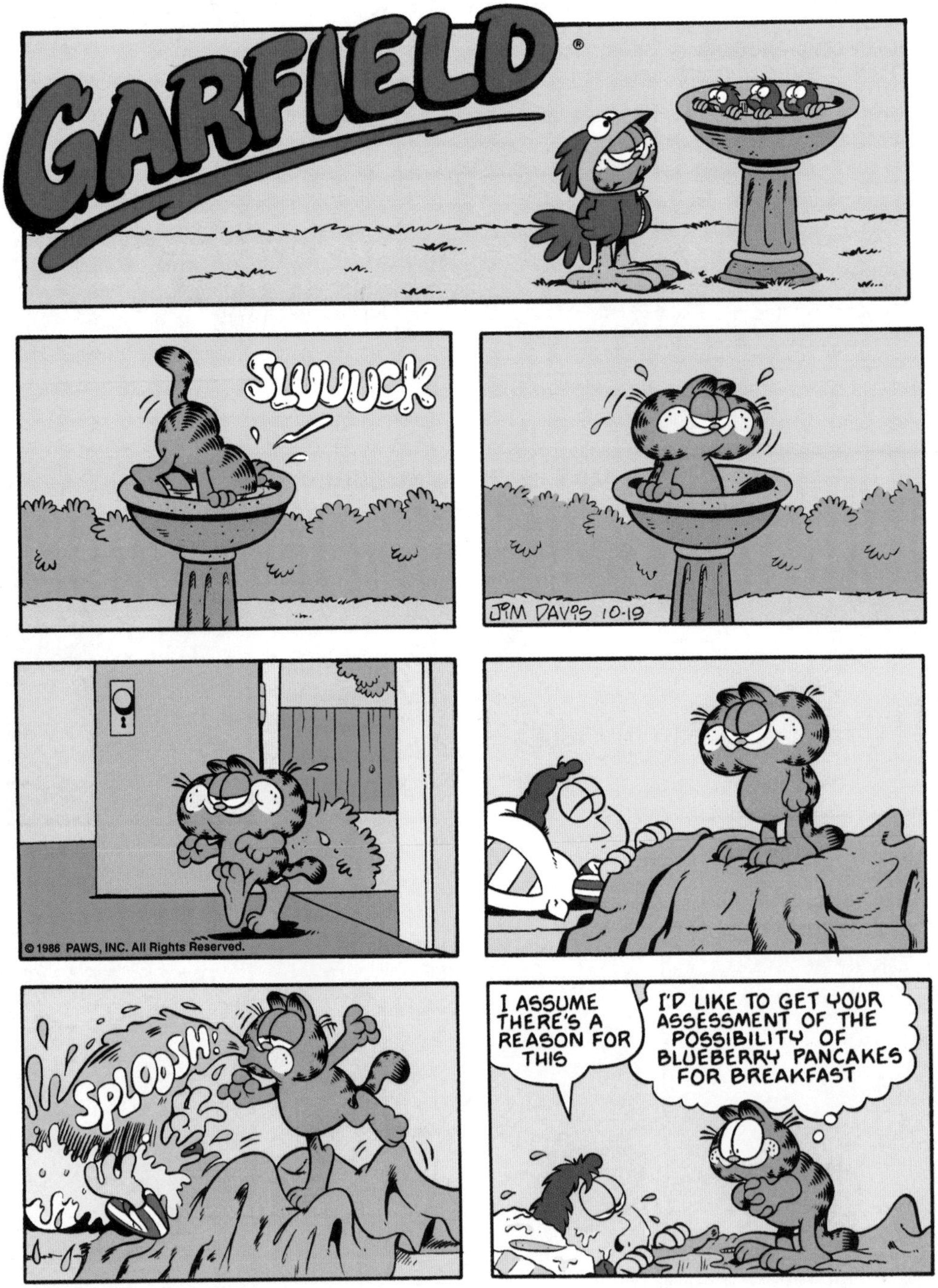
GARFIELD
SLUUUCK
JIM DAVIS 10-19
© 1986 PAWS, INC. All Rights Reserved.
SPLOOSH!
I ASSUME THERE'S A REASON FOR THIS
I'D LIKE TO GET YOUR ASSESSMENT OF THE POSSIBILITY OF BLUEBERRY PANCAKES FOR BREAKFAST

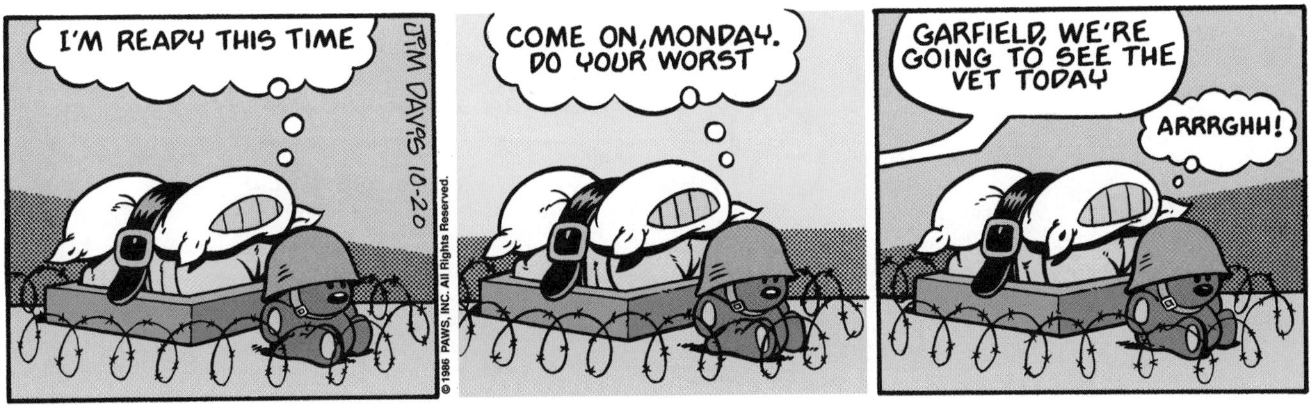
I'M READY THIS TIME
JIM DAVIS 10-20
COME ON, MONDAY. DO YOUR WORST
GARFIELD, WE'RE GOING TO SEE THE VET TODAY
ARRRGHH!

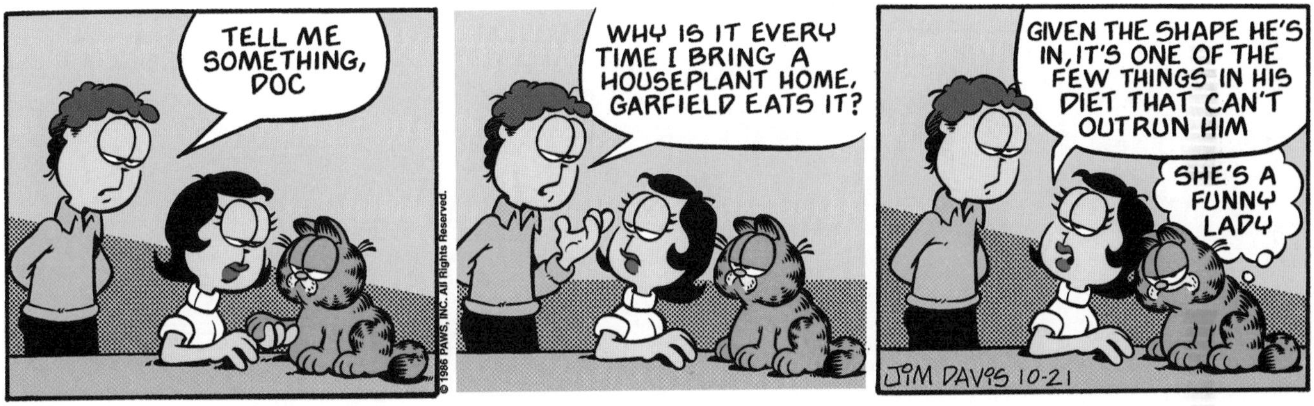
TELL ME SOMETHING, DOC
WHY IS IT EVERY TIME I BRING A HOUSEPLANT HOME, GARFIELD EATS IT?
GIVEN THE SHAPE HE'S IN, IT'S ONE OF THE FEW THINGS IN HIS DIET THAT CAN'T OUTRUN HIM
SHE'S A FUNNY LADY
JIM DAVIS 10-21

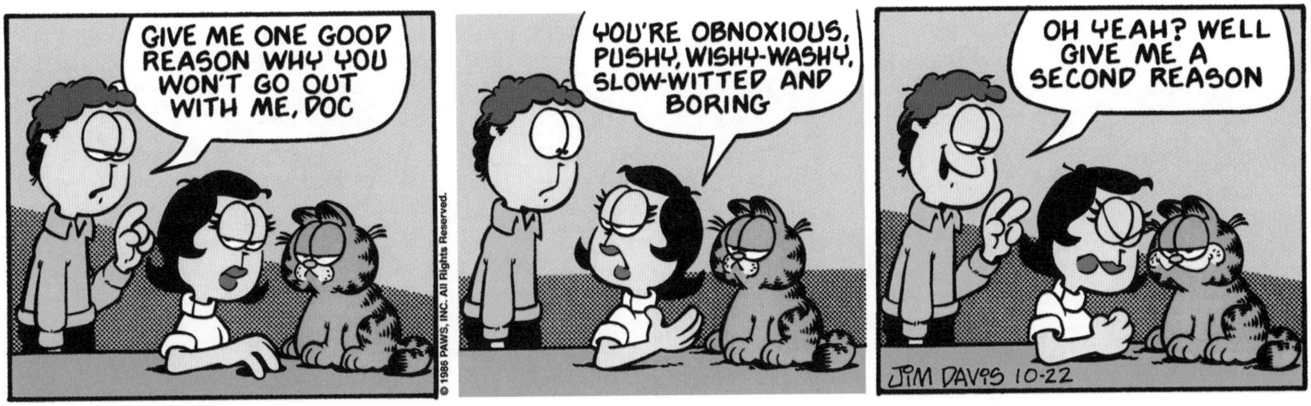
GIVE ME ONE GOOD REASON WHY YOU WON'T GO OUT WITH ME, DOC
YOU'RE OBNOXIOUS, PUSHY, WISHY-WASHY, SLOW-WITTED AND BORING
OH YEAH? WELL GIVE ME A SECOND REASON
JIM DAVIS 10-22

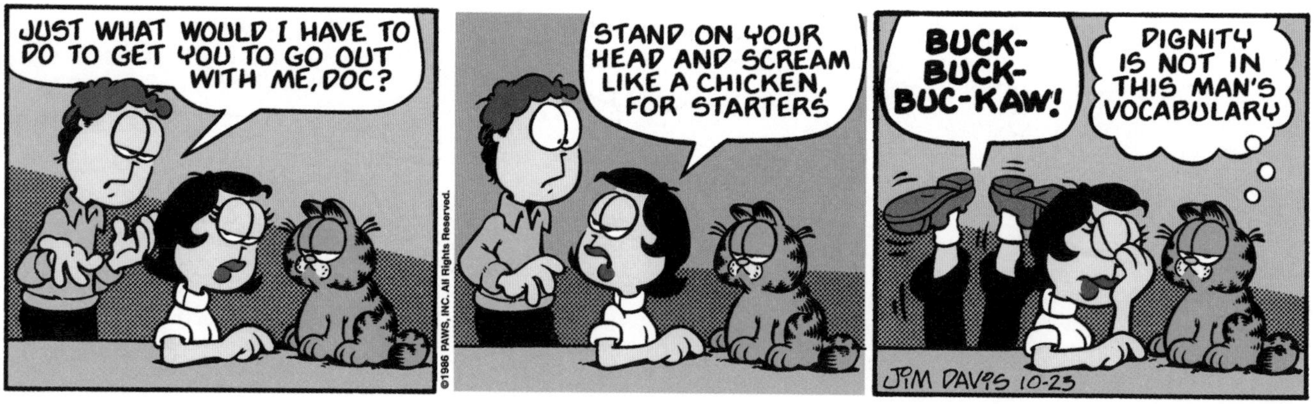
JUST WHAT WOULD I HAVE TO DO TO GET YOU TO GO OUT WITH ME, DOC?
©1986 PAWS, INC. All Rights Reserved.
STAND ON YOUR HEAD AND SCREAM LIKE A CHICKEN, FOR STARTERS
BUCK-BUCK-BUC-KAW!
DIGNITY IS NOT IN THIS MAN'S VOCABULARY
JIM DAVIS 10-23

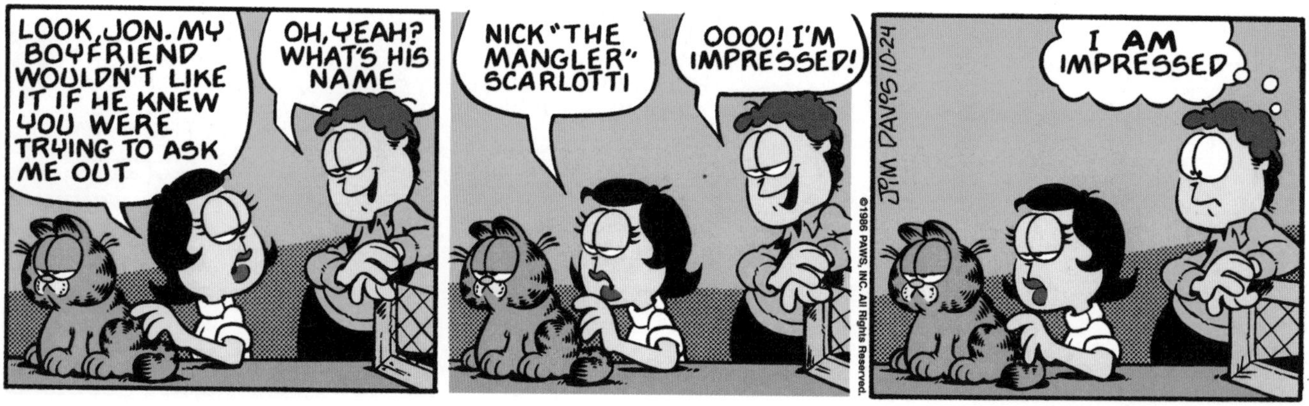
LOOK, JON. MY BOYFRIEND WOULDN'T LIKE IT IF HE KNEW YOU WERE TRYING TO ASK ME OUT
OH, YEAH? WHAT'S HIS NAME
NICK "THE MANGLER" SCARLOTTI
OOOO! I'M IMPRESSED!
©1986 PAWS, INC. All Rights Reserved.
JIM DAVIS 10-24
I AM IMPRESSED

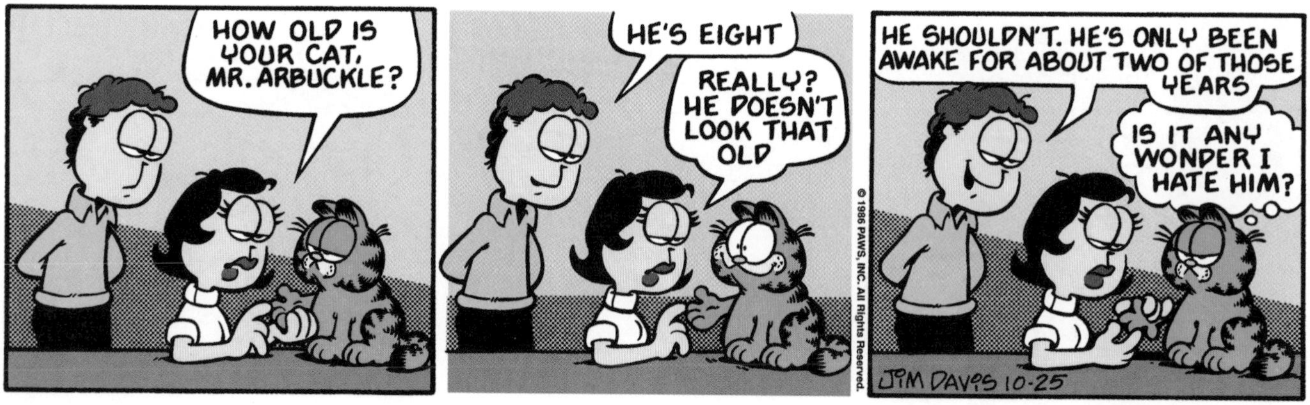
HOW OLD IS YOUR CAT, MR. ARBUCKLE?
HE'S EIGHT
REALLY? HE DOESN'T LOOK THAT OLD
© 1986 PAWS, INC. All Rights Reserved.
HE SHOULDN'T. HE'S ONLY BEEN AWAKE FOR ABOUT TWO OF THOSE YEARS
IS IT ANY WONDER I HATE HIM?
JIM DAVIS 10-25

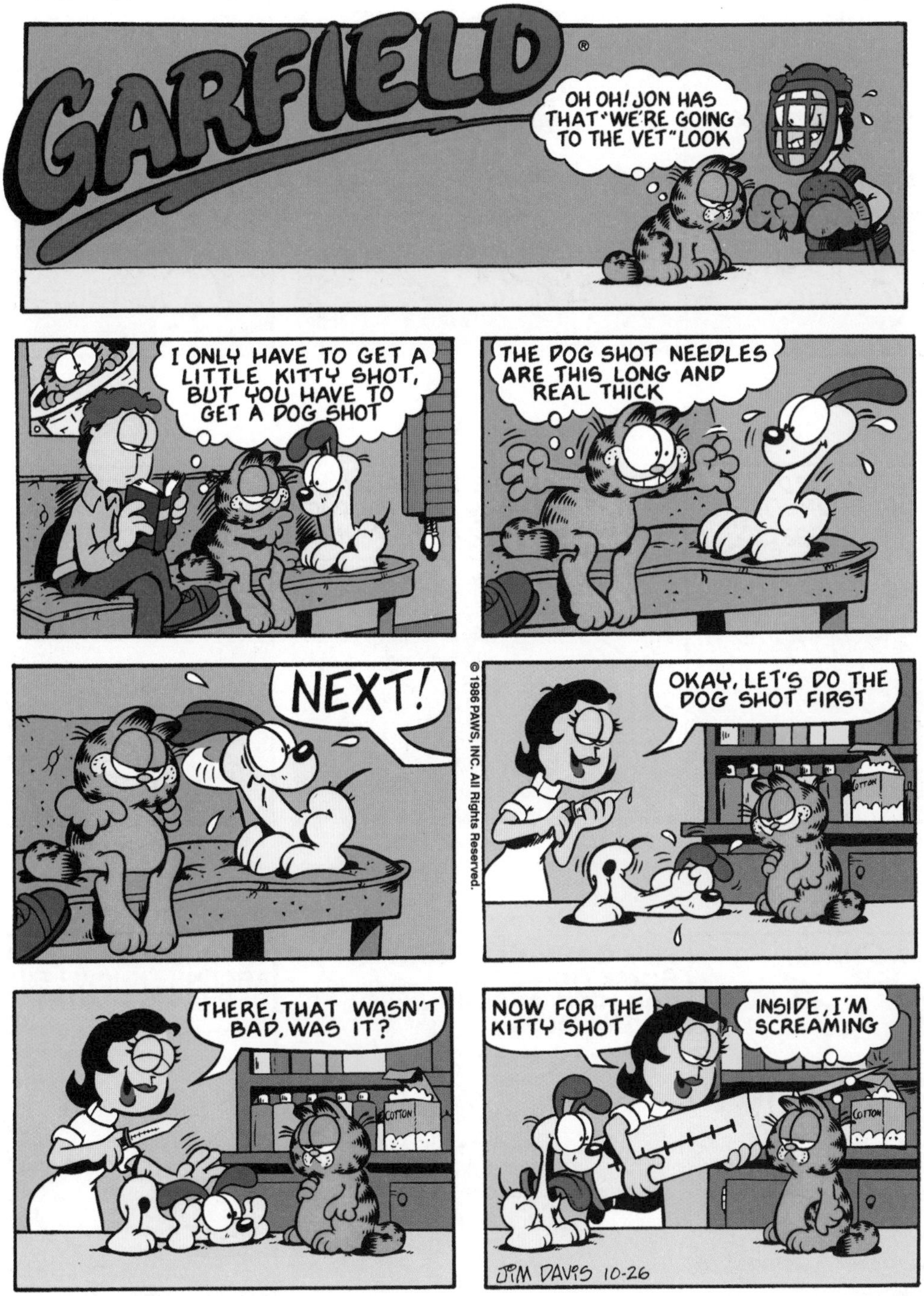
GARFIELD®
OH OH! JON HAS THAT "WE'RE GOING TO THE VET" LOOK
I ONLY HAVE TO GET A LITTLE KITTY SHOT, BUT YOU HAVE TO GET A DOG SHOT
THE DOG SHOT NEEDLES ARE THIS LONG AND REAL THICK
NEXT!
OKAY, LET'S DO THE DOG SHOT FIRST
COTTON
THERE, THAT WASN'T BAD, WAS IT?
COTTON
NOW FOR THE KITTY SHOT
INSIDE, I'M SCREAMING
COTTON
JIM DAVIS 10-26
© 1986 PAWS, INC. All Rights Reserved.

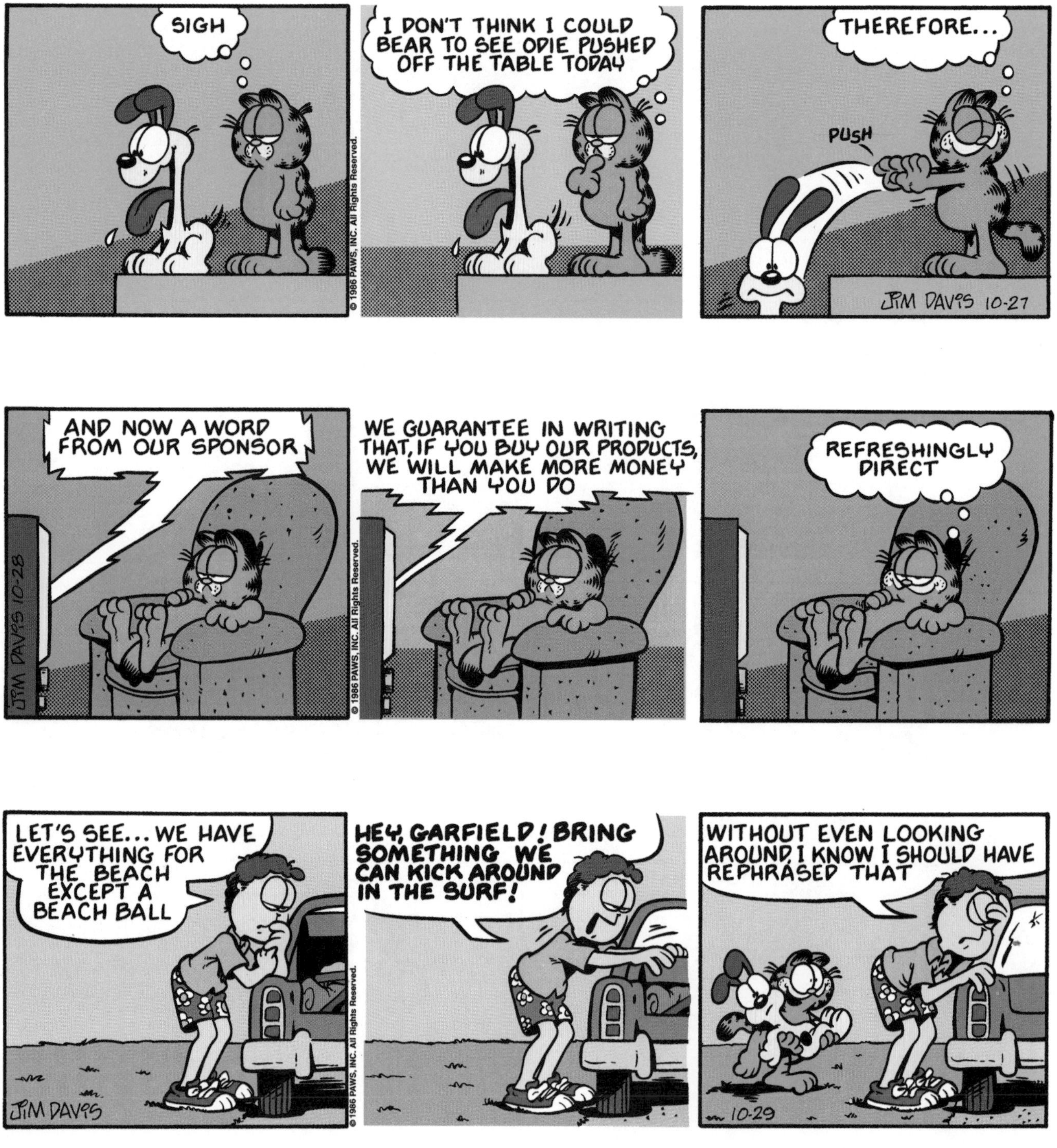
SIGH
I DON'T THINK I COULD BEAR TO SEE ODIE PUSHED OFF THE TABLE TODAY
THEREFORE...
PUSH
JIM DAVIS 10-27
© 1986 PAWS, INC. All Rights Reserved.
AND NOW A WORD FROM OUR SPONSOR
WE GUARANTEE IN WRITING THAT, IF YOU BUY OUR PRODUCTS, WE WILL MAKE MORE MONEY THAN YOU DO
REFRESHINGLY DIRECT
JIM DAVIS 10-28
© 1986 PAWS, INC. All Rights Reserved.
LET'S SEE... WE HAVE EVERYTHING FOR THE BEACH EXCEPT A BEACH BALL
HEY, GARFIELD! BRING SOMETHING WE CAN KICK AROUND IN THE SURF!
WITHOUT EVEN LOOKING AROUND, I KNOW I SHOULD HAVE REPHRASED THAT
JIM DAVIS
10-29
© 1986 PAWS, INC. All Rights Reserved.

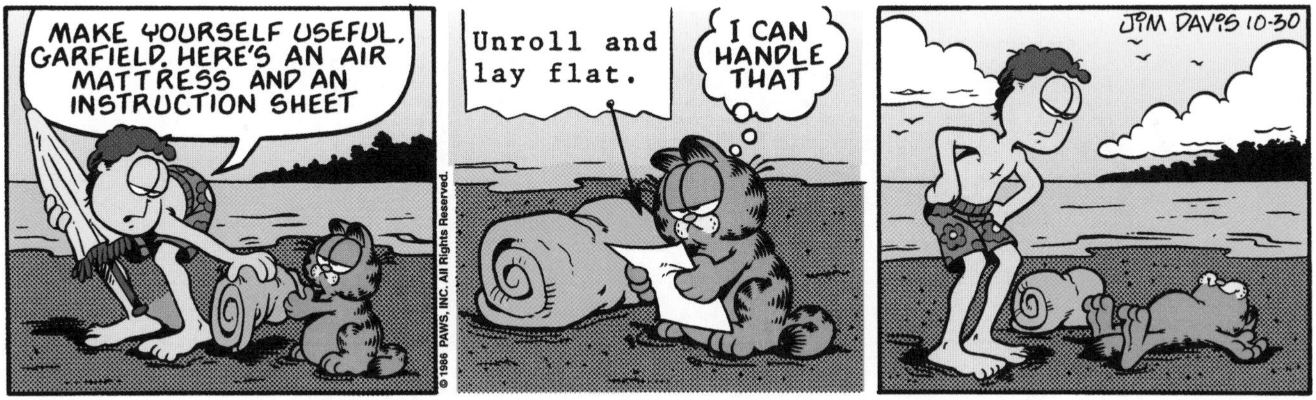
MAKE YOURSELF USEFUL, GARFIELD. HERE'S AN AIR MATTRESS AND AN INSTRUCTION SHEET
© 1986 PAWS, INC. All Rights Reserved.
Unroll and lay flat.
I CAN HANDLE THAT
JIM DAVIS 10-30

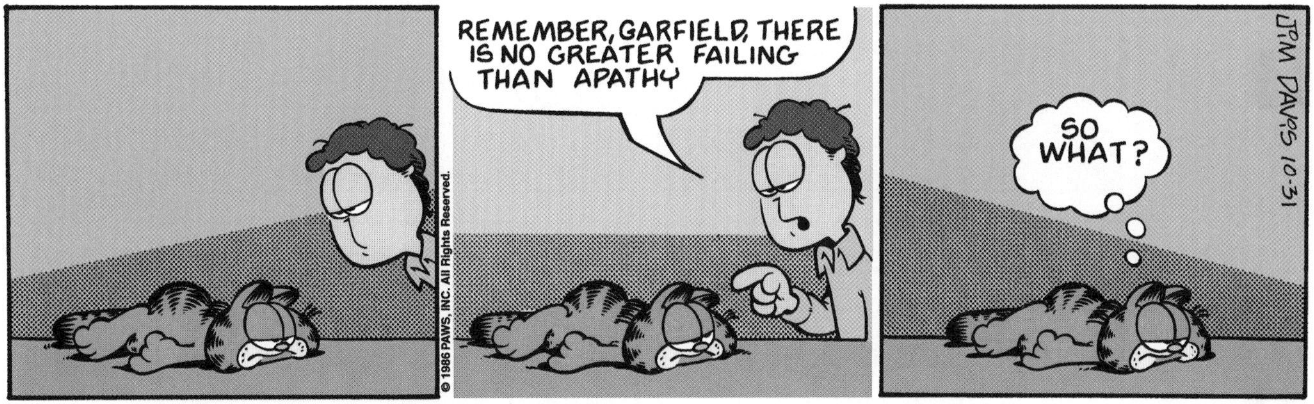
© 1986 PAWS, INC. All Rights Reserved.
REMEMBER, GARFIELD, THERE IS NO GREATER FAILING THAN APATHY
SO WHAT?
JIM DAVIS 10-31

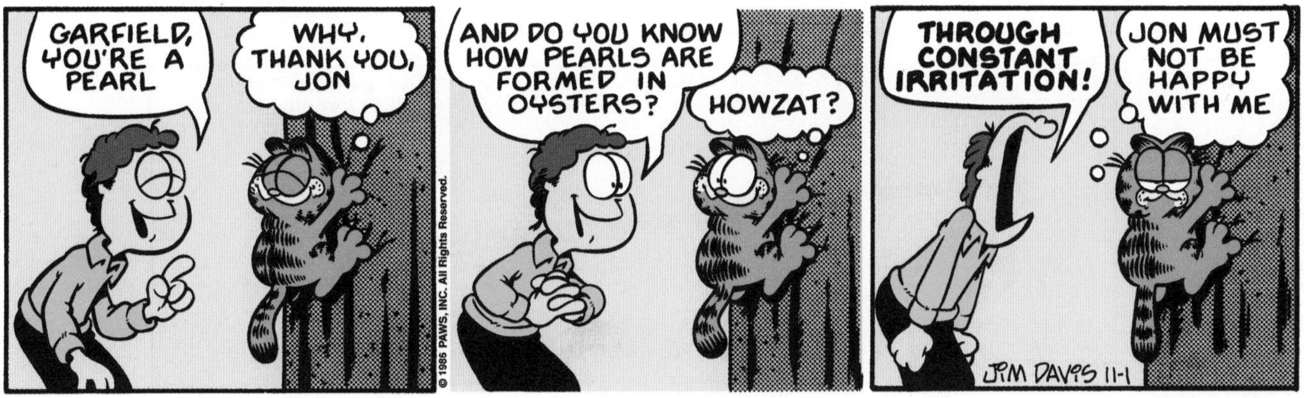
GARFIELD, YOU'RE A PEARL
WHY, THANK YOU, JON
© 1986 PAWS, INC. All Rights Reserved.
AND DO YOU KNOW HOW PEARLS ARE FORMED IN OYSTERS?
HOWZAT?
THROUGH CONSTANT IRRITATION!
JON MUST NOT BE HAPPY WITH ME
JIM DAVIS 11-1

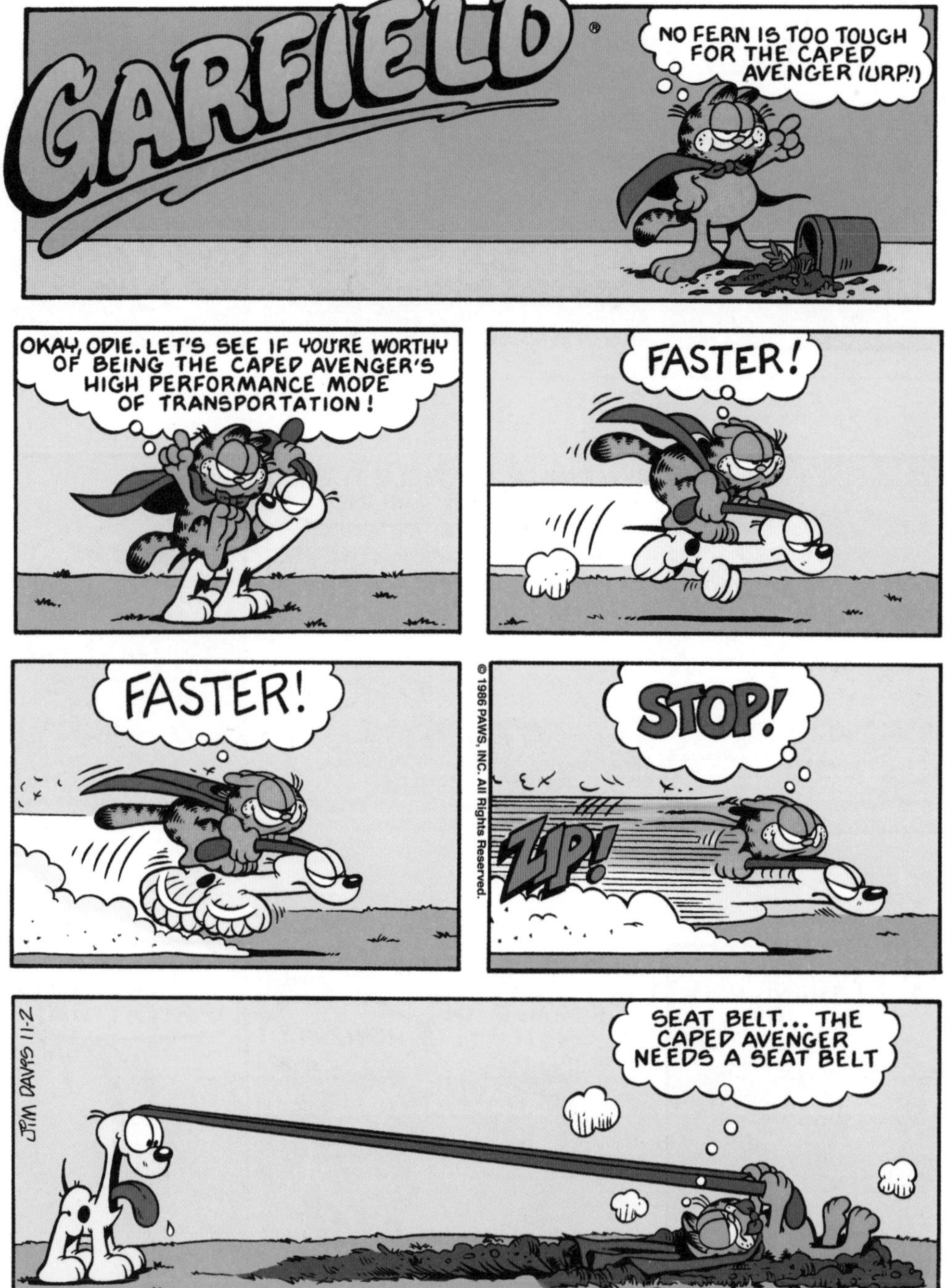
GARFIELD®
NO FERN IS TOO TOUGH FOR THE CAPED AVENGER (URP!)
OKAY, ODIE. LET'S SEE IF YOU'RE WORTHY OF BEING THE CAPED AVENGER'S HIGH PERFORMANCE MODE OF TRANSPORTATION!
FASTER!
FASTER!
STOP!
ZIP!
SEAT BELT... THE CAPED AVENGER NEEDS A SEAT BELT
JIM DAVIS 11-2

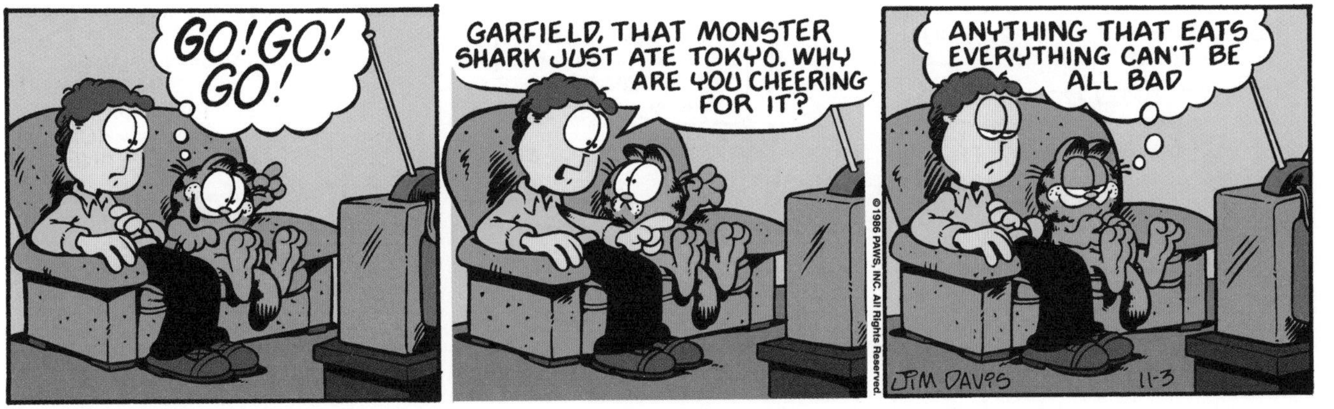
GO! GO! GO!
GARFIELD, THAT MONSTER SHARK JUST ATE TOKYO. WHY ARE YOU CHEERING FOR IT?
ANYTHING THAT EATS EVERYTHING CAN'T BE ALL BAD
© 1986 PAWS, INC. All Rights Reserved.
JIM DAVIS 11-3

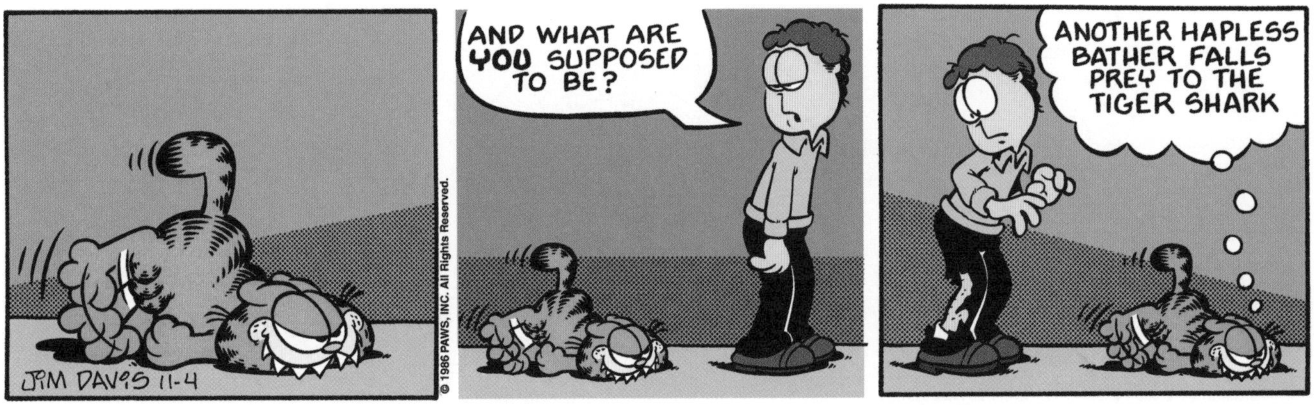
JIM DAVIS 11-4
© 1986 PAWS, INC. All Rights Reserved.
AND WHAT ARE **YOU** SUPPOSED TO BE?
ANOTHER HAPLESS BATHER FALLS PREY TO THE TIGER SHARK

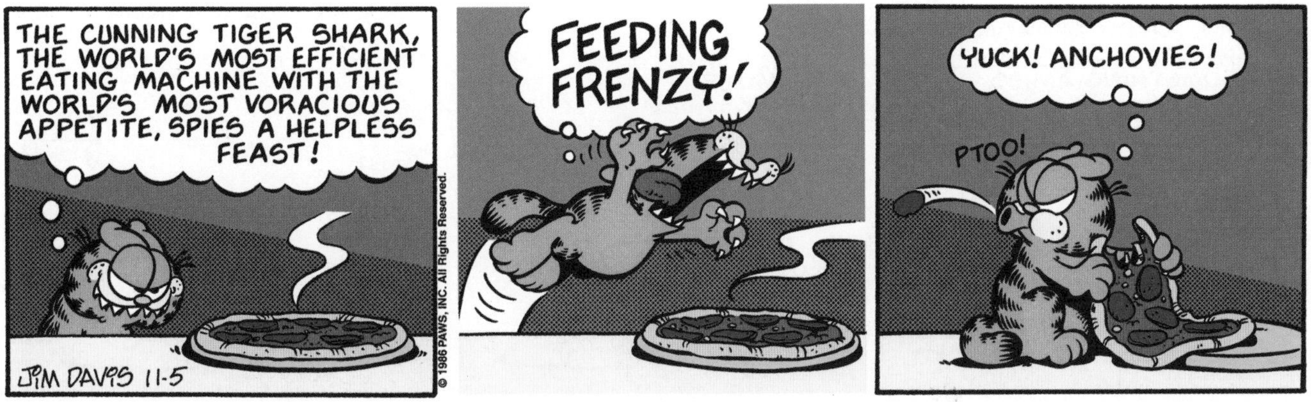
THE CUNNING TIGER SHARK, THE WORLD'S MOST EFFICIENT EATING MACHINE WITH THE WORLD'S MOST VORACIOUS APPETITE, SPIES A HELPLESS FEAST!
JIM DAVIS 11-5
© 1986 PAWS, INC. All Rights Reserved.
FEEDING FRENZY!
YUCK! ANCHOVIES!
PTOO!

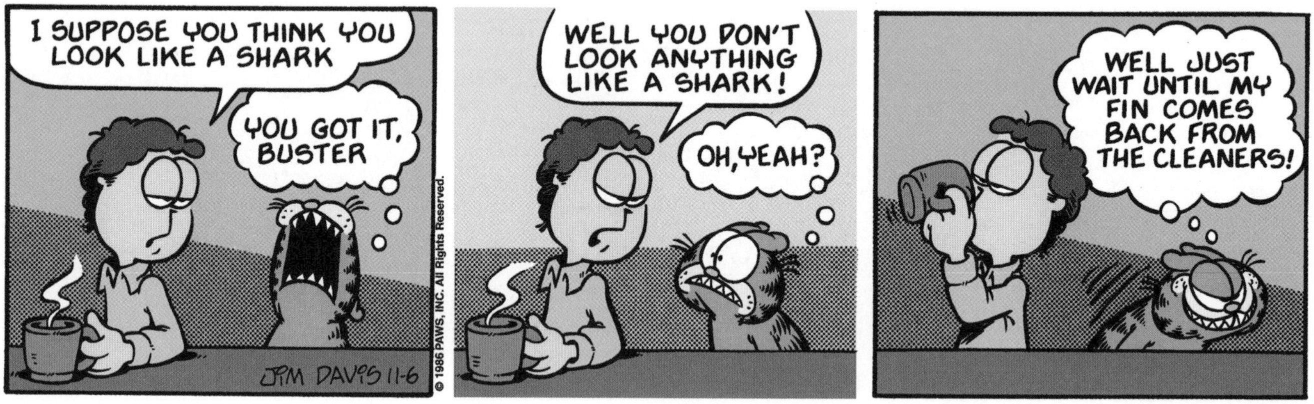
I SUPPOSE YOU THINK YOU LOOK LIKE A SHARK
YOU GOT IT, BUSTER
JIM DAVIS 11-6
© 1986 PAWS, INC. All Rights Reserved.
WELL YOU DON'T LOOK ANYTHING LIKE A SHARK!
OH, YEAH?
WELL JUST WAIT UNTIL MY FIN COMES BACK FROM THE CLEANERS!

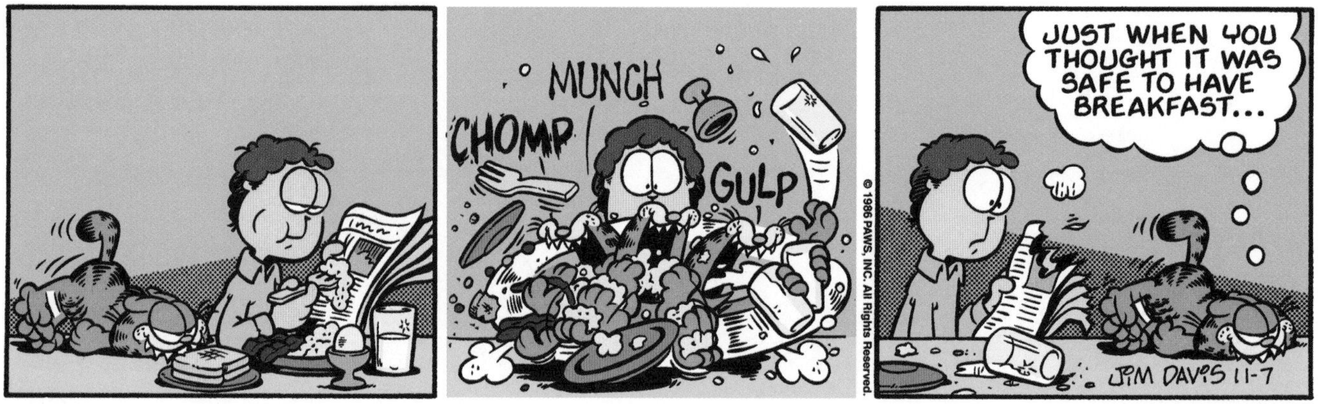
MUNCH
CHOMP
GULP
© 1986 PAWS, INC. All Rights Reserved.
JUST WHEN YOU THOUGHT IT WAS SAFE TO HAVE BREAKFAST...
JIM DAVIS 11-7

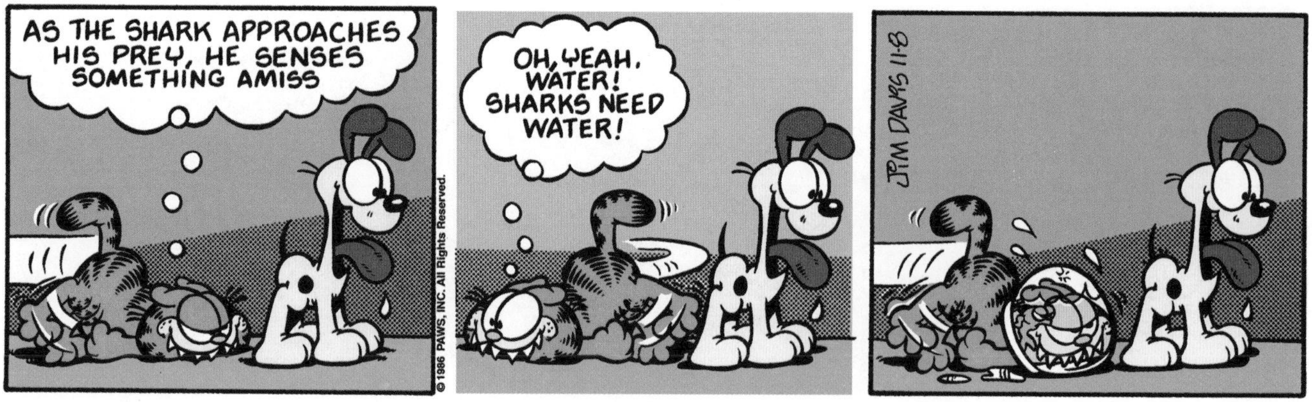
AS THE SHARK APPROACHES HIS PREY, HE SENSES SOMETHING AMISS
© 1986 PAWS, INC. All Rights Reserved.
OH, YEAH. WATER! SHARKS NEED WATER!
JIM DAVIS 11-8

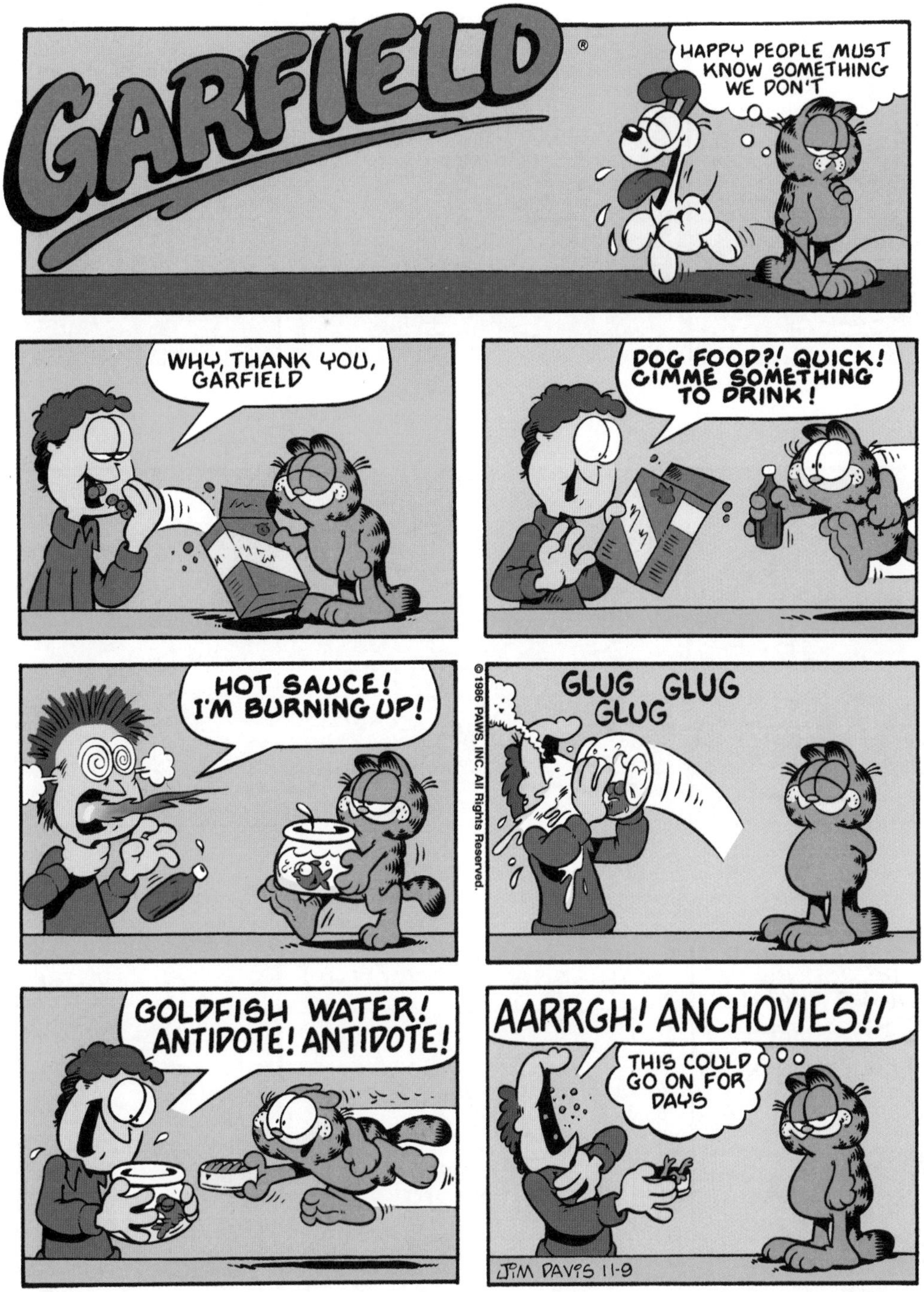
GARFIELD®
HAPPY PEOPLE MUST KNOW SOMETHING WE DON'T
WHY, THANK YOU, GARFIELD
DOG FOOD?! QUICK! GIMME SOMETHING TO DRINK!
HOT SAUCE! I'M BURNING UP!
© 1986 PAWS, INC. All Rights Reserved.
GLUG GLUG GLUG
GOLDFISH WATER! ANTIDOTE! ANTIDOTE!
AARRGH! ANCHOVIES!!
THIS COULD GO ON FOR DAYS
JIM DAVIS 11-9

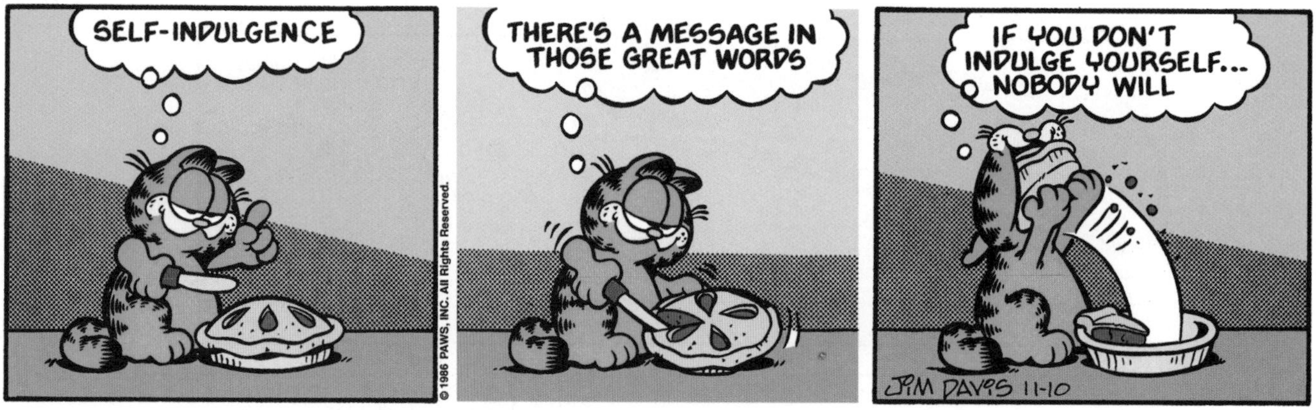
SELF-INDULGENCE
THERE'S A MESSAGE IN THOSE GREAT WORDS
IF YOU DON'T INDULGE YOURSELF... NOBODY WILL
© 1986 PAWS, INC. All Rights Reserved.
JIM DAVIS 11-10

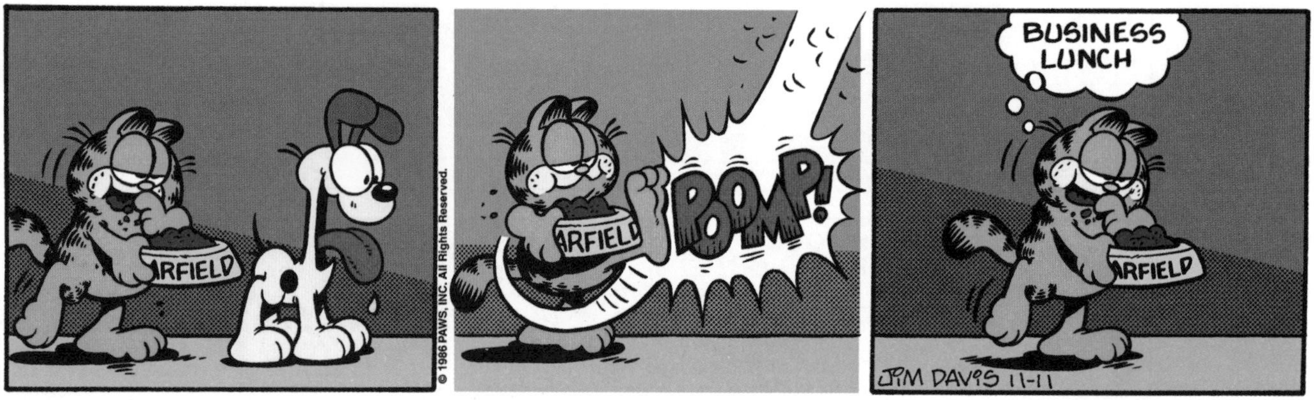
ARFIELD
ARFIELD
BOMP!
BUSINESS LUNCH
ARFIELD
© 1986 PAWS, INC. All Rights Reserved.
JIM DAVIS 11-11

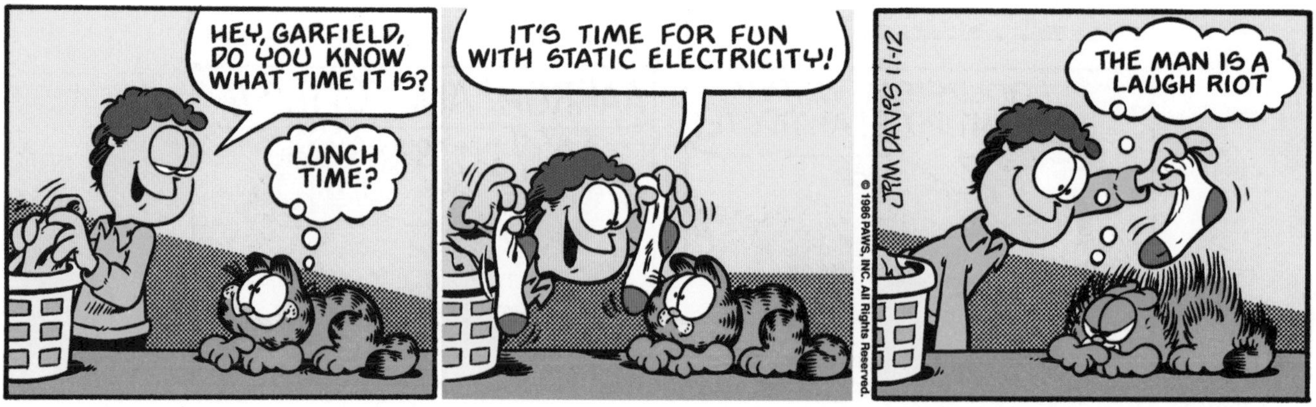
HEY, GARFIELD, DO YOU KNOW WHAT TIME IT IS?
LUNCH TIME?
IT'S TIME FOR FUN WITH STATIC ELECTRICITY!
JIM DAVIS 11-12
© 1986 PAWS, INC. All Rights Reserved.
THE MAN IS A LAUGH RIOT

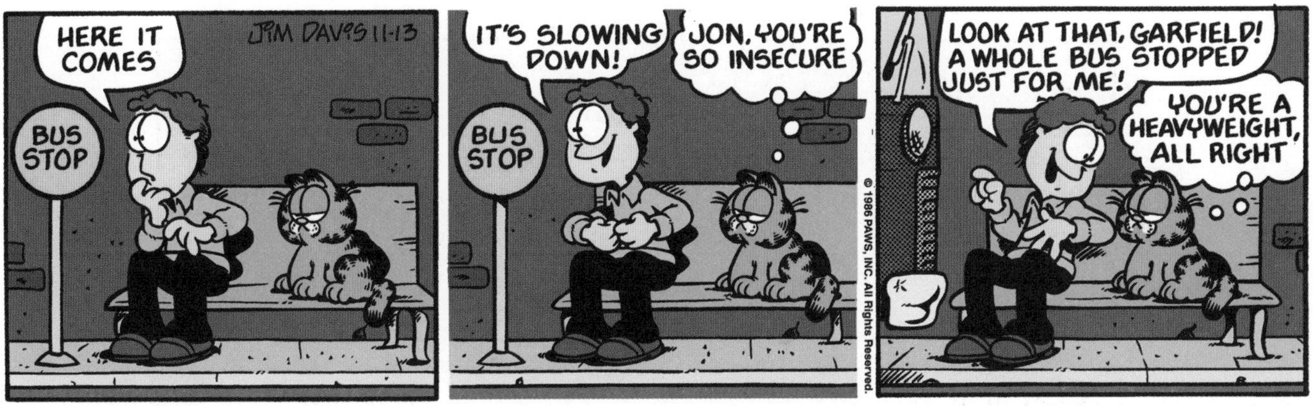
JIM DAVIS 11-13
BUS STOP
HERE IT COMES
IT'S SLOWING DOWN!
JON, YOU'RE SO INSECURE
© 1986 PAWS, INC. All Rights Reserved.
LOOK AT THAT, GARFIELD! A WHOLE BUS STOPPED JUST FOR ME!
YOU'RE A HEAVYWEIGHT, ALL RIGHT

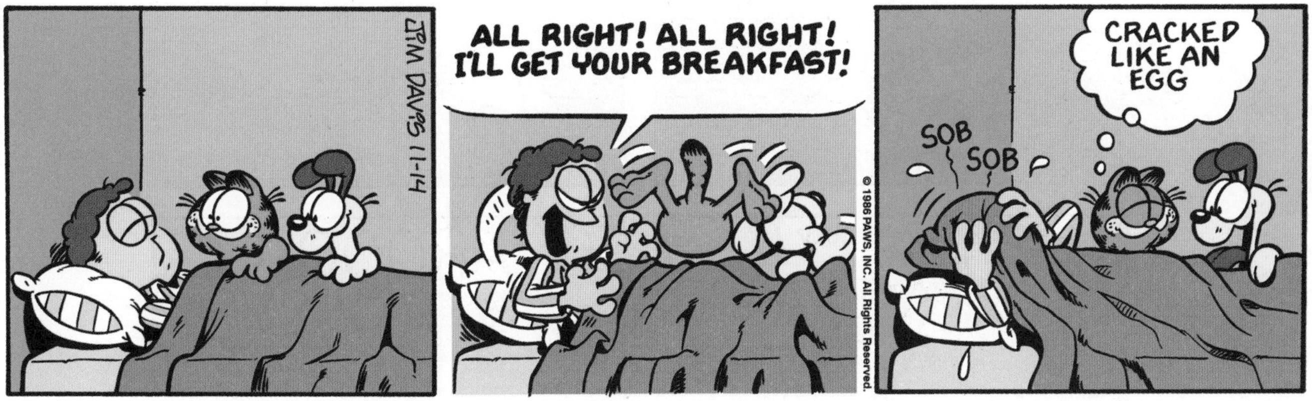
JIM DAVIS 11-14
ALL RIGHT! ALL RIGHT! I'LL GET YOUR BREAKFAST!
© 1986 PAWS, INC. All Rights Reserved.
SOB SOB
CRACKED LIKE AN EGG

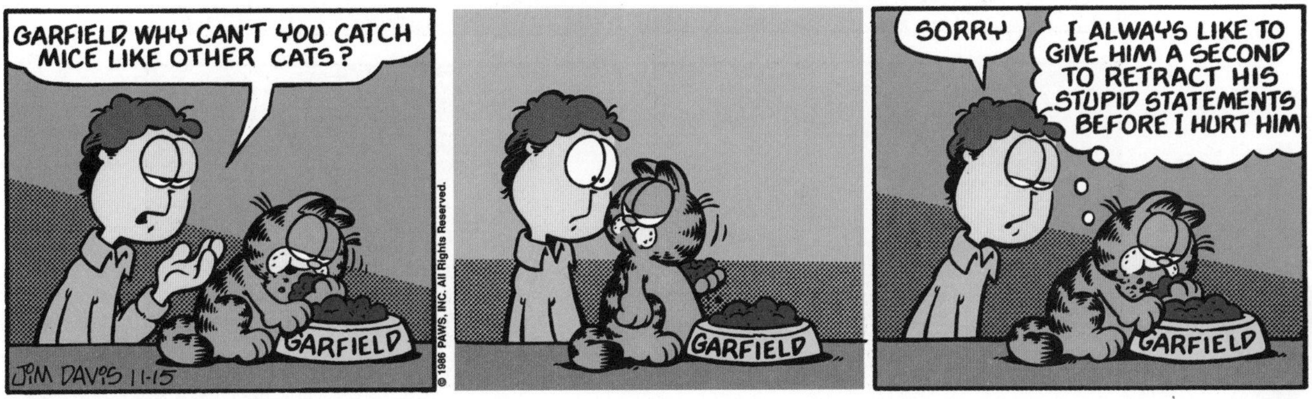
GARFIELD, WHY CAN'T YOU CATCH MICE LIKE OTHER CATS?
GARFIELD
JIM DAVIS 11-15
© 1986 PAWS, INC. All Rights Reserved.
GARFIELD
SORRY
I ALWAYS LIKE TO GIVE HIM A SECOND TO RETRACT HIS STUPID STATEMENTS BEFORE I HURT HIM
GARFIELD

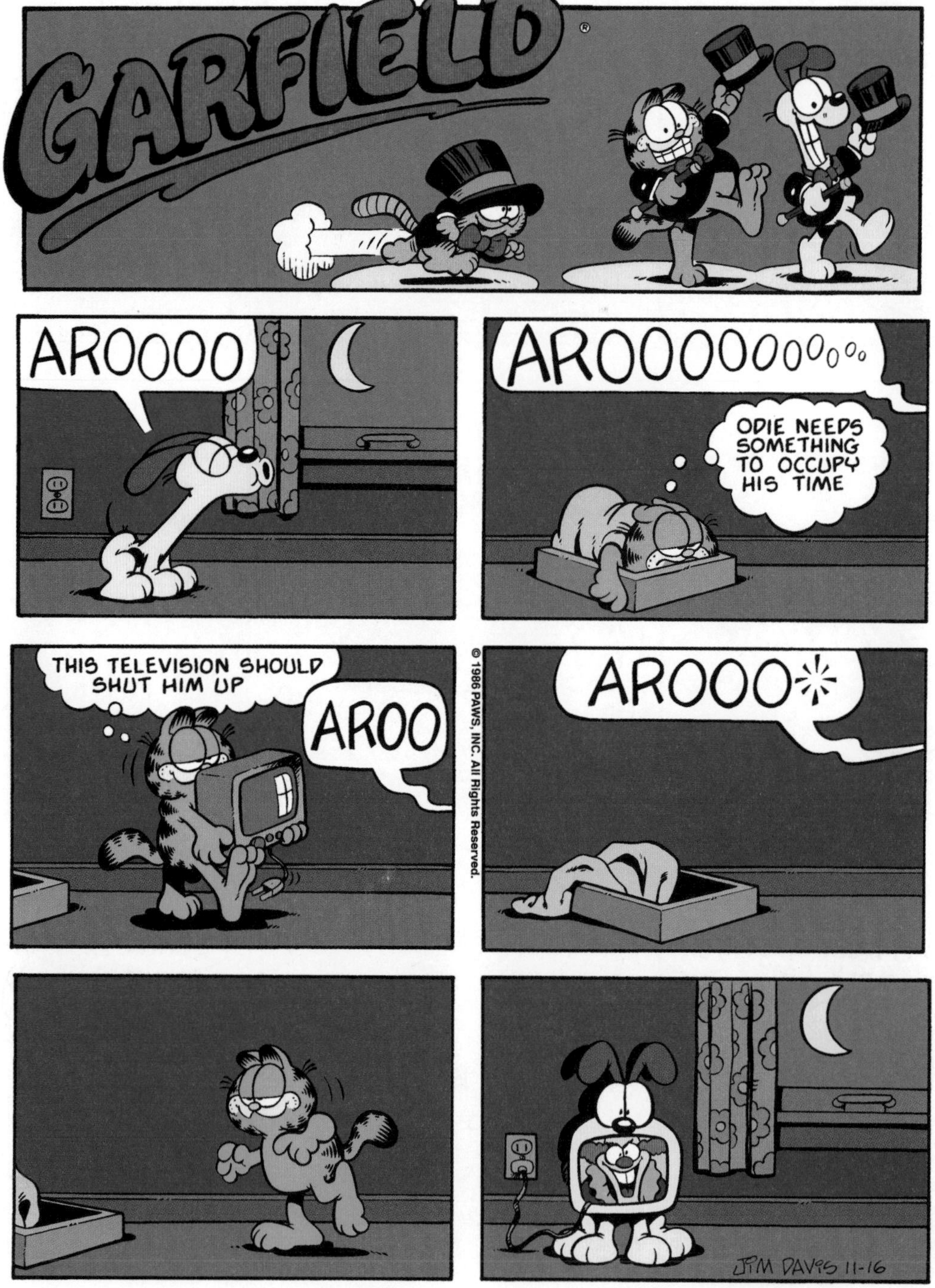
GARFIELD®
AROOOO
AROOOOOOOOOoo
ODIE NEEDS SOMETHING TO OCCUPY HIS TIME
THIS TELEVISION SHOULD SHUT HIM UP
AROO
© 1986 PAWS, INC. All Rights Reserved.
AROOO
JIM DAVIS 11-16

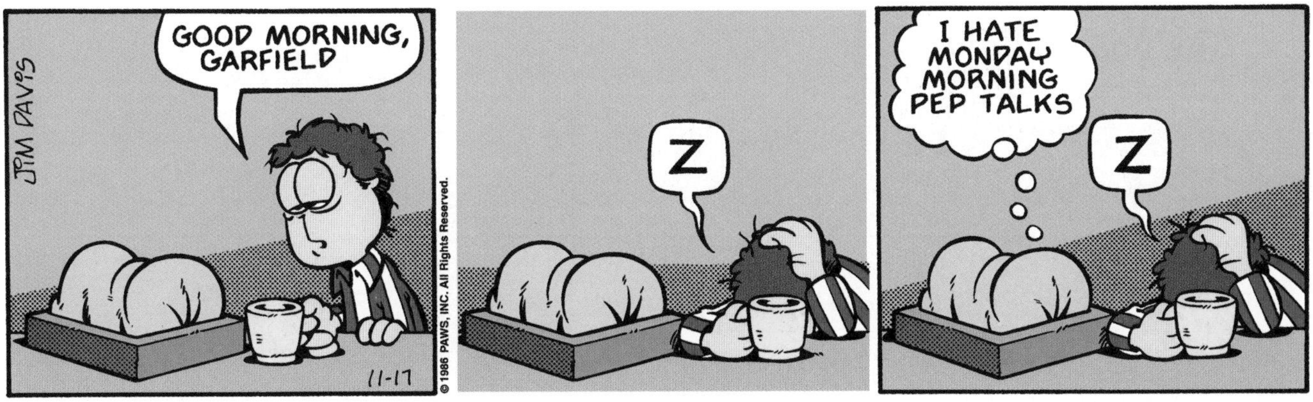
JIM DAVIS
GOOD MORNING, GARFIELD
11-17
Z
I HATE MONDAY MORNING PEP TALKS
Z

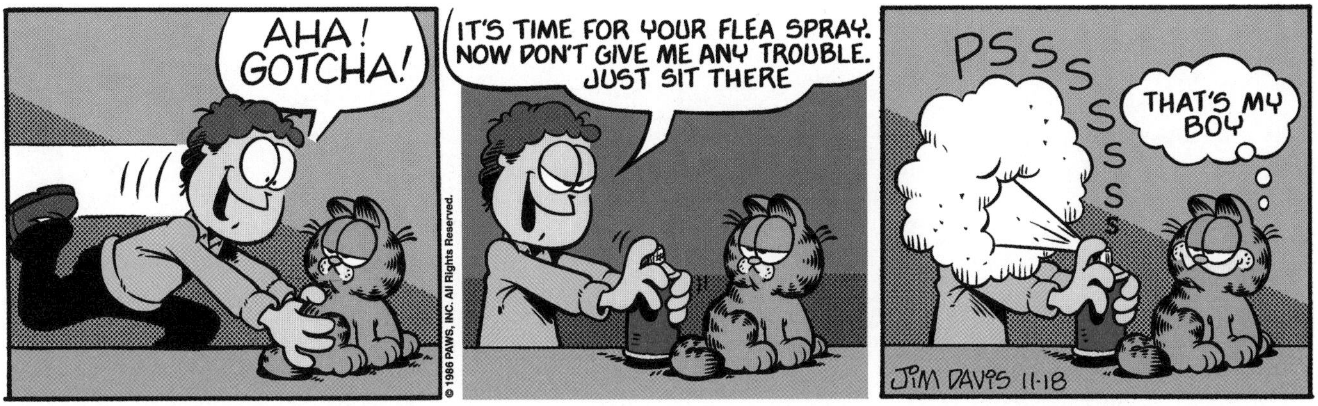
AHA! GOTCHA!
IT'S TIME FOR YOUR FLEA SPRAY. NOW DON'T GIVE ME ANY TROUBLE. JUST SIT THERE
PSSSSSSSS
THAT'S MY BOY
JIM DAVIS 11-18

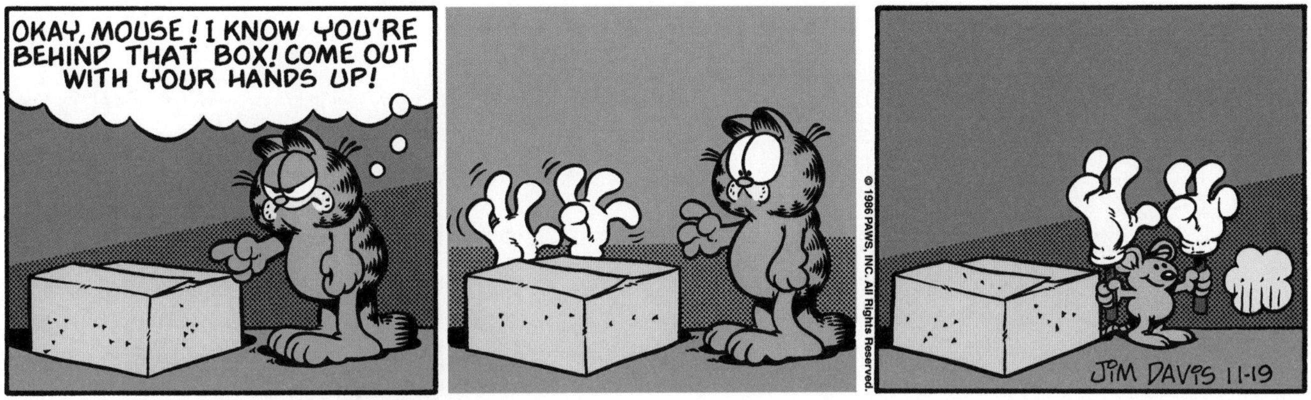
OKAY, MOUSE! I KNOW YOU'RE BEHIND THAT BOX! COME OUT WITH YOUR HANDS UP!
JIM DAVIS 11-19

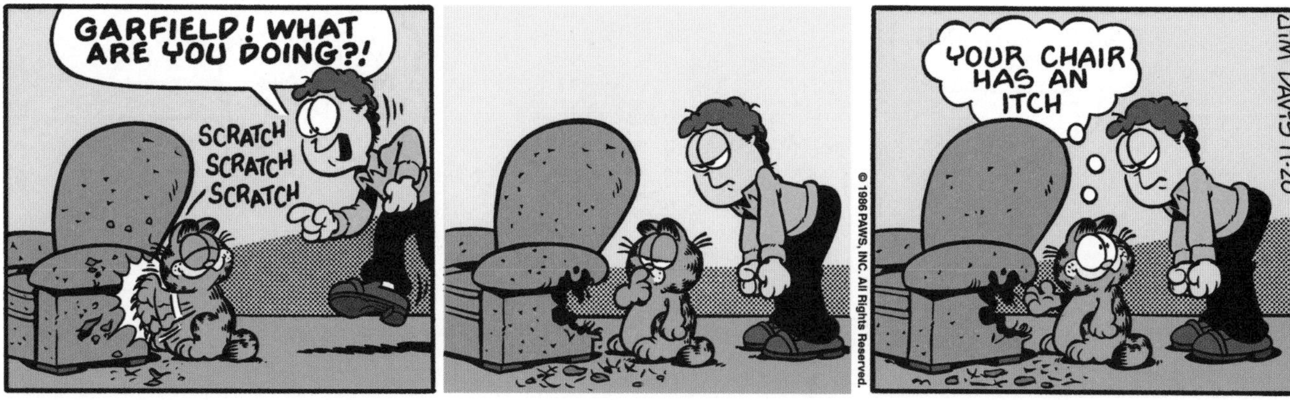
GARFIELD! WHAT ARE YOU DOING?!
SCRATCH SCRATCH SCRATCH
YOUR CHAIR HAS AN ITCH
JIM DAVIS 11-20
© 1986 PAWS, INC. All Rights Reserved.

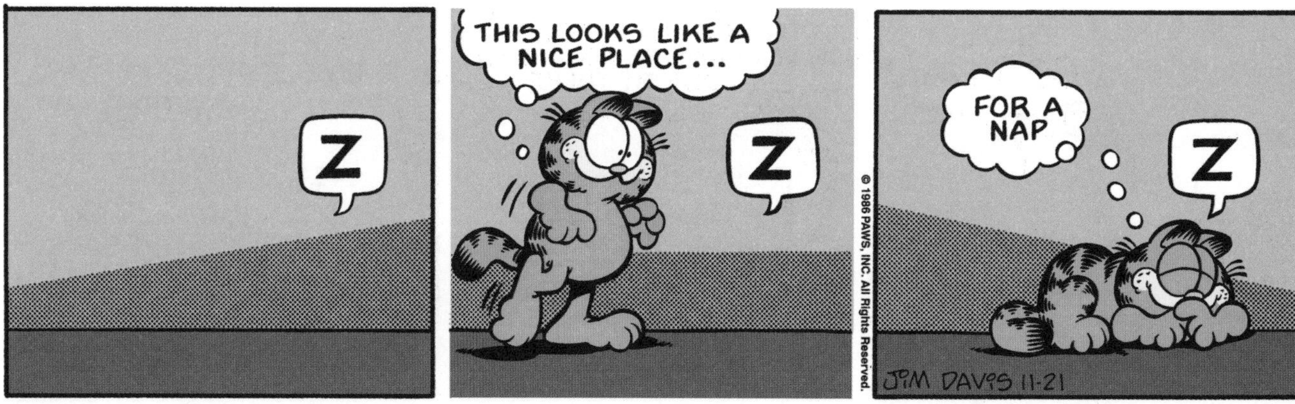
Z
THIS LOOKS LIKE A NICE PLACE...
Z
FOR A NAP
Z
JIM DAVIS 11-21
© 1986 PAWS, INC. All Rights Reserved.

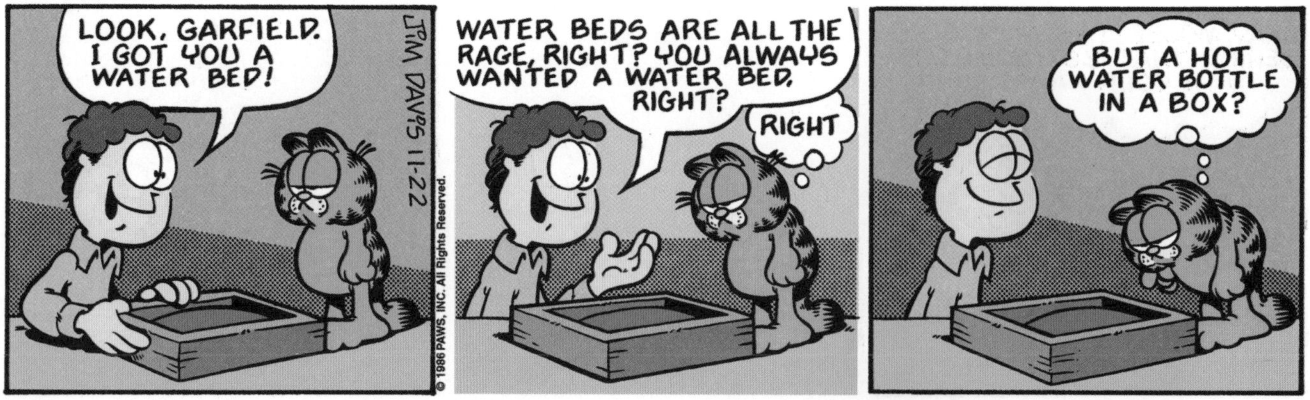
LOOK, GARFIELD. I GOT YOU A WATER BED!
WATER BEDS ARE ALL THE RAGE, RIGHT? YOU ALWAYS WANTED A WATER BED. RIGHT?
RIGHT
BUT A HOT WATER BOTTLE IN A BOX?
JIM DAVIS 11-22
© 1986 PAWS, INC. All Rights Reserved.

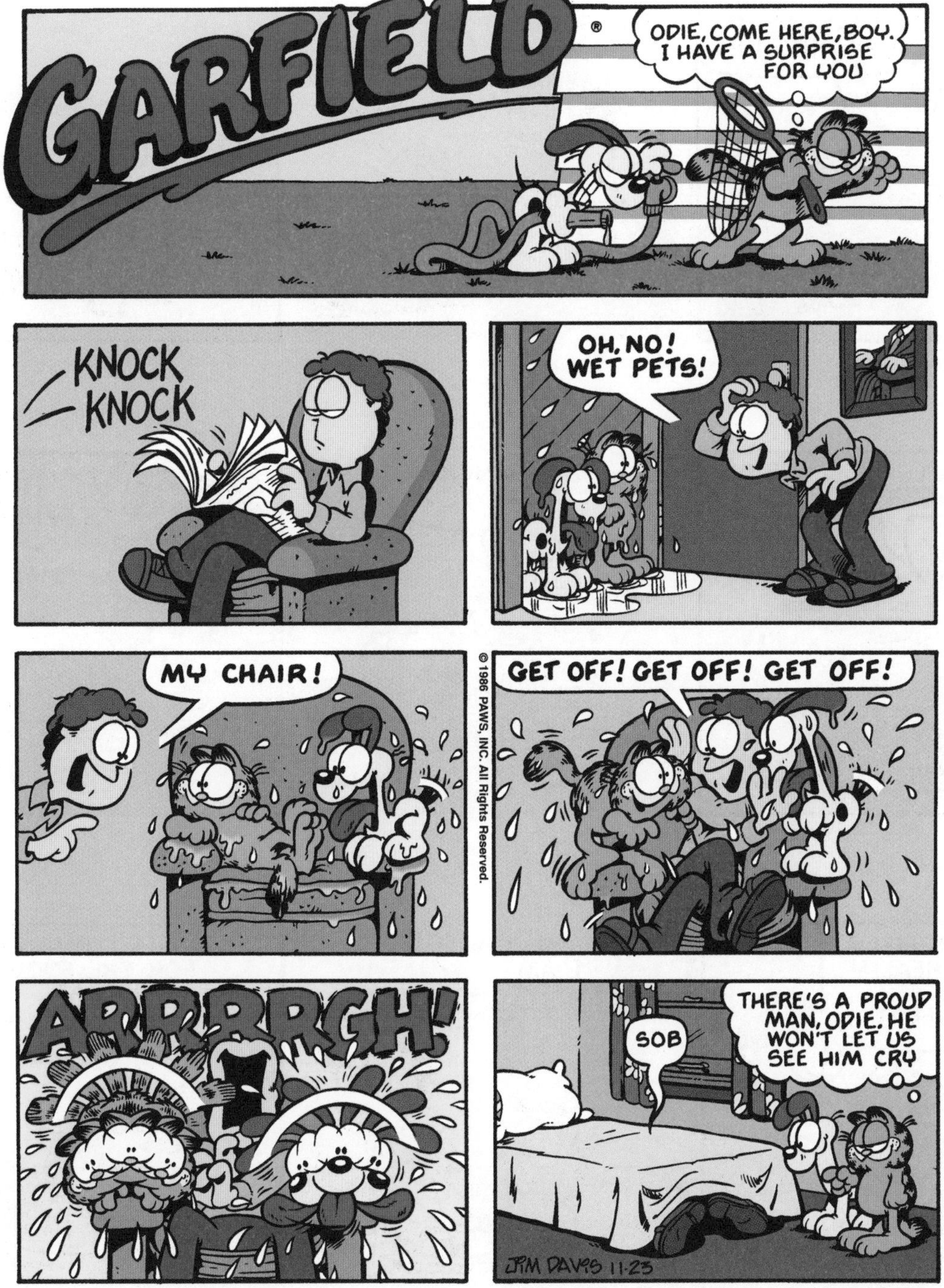
GARFIELD®
ODIE, COME HERE, BOY. I HAVE A SURPRISE FOR YOU
KNOCK KNOCK
OH, NO! WET PETS!
MY CHAIR!
GET OFF! GET OFF! GET OFF!
ARRRRGH!
SOB
THERE'S A PROUD MAN, ODIE. HE WON'T LET US SEE HIM CRY
JIM DAVIS 11-23

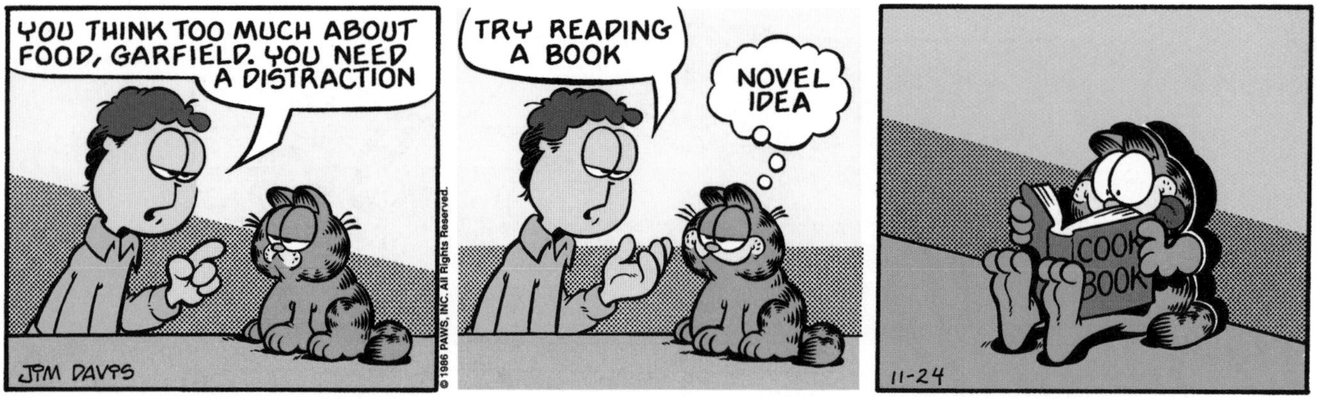
YOU THINK TOO MUCH ABOUT FOOD, GARFIELD. YOU NEED A DISTRACTION
JIM DAVIS
© 1986 PAWS, INC. All Rights Reserved.
TRY READING A BOOK
NOVEL IDEA
COOK BOOK
11-24

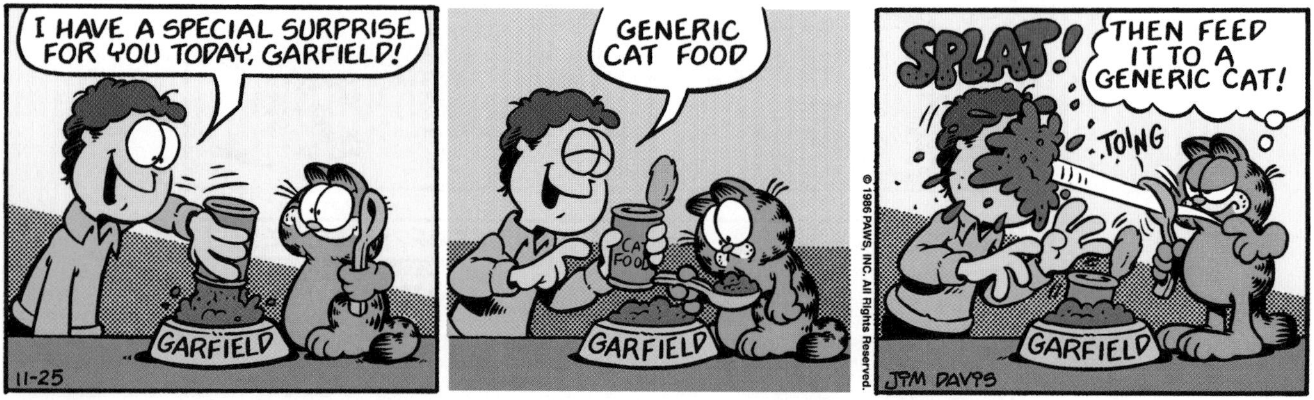
I HAVE A SPECIAL SURPRISE FOR YOU TODAY, GARFIELD!
GARFIELD
11-25
GENERIC CAT FOOD
CAT FOOD
GARFIELD
© 1986 PAWS, INC. All Rights Reserved.
SPLAT!
THEN FEED IT TO A GENERIC CAT!
TOING
GARFIELD
JIM DAVIS

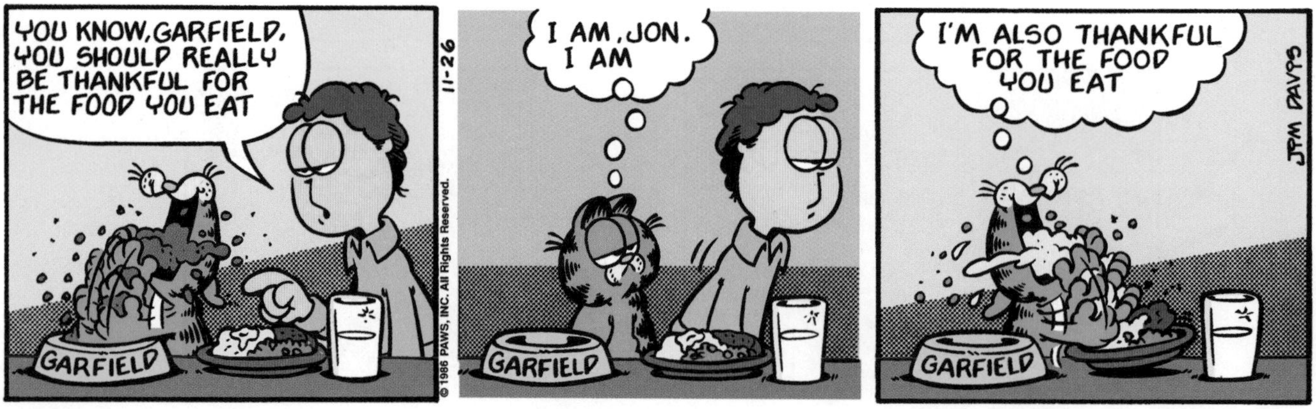
YOU KNOW, GARFIELD, YOU SHOULD REALLY BE THANKFUL FOR THE FOOD YOU EAT
GARFIELD
11-26
© 1986 PAWS, INC. All Rights Reserved.
I AM, JON. I AM
GARFIELD
I'M ALSO THANKFUL FOR THE FOOD YOU EAT
JIM DAVIS
GARFIELD

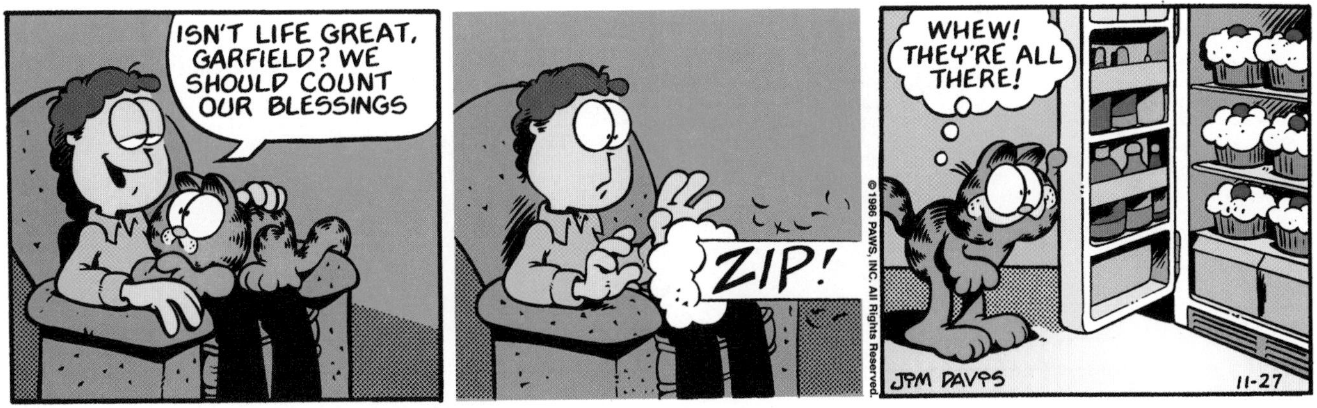
ISN'T LIFE GREAT, GARFIELD? WE SHOULD COUNT OUR BLESSINGS
ZIP!
© 1986 PAWS, INC. All Rights Reserved.
WHEW! THEY'RE ALL THERE!
JIM DAVIS
11-27

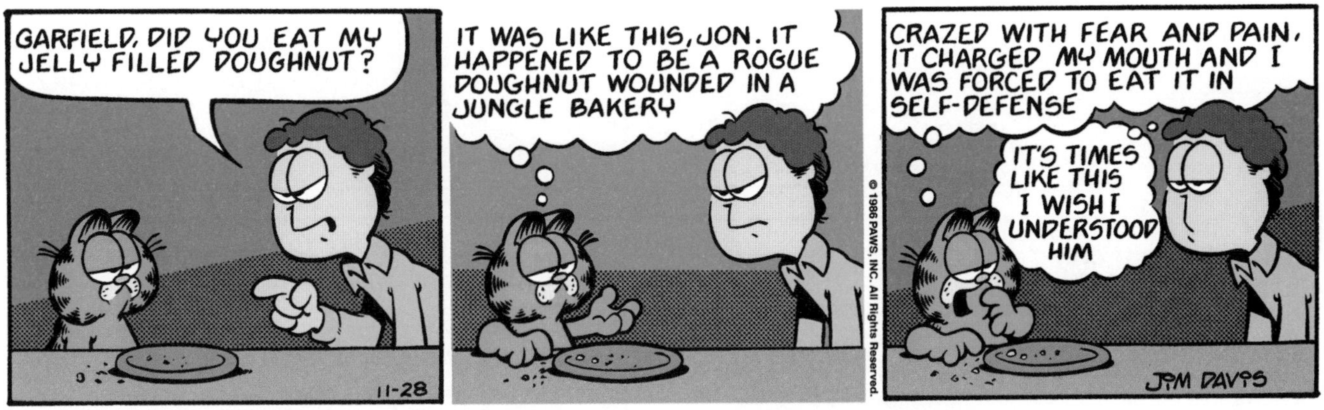
GARFIELD, DID YOU EAT MY JELLY FILLED DOUGHNUT?
11-28
IT WAS LIKE THIS, JON. IT HAPPENED TO BE A ROGUE DOUGHNUT WOUNDED IN A JUNGLE BAKERY
© 1986 PAWS, INC. All Rights Reserved.
CRAZED WITH FEAR AND PAIN, IT CHARGED MY MOUTH AND I WAS FORCED TO EAT IT IN SELF-DEFENSE
IT'S TIMES LIKE THIS I WISH I UNDERSTOOD HIM
JIM DAVIS

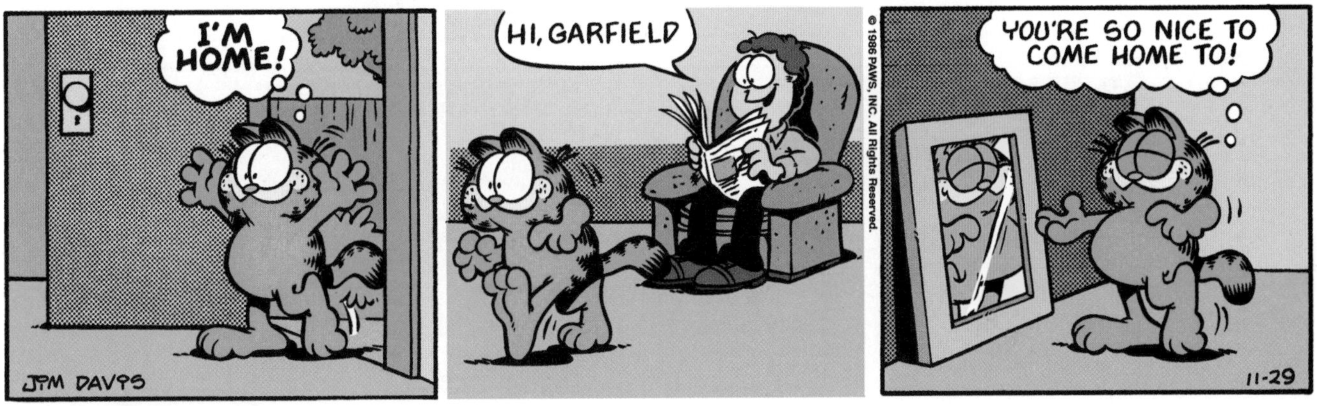
I'M HOME!
JIM DAVIS
HI, GARFIELD
© 1986 PAWS, INC. All Rights Reserved.
YOU'RE SO NICE TO COME HOME TO!
11-29

GARFIELD®
NUTS! STUCK AGAIN!
SCREEEE
GARFIELD
GULP
GARFIELD, YOU CAN'T STILL BE HUNGRY
© 1986 PAWS, INC. All Rights Reserved.
YOU HAVE TO LOSE WEIGHT. NO MORE FOOD UNTIL BREAKFAST
DO YOU REALLY WANT THAT, JON? DO YOU KNOW WHAT HAPPENS TO SKINNY PEOPLE?
JIM DAVIS 11-30
THEY BECOME MIMES, JON. IS THAT WHAT YOU WANT?!! A MIME?!

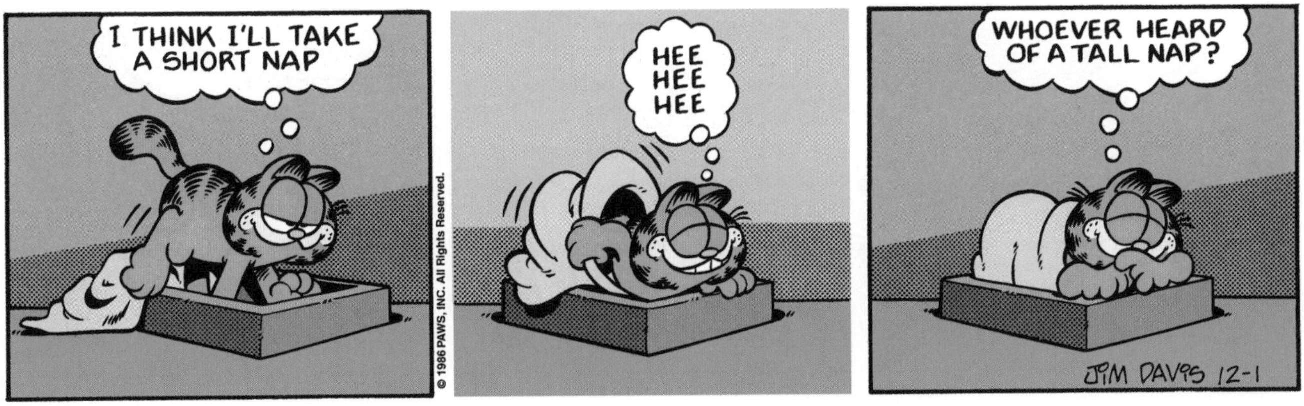
I THINK I'LL TAKE A SHORT NAP
© 1986 PAWS, INC. All Rights Reserved.
HEE HEE HEE
WHOEVER HEARD OF A TALL NAP?
JIM DAVIS 12-1

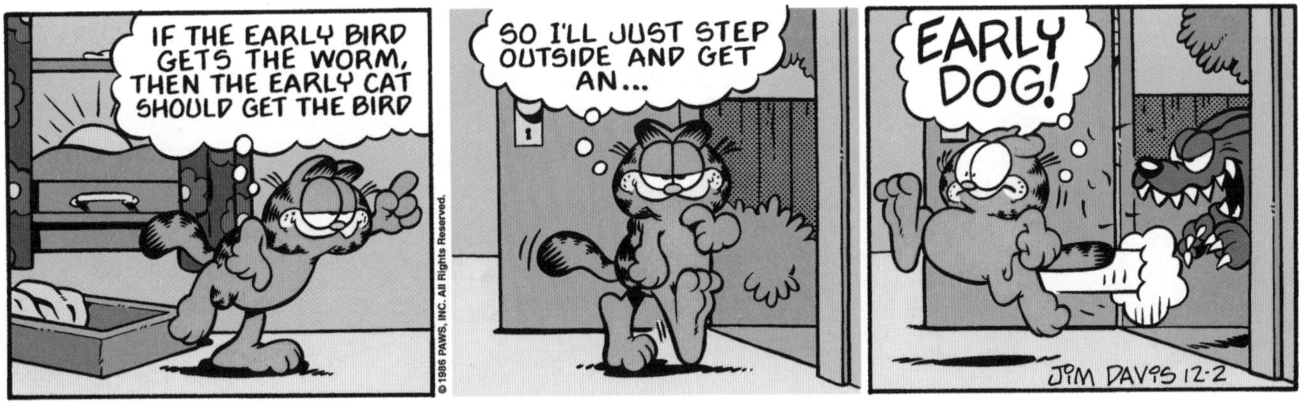
IF THE EARLY BIRD GETS THE WORM, THEN THE EARLY CAT SHOULD GET THE BIRD
© 1986 PAWS, INC. All Rights Reserved.
SO I'LL JUST STEP OUTSIDE AND GET AN...
EARLY DOG!
JIM DAVIS 12-2

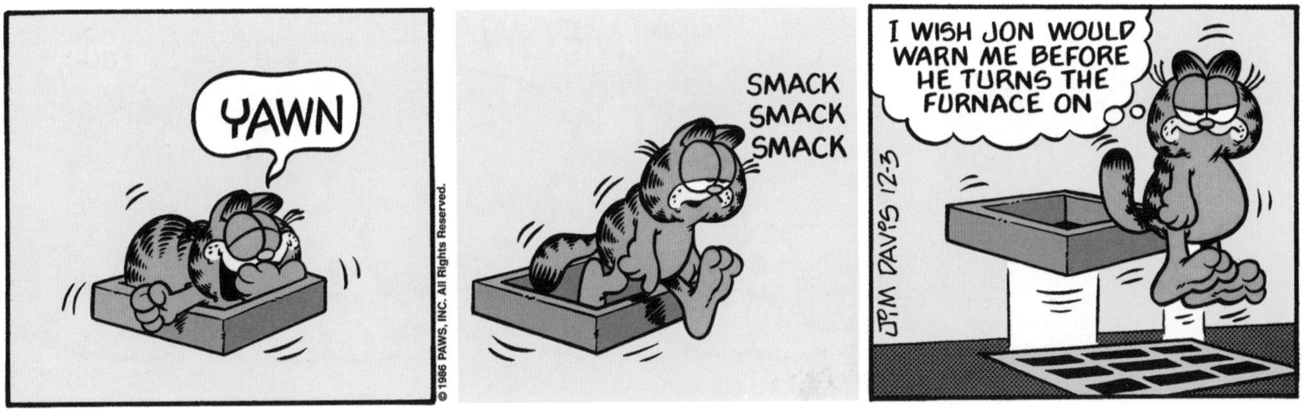
YAWN
© 1986 PAWS, INC. All Rights Reserved.
SMACK
SMACK
SMACK
I WISH JON WOULD WARN ME BEFORE HE TURNS THE FURNACE ON
JIM DAVIS 12-3

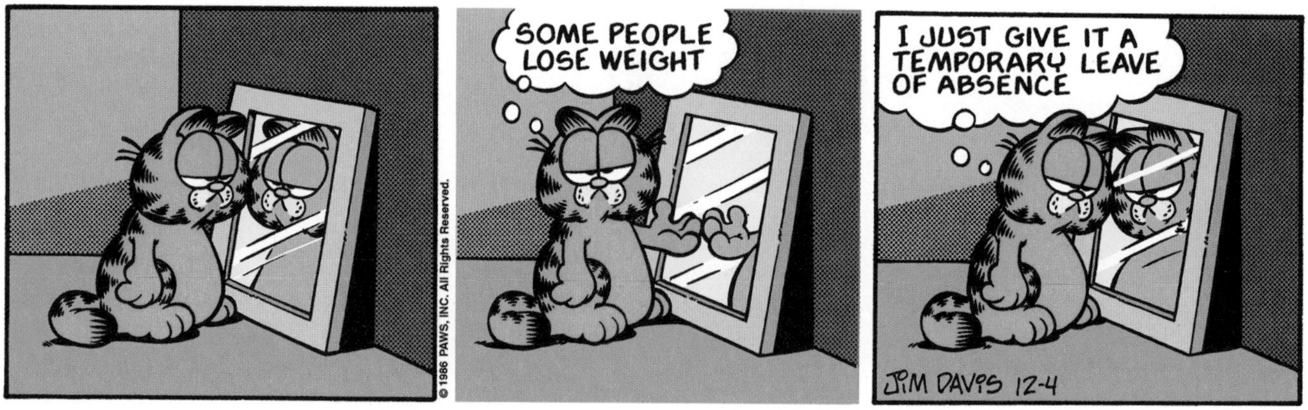
© 1986 PAWS, INC. All Rights Reserved.
SOME PEOPLE LOSE WEIGHT
I JUST GIVE IT A TEMPORARY LEAVE OF ABSENCE
JIM DAVIS 12-4

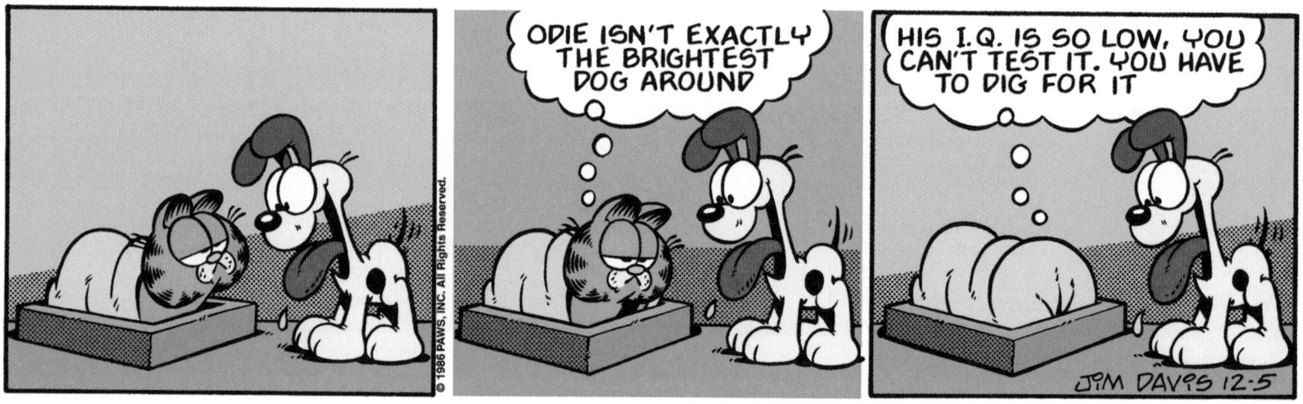
© 1986 PAWS, INC. All Rights Reserved.
ODIE ISN'T EXACTLY THE BRIGHTEST DOG AROUND
HIS I.Q. IS SO LOW, YOU CAN'T TEST IT. YOU HAVE TO DIG FOR IT
JIM DAVIS 12-5

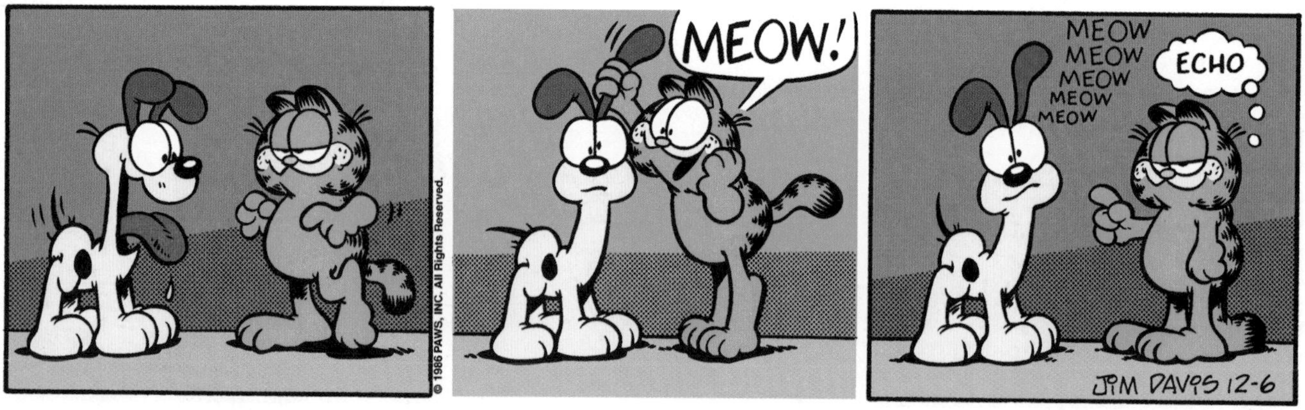
© 1986 PAWS, INC. All Rights Reserved.
MEOW!
MEOW MEOW MEOW MEOW MEOW
ECHO
JIM DAVIS 12-6

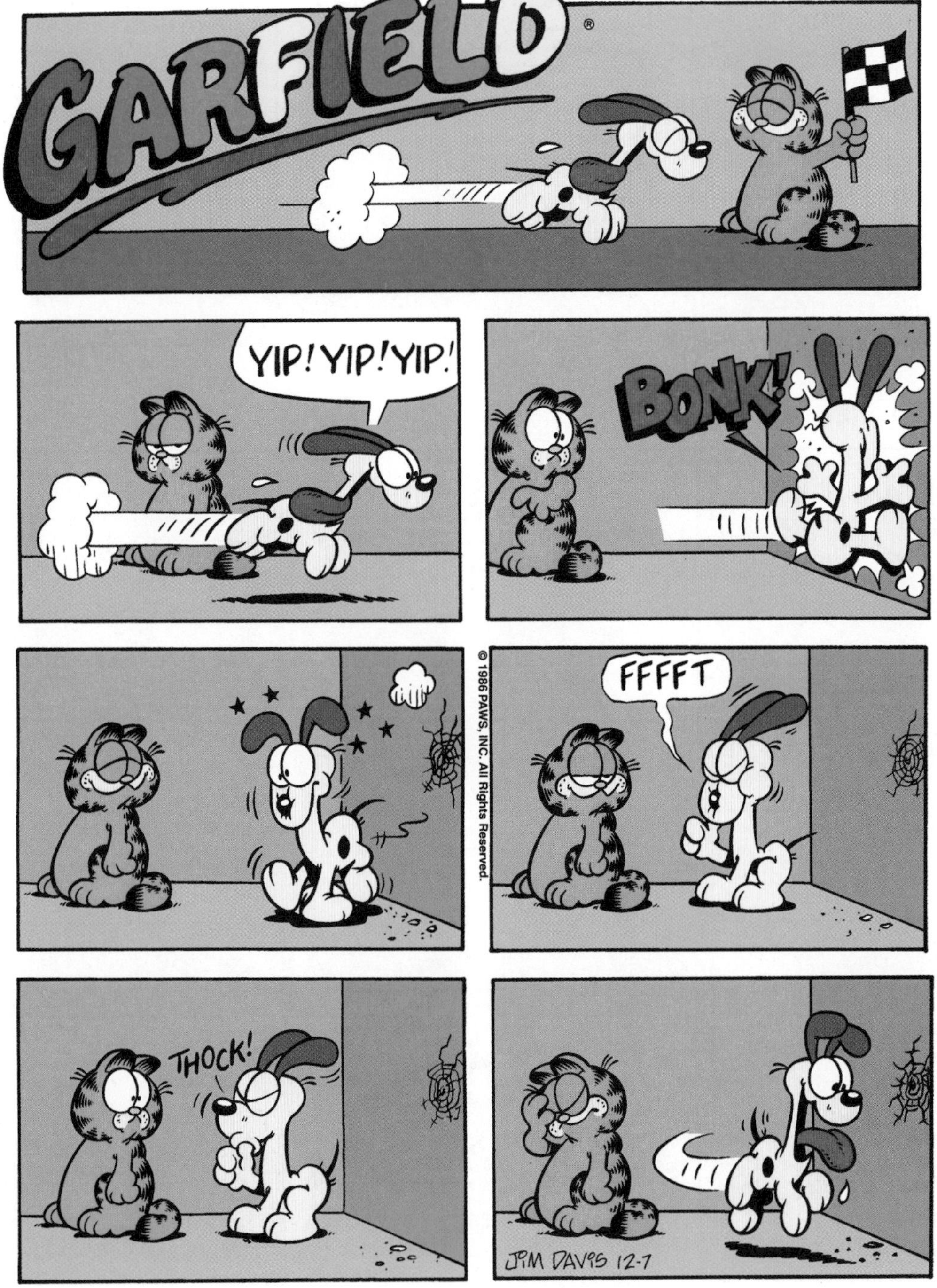
GARFIELD®
YIP! YIP! YIP!
BONK!
© 1986 PAWS, INC. All Rights Reserved.
FFFFT
THOCK!
JIM DAVIS 12-7

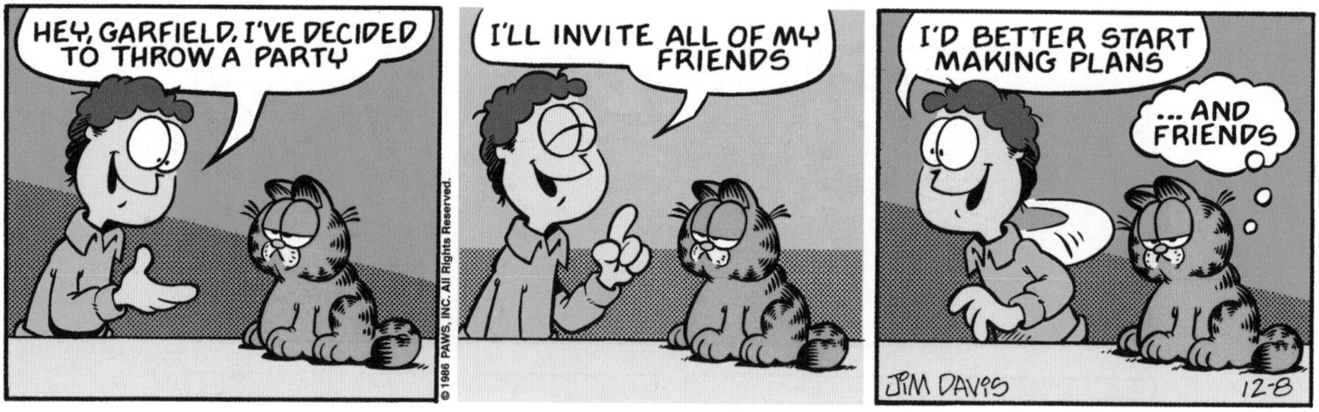
HEY, GARFIELD, I'VE DECIDED TO THROW A PARTY
I'LL INVITE ALL OF MY FRIENDS
I'D BETTER START MAKING PLANS
... AND FRIENDS
© 1986 PAWS, INC. All Rights Reserved.
JIM DAVIS 12-8

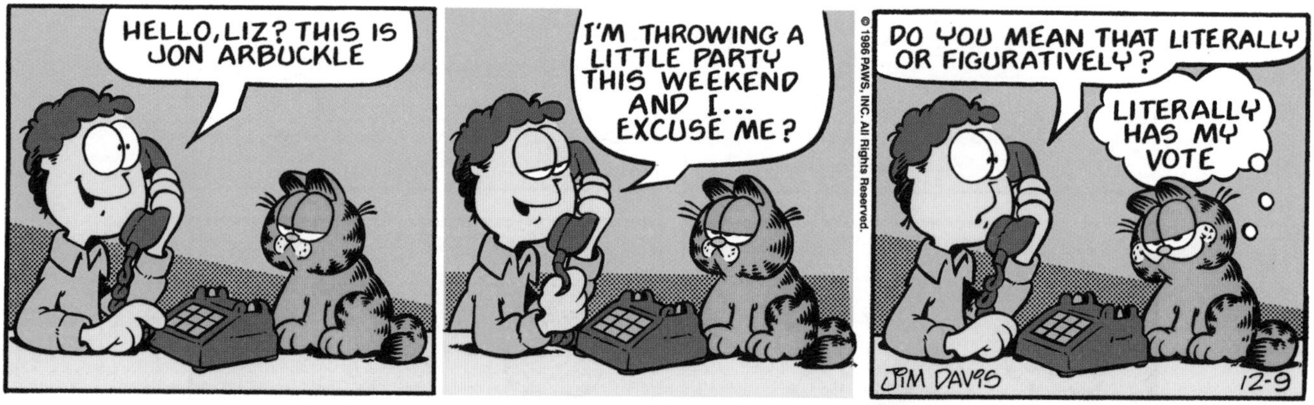
HELLO, LIZ? THIS IS JON ARBUCKLE
I'M THROWING A LITTLE PARTY THIS WEEKEND AND I... EXCUSE ME?
DO YOU MEAN THAT LITERALLY OR FIGURATIVELY?
LITERALLY HAS MY VOTE
© 1986 PAWS, INC. All Rights Reserved.
JIM DAVIS 12-9

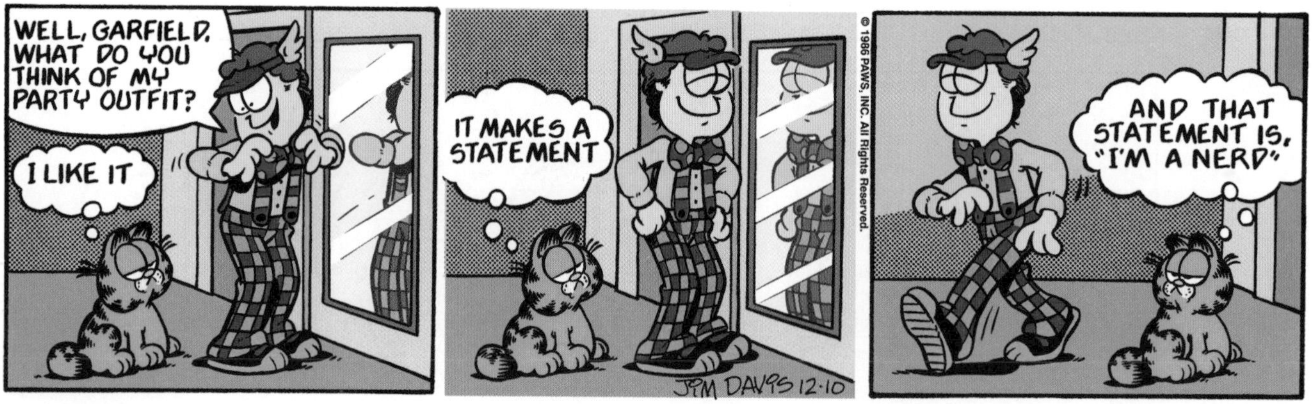
WELL, GARFIELD, WHAT DO YOU THINK OF MY PARTY OUTFIT?
I LIKE IT
IT MAKES A STATEMENT
AND THAT STATEMENT IS, "I'M A NERD"
© 1986 PAWS, INC. All Rights Reserved.
JIM DAVIS 12-10

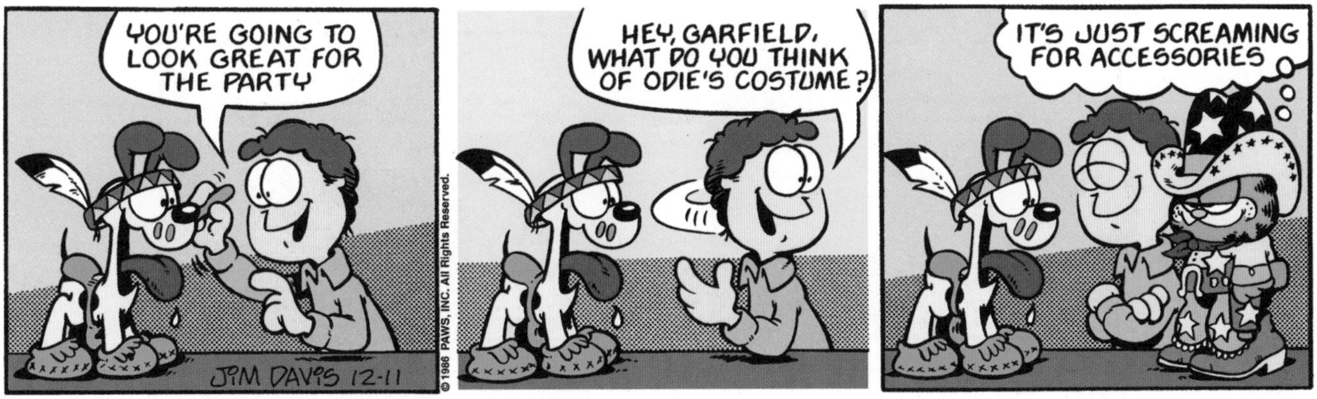
YOU'RE GOING TO LOOK GREAT FOR THE PARTY
JIM DAVIS 12-11
© 1986 PAWS, INC. All Rights Reserved.
HEY, GARFIELD, WHAT DO YOU THINK OF ODIE'S COSTUME?
IT'S JUST SCREAMING FOR ACCESSORIES

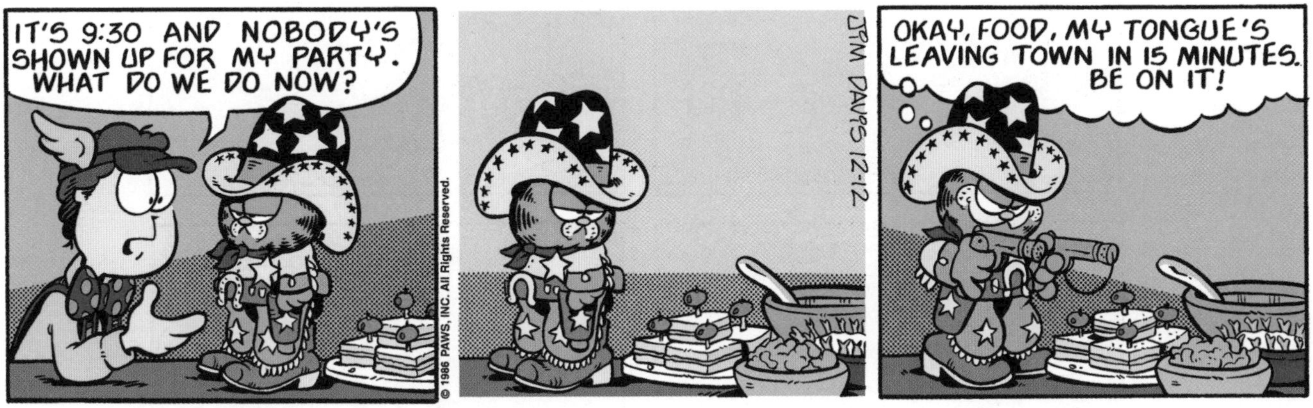
IT'S 9:30 AND NOBODY'S SHOWN UP FOR MY PARTY. WHAT DO WE DO NOW?
© 1986 PAWS, INC. All Rights Reserved.
JIM DAVIS 12-12
OKAY, FOOD, MY TONGUE'S LEAVING TOWN IN 15 MINUTES. BE ON IT!

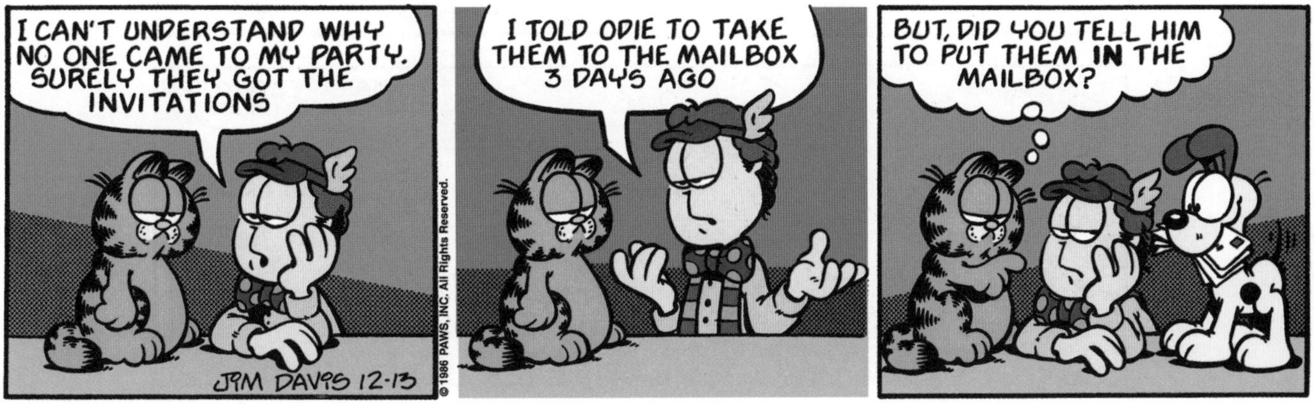
I CAN'T UNDERSTAND WHY NO ONE CAME TO MY PARTY. SURELY THEY GOT THE INVITATIONS
JIM DAVIS 12-13
© 1986 PAWS, INC. All Rights Reserved.
I TOLD ODIE TO TAKE THEM TO THE MAILBOX 3 DAYS AGO
BUT, DID YOU TELL HIM TO PUT THEM IN THE MAILBOX?

GARFIELD®
GARFIELD, DON'T EAT THIS FOOD. IT'S FOR MY PARTY
OKAY, ODIE. TAKE THESE PARTY INVITATIONS AND PUT THEM IN THE MAILBOX
© 1986 PAWS, INC. All Rights Reserved.
JIM DAVIS 12-14
COME ON, GARFIELD. THE SOCIAL EVENT OF THE SEASON HAS ARRIVED
DING DONG
I WAS EXPECTING THE UPPER CRUST
AND YOU GOT THE CRUMBS

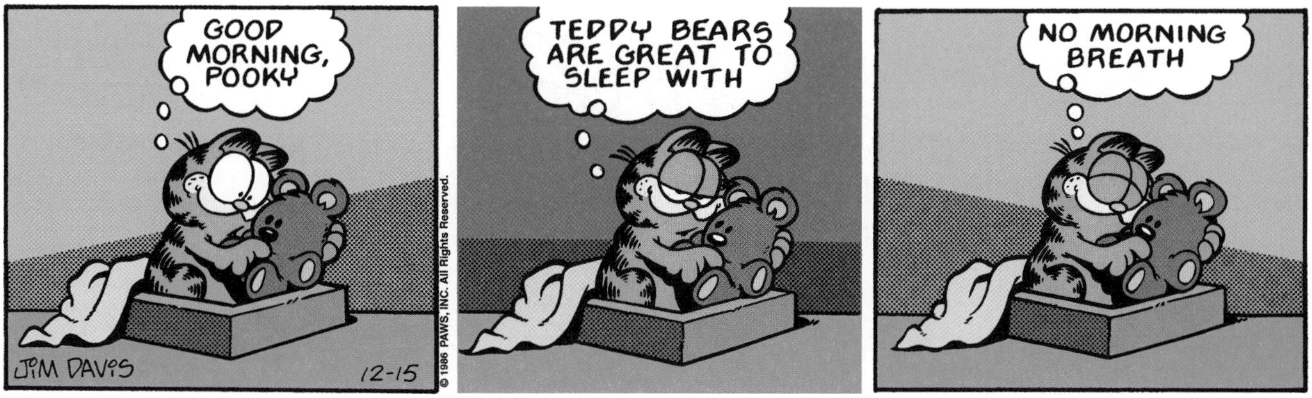
GOOD MORNING, POOKY
TEDDY BEARS ARE GREAT TO SLEEP WITH
NO MORNING BREATH
JIM DAVIS 12-15

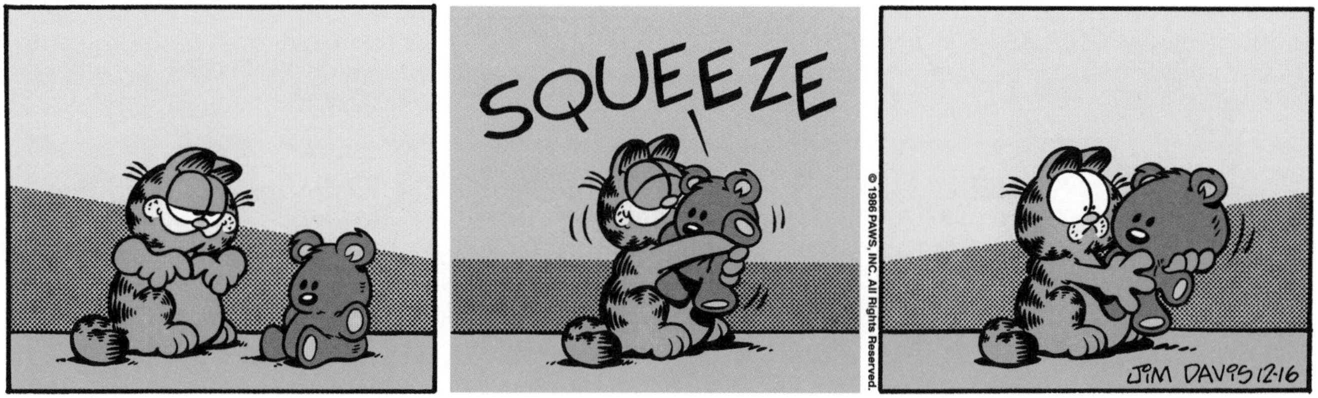
SQUEEZE
JIM DAVIS 12-16

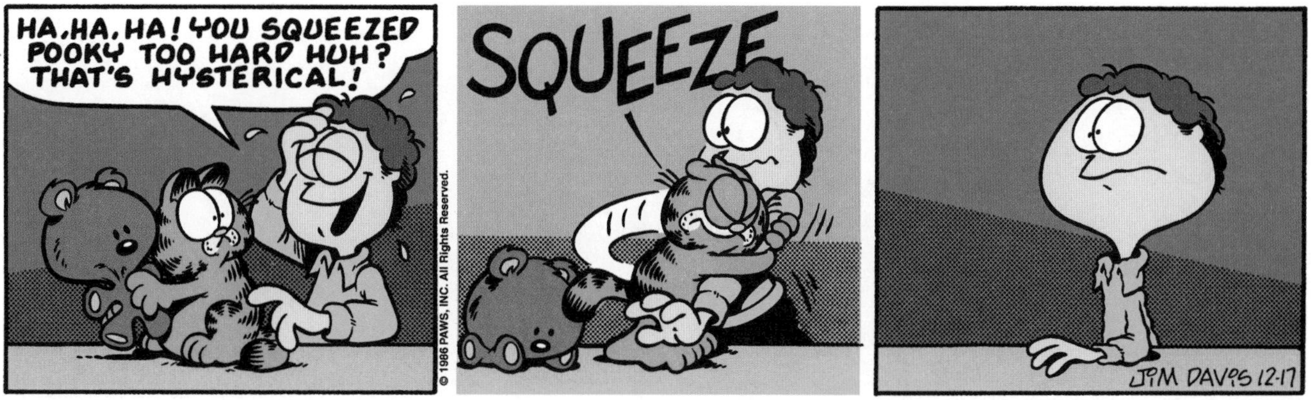
HA, HA, HA! YOU SQUEEZED POOKY TOO HARD HUH? THAT'S HYSTERICAL!
SQUEEZE
JIM DAVIS 12-17

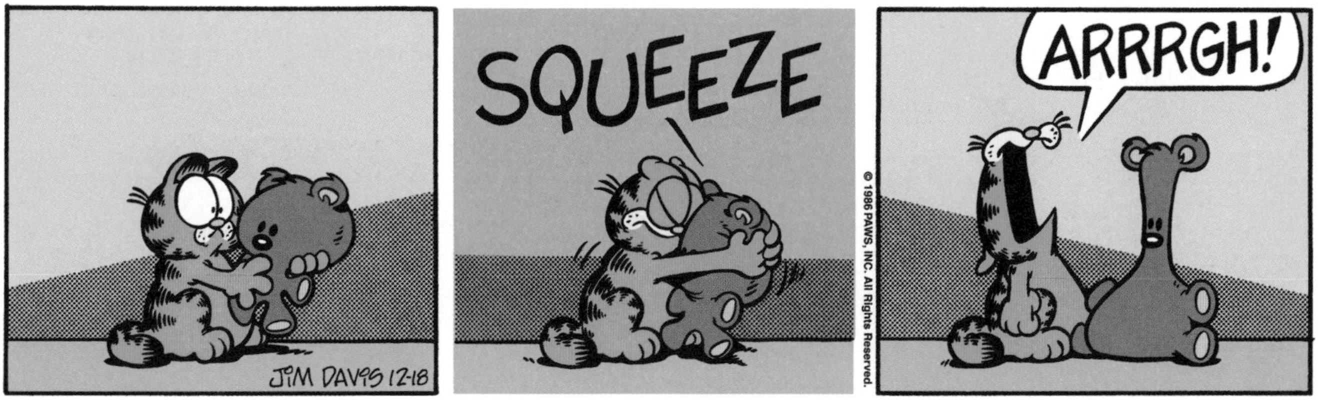
SQUEEZE
ARRRGH!
JIM DAVIS 12-18
© 1986 PAWS, INC. All Rights Reserved.

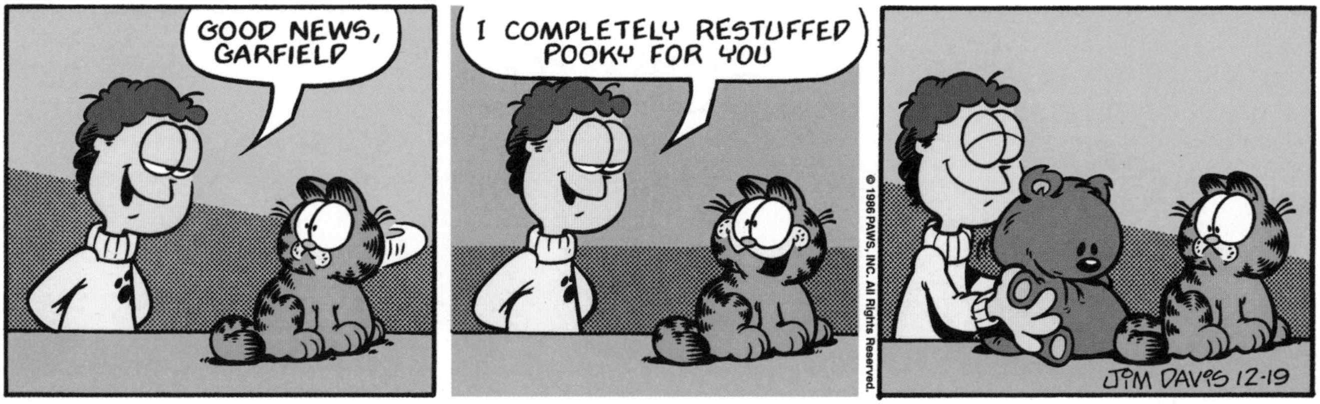
GOOD NEWS, GARFIELD
I COMPLETELY RESTUFFED POOKY FOR YOU
JIM DAVIS 12-19
© 1986 PAWS, INC. All Rights Reserved.

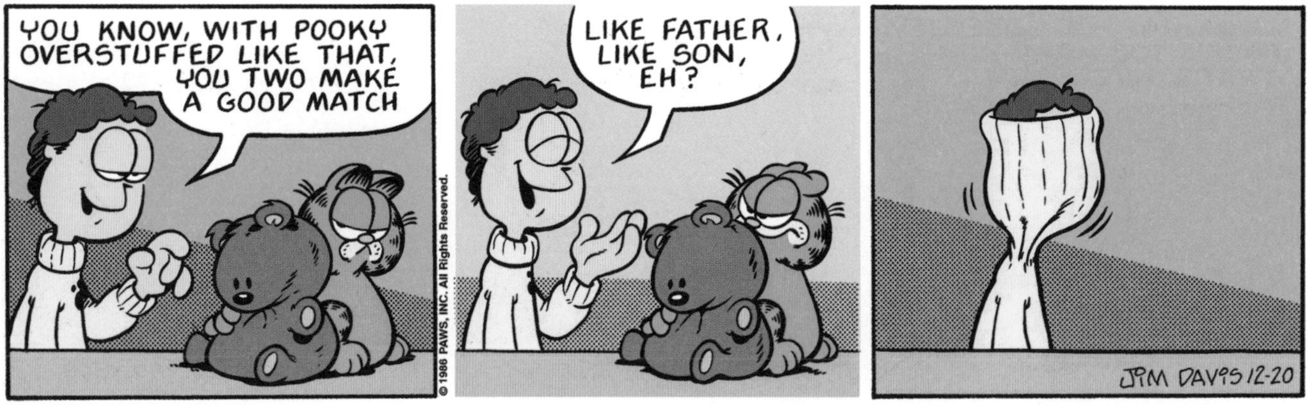
YOU KNOW, WITH POOKY OVERSTUFFED LIKE THAT, YOU TWO MAKE A GOOD MATCH
LIKE FATHER, LIKE SON, EH?
JIM DAVIS 12-20
© 1986 PAWS, INC. All Rights Reserved.

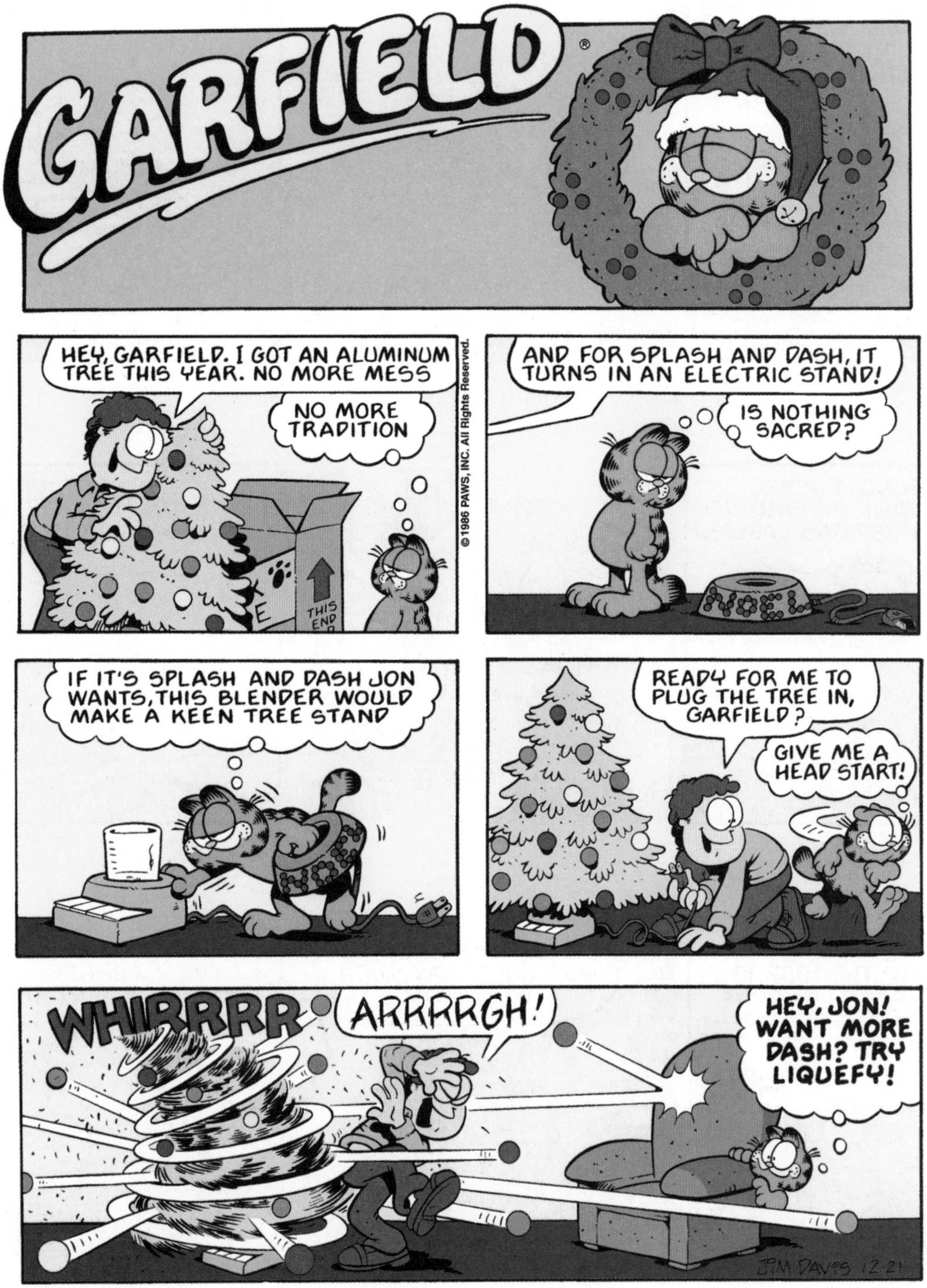
GARFIELD®
HEY, GARFIELD. I GOT AN ALUMINUM TREE THIS YEAR. NO MORE MESS
NO MORE TRADITION
THIS END
© 1986 PAWS, INC. All Rights Reserved.
AND FOR SPLASH AND DASH, IT TURNS IN AN ELECTRIC STAND!
IS NOTHING SACRED?
NOEL
IF IT'S SPLASH AND DASH JON WANTS, THIS BLENDER WOULD MAKE A KEEN TREE STAND
READY FOR ME TO PLUG THE TREE IN, GARFIELD?
GIVE ME A HEAD START!
WHIRRRR
ARRRRGH!
HEY, JON! WANT MORE DASH? TRY LIQUEFY!
JIM DAVIS 12-21

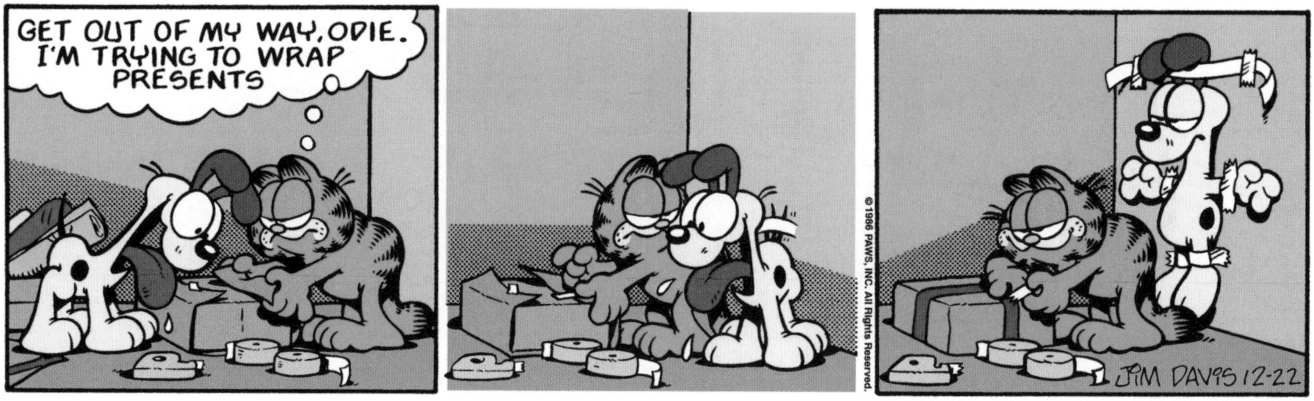
GET OUT OF MY WAY, ODIE. I'M TRYING TO WRAP PRESENTS
© 1986 PAWS, INC. All Rights Reserved.
JIM DAVIS 12-22

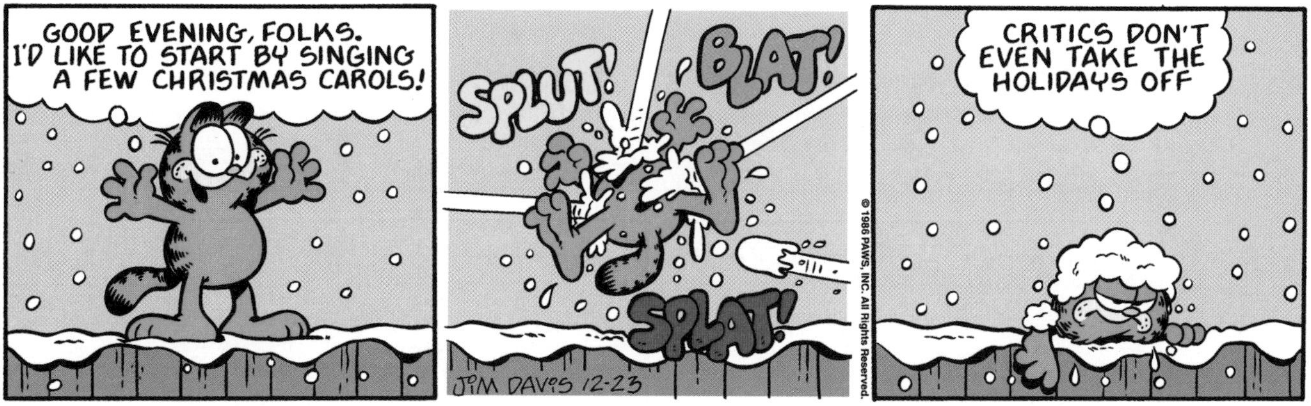
GOOD EVENING, FOLKS. I'D LIKE TO START BY SINGING A FEW CHRISTMAS CAROLS!
SPLUT!
BLAT!
SPLAT!
JIM DAVIS 12-23
© 1986 PAWS, INC. All Rights Reserved.
CRITICS DON'T EVEN TAKE THE HOLIDAYS OFF

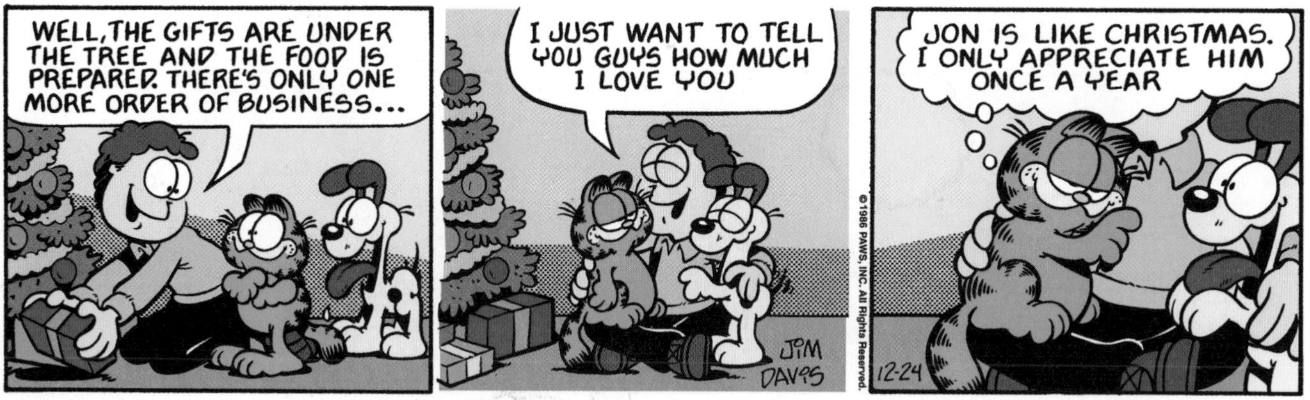
WELL, THE GIFTS ARE UNDER THE TREE AND THE FOOD IS PREPARED. THERE'S ONLY ONE MORE ORDER OF BUSINESS...
I JUST WANT TO TELL YOU GUYS HOW MUCH I LOVE YOU
JIM DAVIS
© 1986 PAWS, INC. All Rights Reserved.
JON IS LIKE CHRISTMAS. I ONLY APPRECIATE HIM ONCE A YEAR
12-24

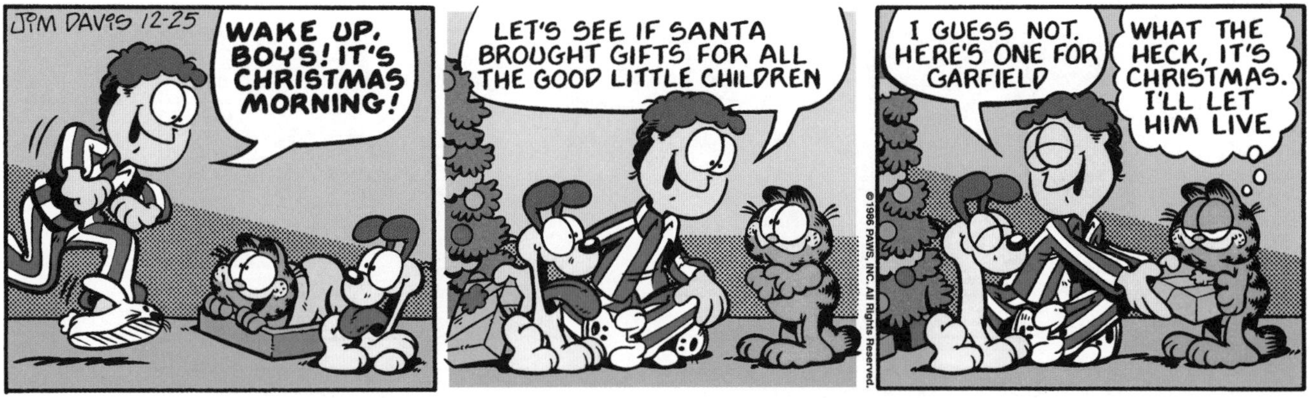
JIM DAVIS 12-25
WAKE UP, BOYS! IT'S CHRISTMAS MORNING!
LET'S SEE IF SANTA BROUGHT GIFTS FOR ALL THE GOOD LITTLE CHILDREN
© 1986 PAWS, INC. All Rights Reserved.
I GUESS NOT. HERE'S ONE FOR GARFIELD
WHAT THE HECK, IT'S CHRISTMAS. I'LL LET HIM LIVE

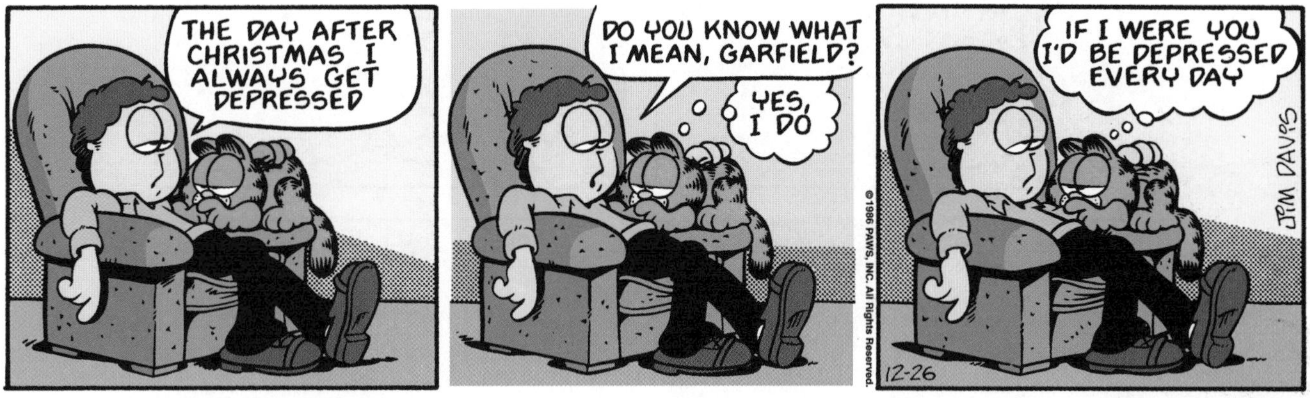
THE DAY AFTER CHRISTMAS I ALWAYS GET DEPRESSED
DO YOU KNOW WHAT I MEAN, GARFIELD?
YES, I DO
© 1986 PAWS, INC. All Rights Reserved.
IF I WERE YOU I'D BE DEPRESSED EVERY DAY
JIM DAVIS
12-26

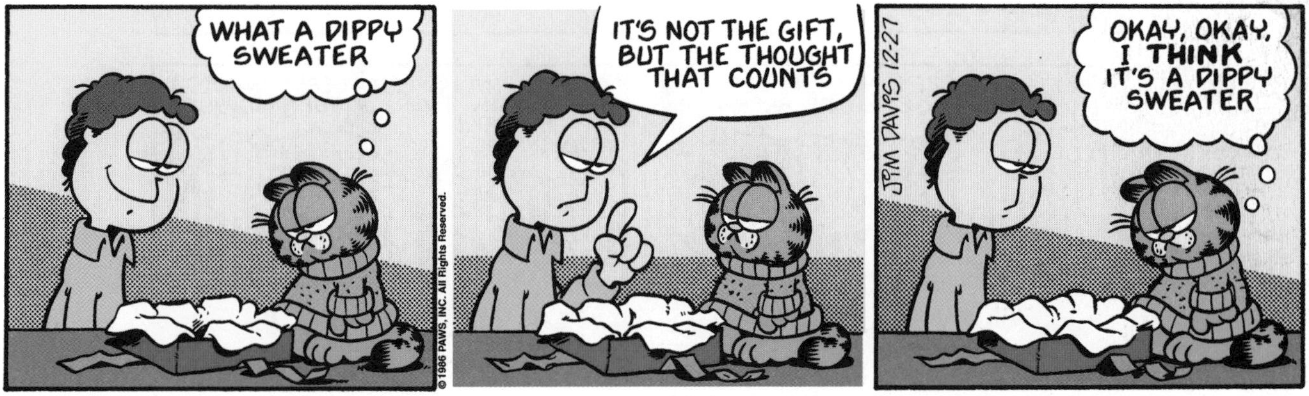
WHAT A DIPPY SWEATER
© 1986 PAWS, INC. All Rights Reserved.
IT'S NOT THE GIFT, BUT THE THOUGHT THAT COUNTS
JIM DAVIS 12-27
OKAY, OKAY, I **THINK** IT'S A DIPPY SWEATER

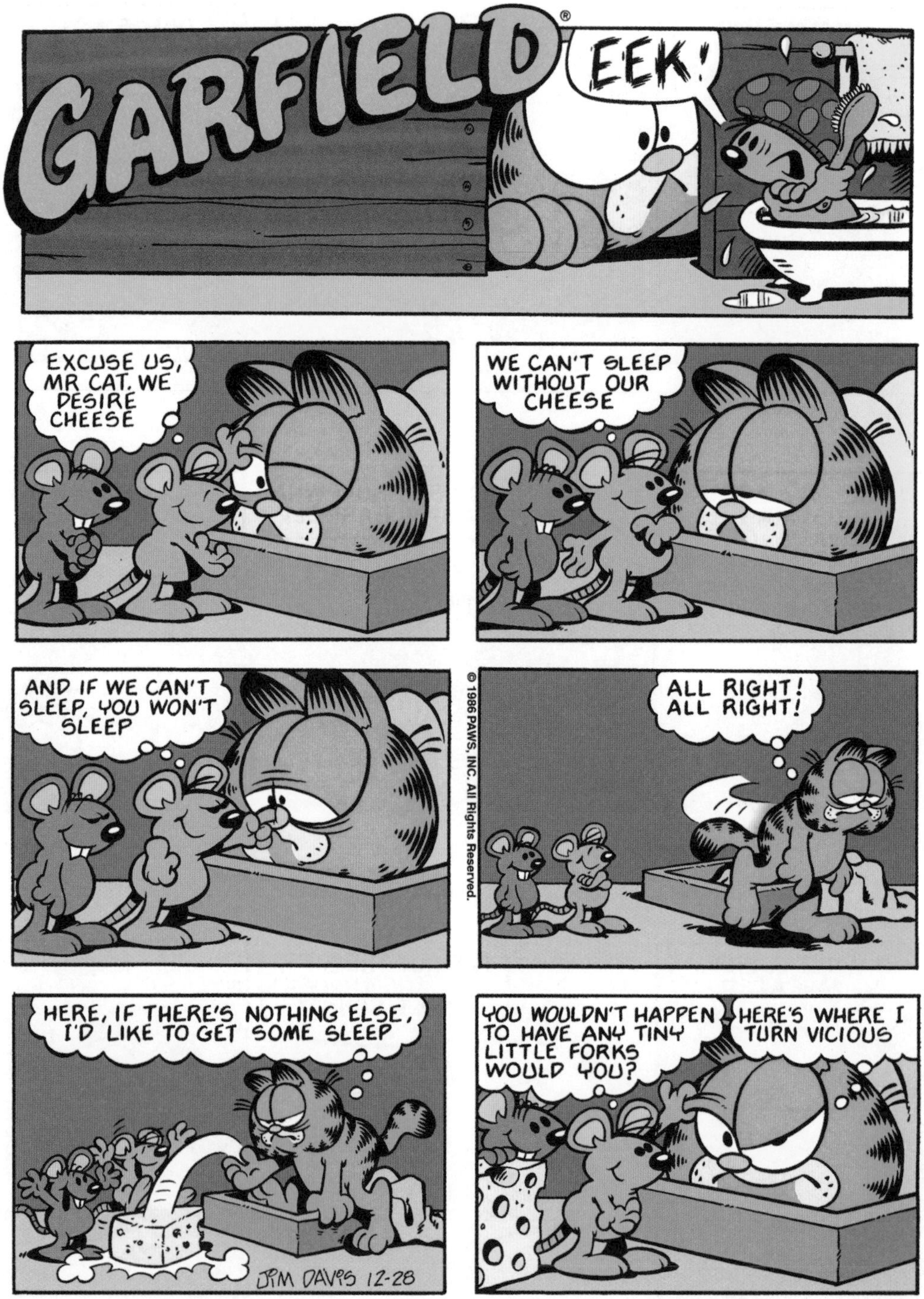
GARFIELD®
EEK!
EXCUSE US, MR CAT. WE DESIRE CHEESE
WE CAN'T SLEEP WITHOUT OUR CHEESE
AND IF WE CAN'T SLEEP, YOU WON'T SLEEP
ALL RIGHT! ALL RIGHT!
HERE, IF THERE'S NOTHING ELSE, I'D LIKE TO GET SOME SLEEP
YOU WOULDN'T HAPPEN TO HAVE ANY TINY LITTLE FORKS WOULD YOU?
HERE'S WHERE I TURN VICIOUS
JIM DAVIS 12-28

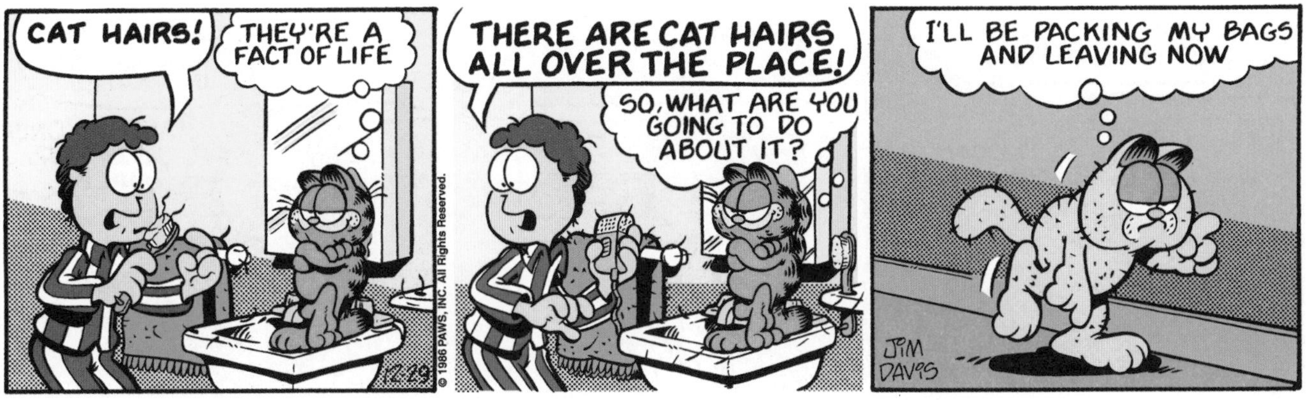
CAT HAIRS!
THEY'RE A FACT OF LIFE
THERE ARE CAT HAIRS ALL OVER THE PLACE!
SO, WHAT ARE YOU GOING TO DO ABOUT IT?
I'LL BE PACKING MY BAGS AND LEAVING NOW
© 1986 PAWS, INC. All Rights Reserved.

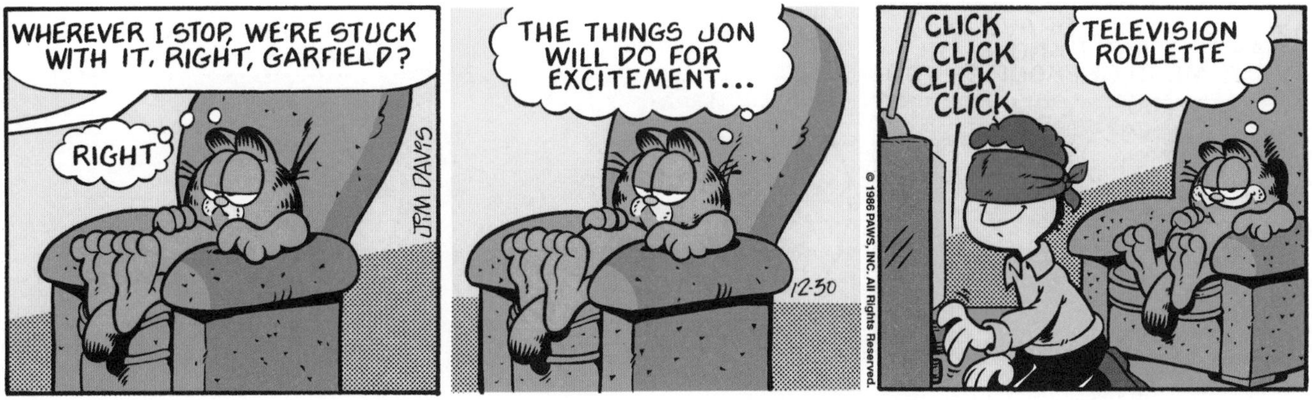
WHEREVER I STOP, WE'RE STUCK WITH IT, RIGHT, GARFIELD?
RIGHT
THE THINGS JON WILL DO FOR EXCITEMENT...
CLICK
CLICK
CLICK
CLICK
TELEVISION ROULETTE
© 1986 PAWS, INC. All Rights Reserved.

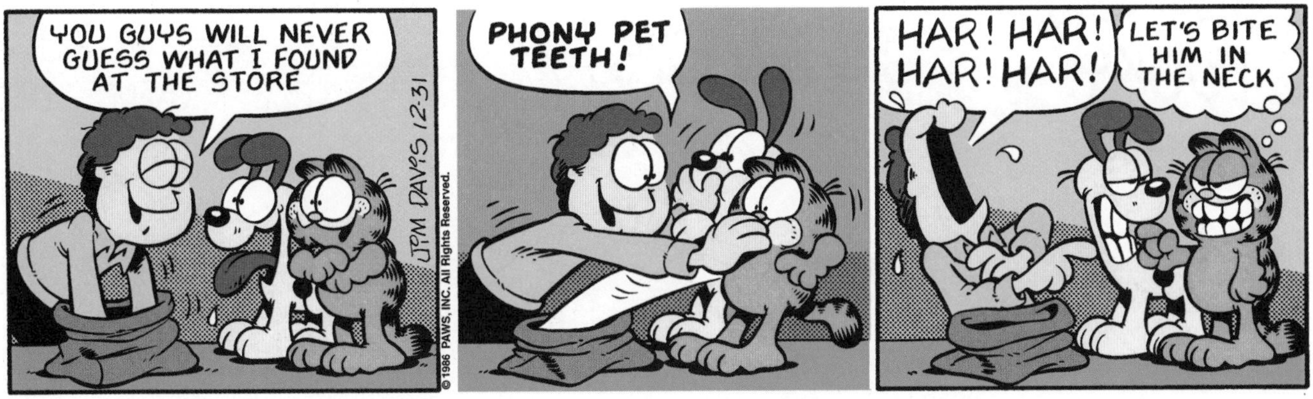
YOU GUYS WILL NEVER GUESS WHAT I FOUND AT THE STORE
PHONY PET TEETH!
HAR! HAR! HAR! HAR!
LET'S BITE HIM IN THE NECK
© 1986 PAWS, INC. All Rights Reserved.

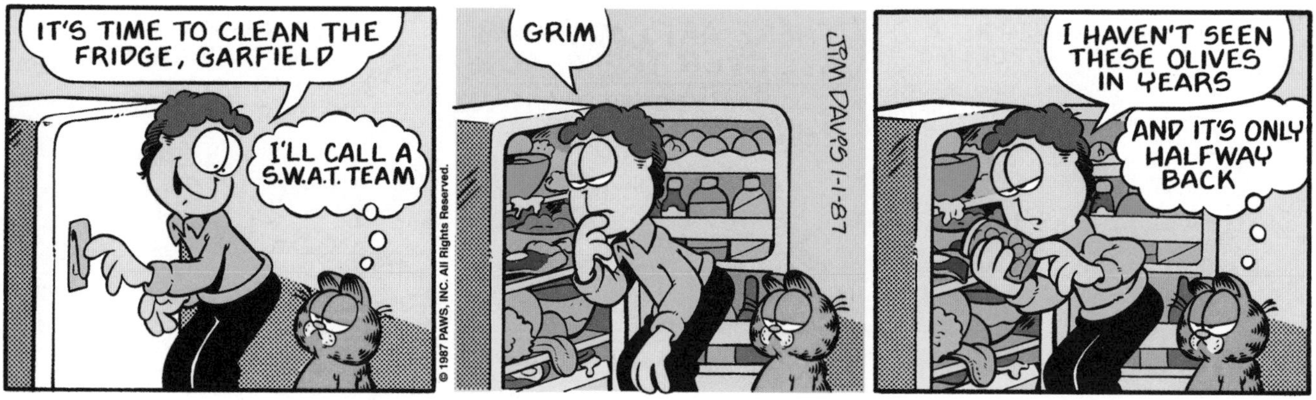
IT'S TIME TO CLEAN THE FRIDGE, GARFIELD
I'LL CALL A S.W.A.T. TEAM
© 1987 PAWS, INC. All Rights Reserved.
GRIM
JIM DAVIS 1-1-87
I HAVEN'T SEEN THESE OLIVES IN YEARS
AND IT'S ONLY HALFWAY BACK

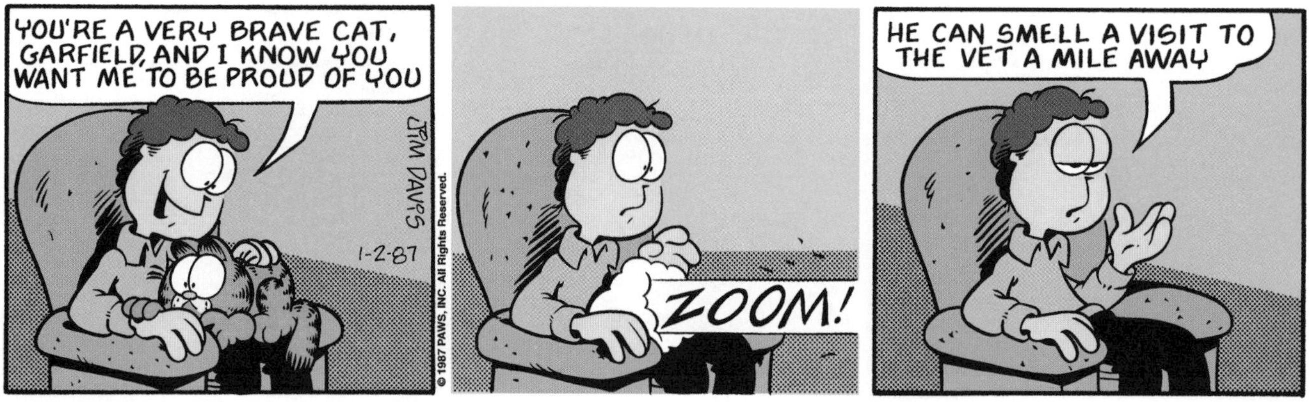
YOU'RE A VERY BRAVE CAT, GARFIELD, AND I KNOW YOU WANT ME TO BE PROUD OF YOU
JIM DAVIS 1-2-87
© 1987 PAWS, INC. All Rights Reserved.
ZOOM!
HE CAN SMELL A VISIT TO THE VET A MILE AWAY

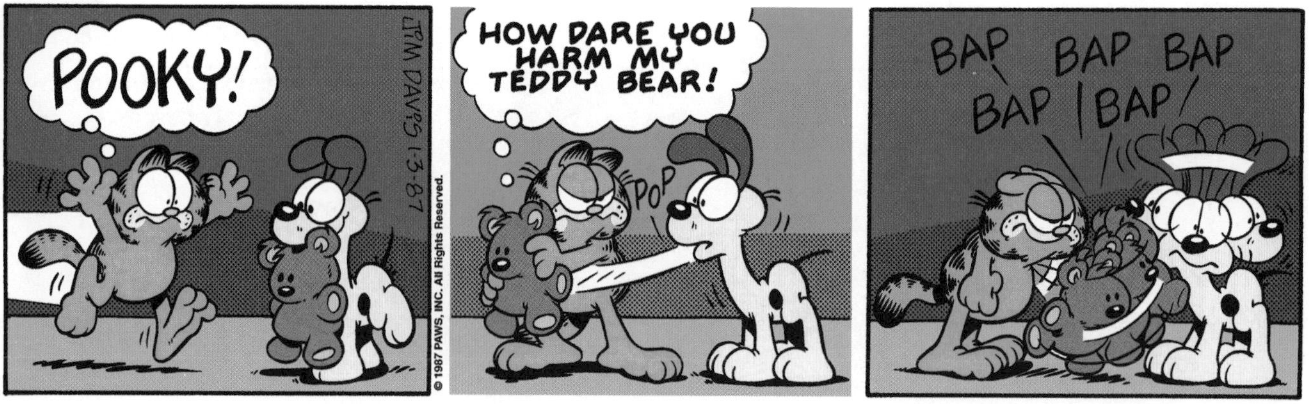
POOKY!
JIM DAVIS 1-3-87
© 1987 PAWS, INC. All Rights Reserved.
HOW DARE YOU HARM MY TEDDY BEAR!
POP
BAP BAP BAP
BAP BAP

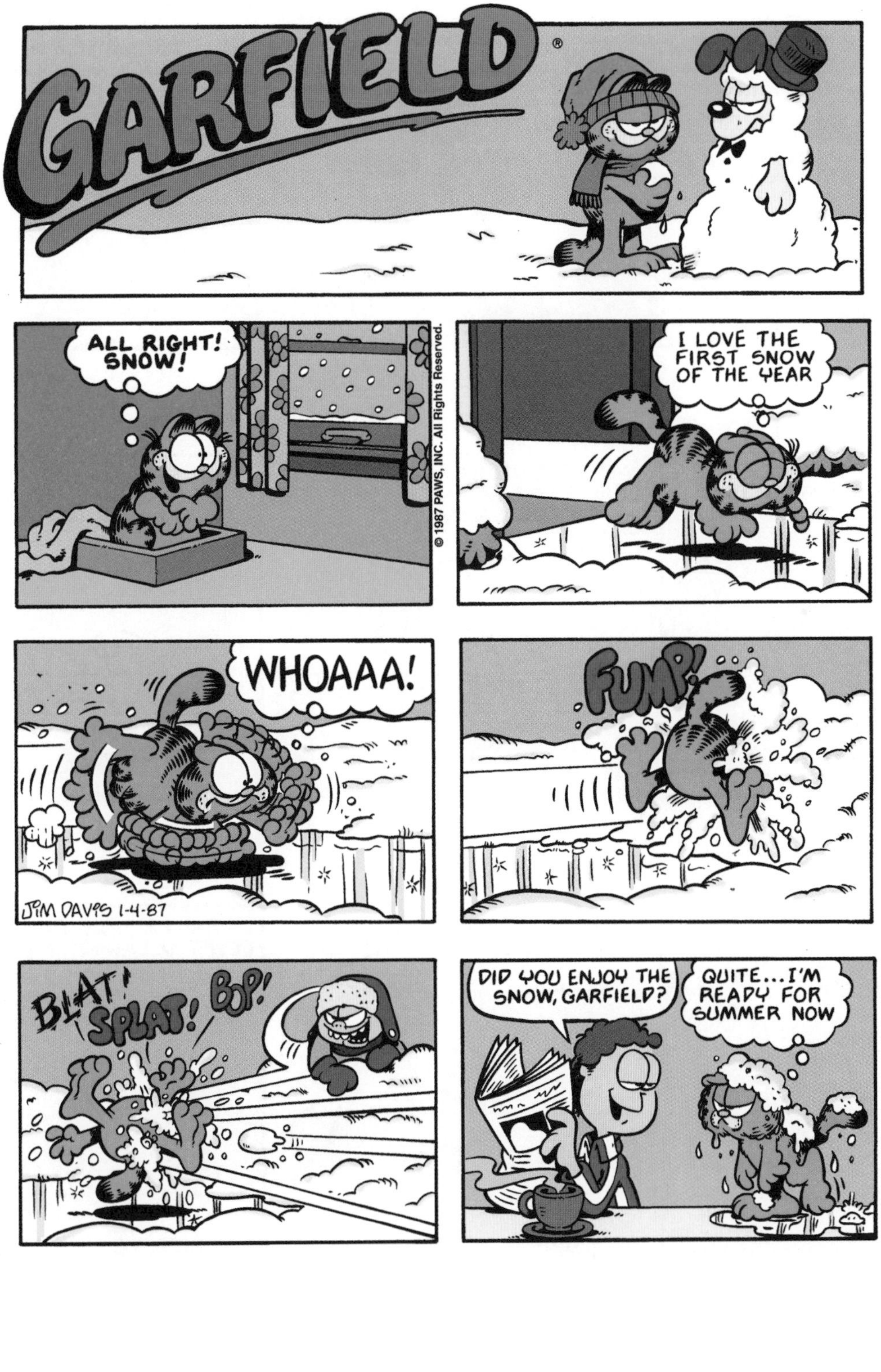
GARFIELD®
© 1987 PAWS, INC. All Rights Reserved.
ALL RIGHT! SNOW!
I LOVE THE FIRST SNOW OF THE YEAR
WHOAAA!
JIM DAVIS 1-4-87
FUMP!
BLAT! SPLAT! BOP!
DID YOU ENJOY THE SNOW, GARFIELD?
QUITE... I'M READY FOR SUMMER NOW

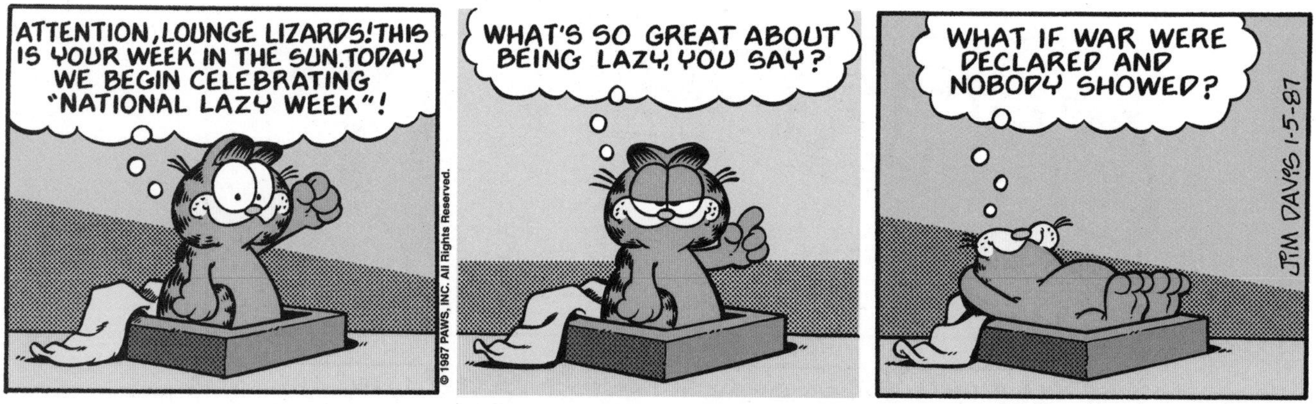
ATTENTION, LOUNGE LIZARDS! THIS IS YOUR WEEK IN THE SUN. TODAY WE BEGIN CELEBRATING "NATIONAL LAZY WEEK"!
WHAT'S SO GREAT ABOUT BEING LAZY, YOU SAY?
WHAT IF WAR WERE DECLARED AND NOBODY SHOWED?
© 1987 PAWS, INC. All Rights Reserved.
JIM DAVIS 1-5-87

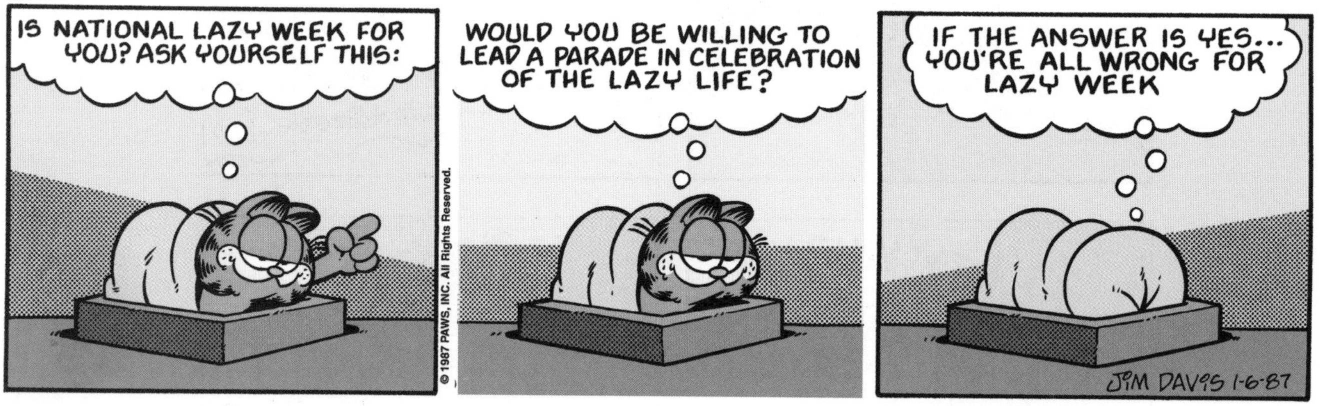
IS NATIONAL LAZY WEEK FOR YOU? ASK YOURSELF THIS:
WOULD YOU BE WILLING TO LEAD A PARADE IN CELEBRATION OF THE LAZY LIFE?
IF THE ANSWER IS YES... YOU'RE ALL WRONG FOR LAZY WEEK
© 1987 PAWS, INC. All Rights Reserved.
JIM DAVIS 1-6-87

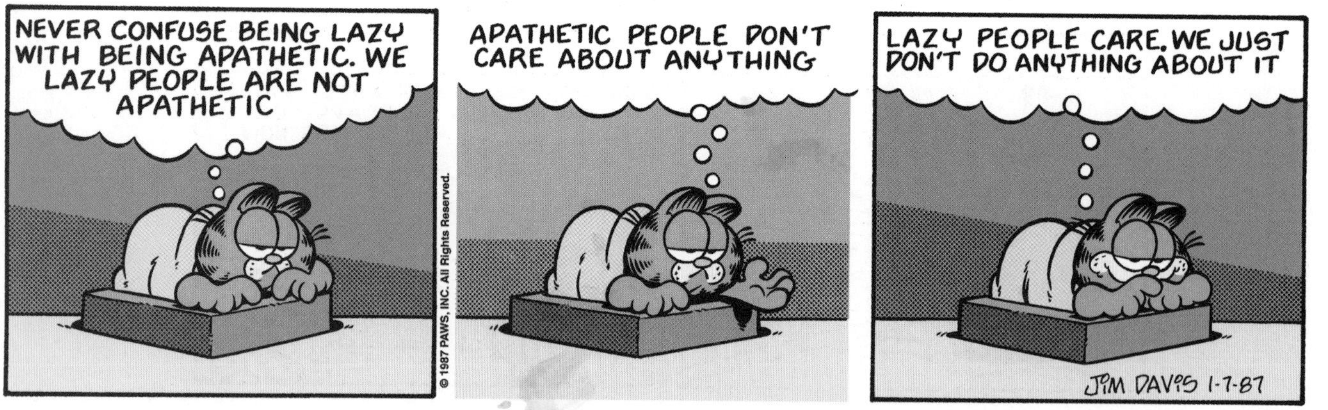
NEVER CONFUSE BEING LAZY WITH BEING APATHETIC. WE LAZY PEOPLE ARE NOT APATHETIC
APATHETIC PEOPLE DON'T CARE ABOUT ANYTHING
LAZY PEOPLE CARE. WE JUST DON'T DO ANYTHING ABOUT IT
© 1987 PAWS, INC. All Rights Reserved.
JIM DAVIS 1-7-87

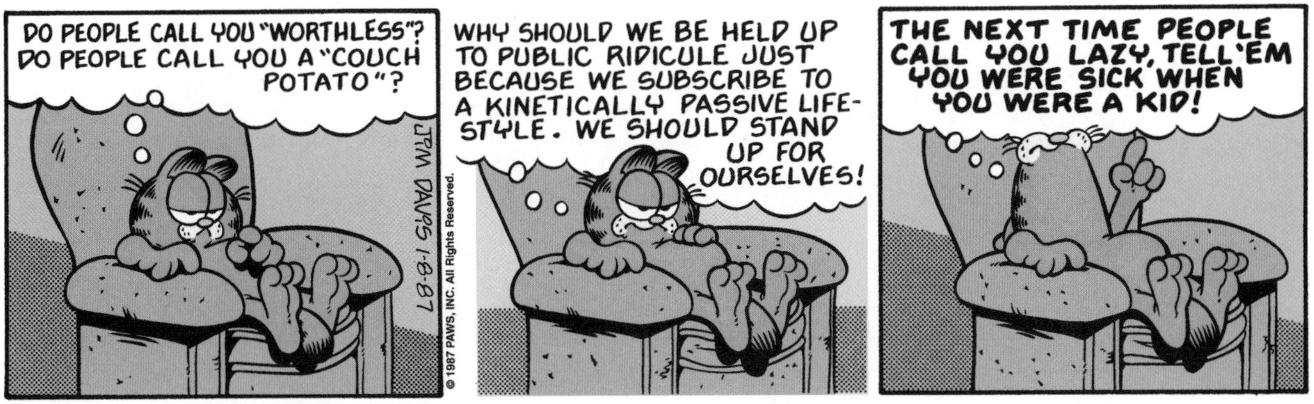
DO PEOPLE CALL YOU "WORTHLESS"? DO PEOPLE CALL YOU A "COUCH POTATO"?
JIM DAVIS 1-8-87
© 1987 PAWS, INC. All Rights Reserved.
WHY SHOULD WE BE HELD UP TO PUBLIC RIDICULE JUST BECAUSE WE SUBSCRIBE TO A KINETICALLY PASSIVE LIFE-STYLE. WE SHOULD STAND UP FOR OURSELVES!
THE NEXT TIME PEOPLE CALL YOU LAZY, TELL 'EM YOU WERE SICK WHEN YOU WERE A KID!

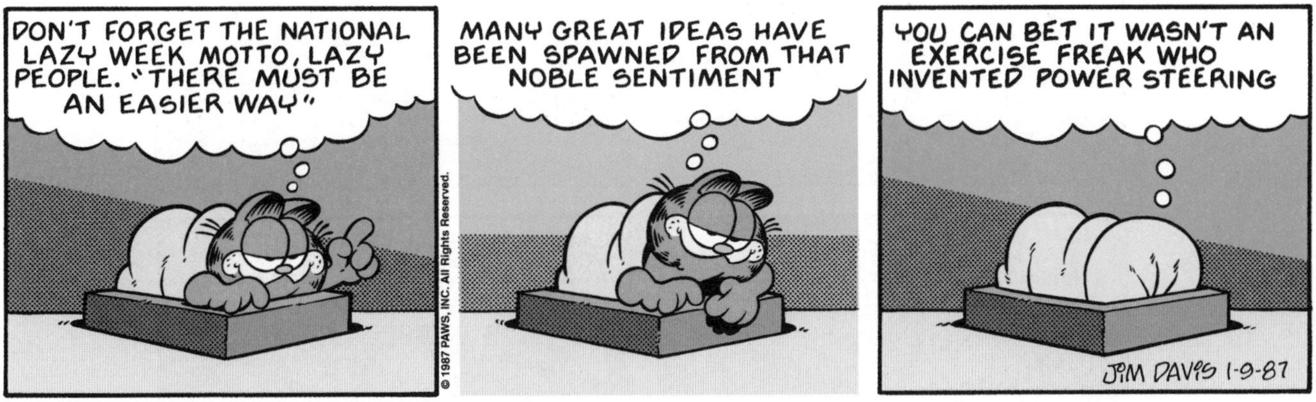
DON'T FORGET THE NATIONAL LAZY WEEK MOTTO, LAZY PEOPLE. "THERE MUST BE AN EASIER WAY"
© 1987 PAWS, INC. All Rights Reserved.
MANY GREAT IDEAS HAVE BEEN SPAWNED FROM THAT NOBLE SENTIMENT
YOU CAN BET IT WASN'T AN EXERCISE FREAK WHO INVENTED POWER STEERING
JIM DAVIS 1-9-87

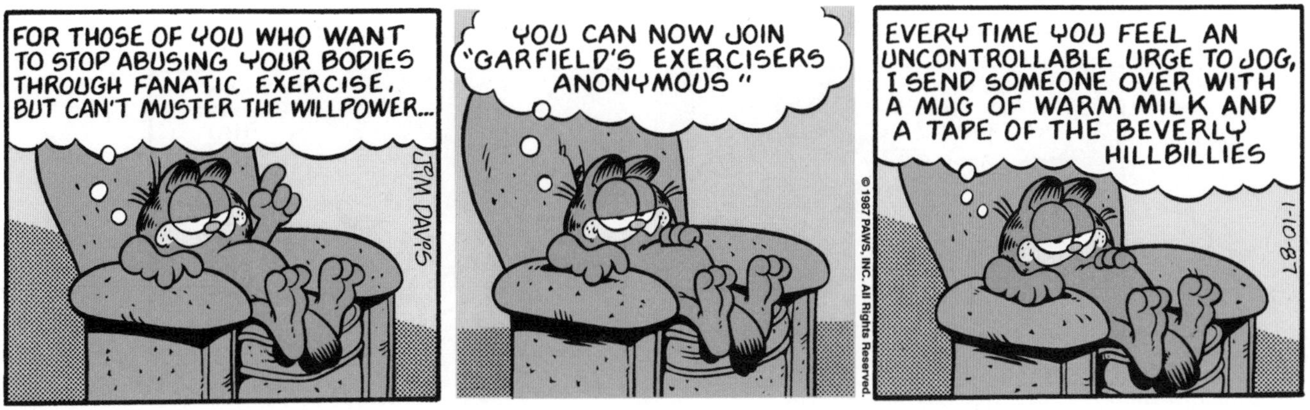
FOR THOSE OF YOU WHO WANT TO STOP ABUSING YOUR BODIES THROUGH FANATIC EXERCISE, BUT CAN'T MUSTER THE WILLPOWER...
JIM DAVIS
YOU CAN NOW JOIN "GARFIELD'S EXERCISERS ANONYMOUS"
© 1987 PAWS, INC. All Rights Reserved.
EVERY TIME YOU FEEL AN UNCONTROLLABLE URGE TO JOG, I SEND SOMEONE OVER WITH A MUG OF WARM MILK AND A TAPE OF THE BEVERLY HILLBILLIES
1-10-87

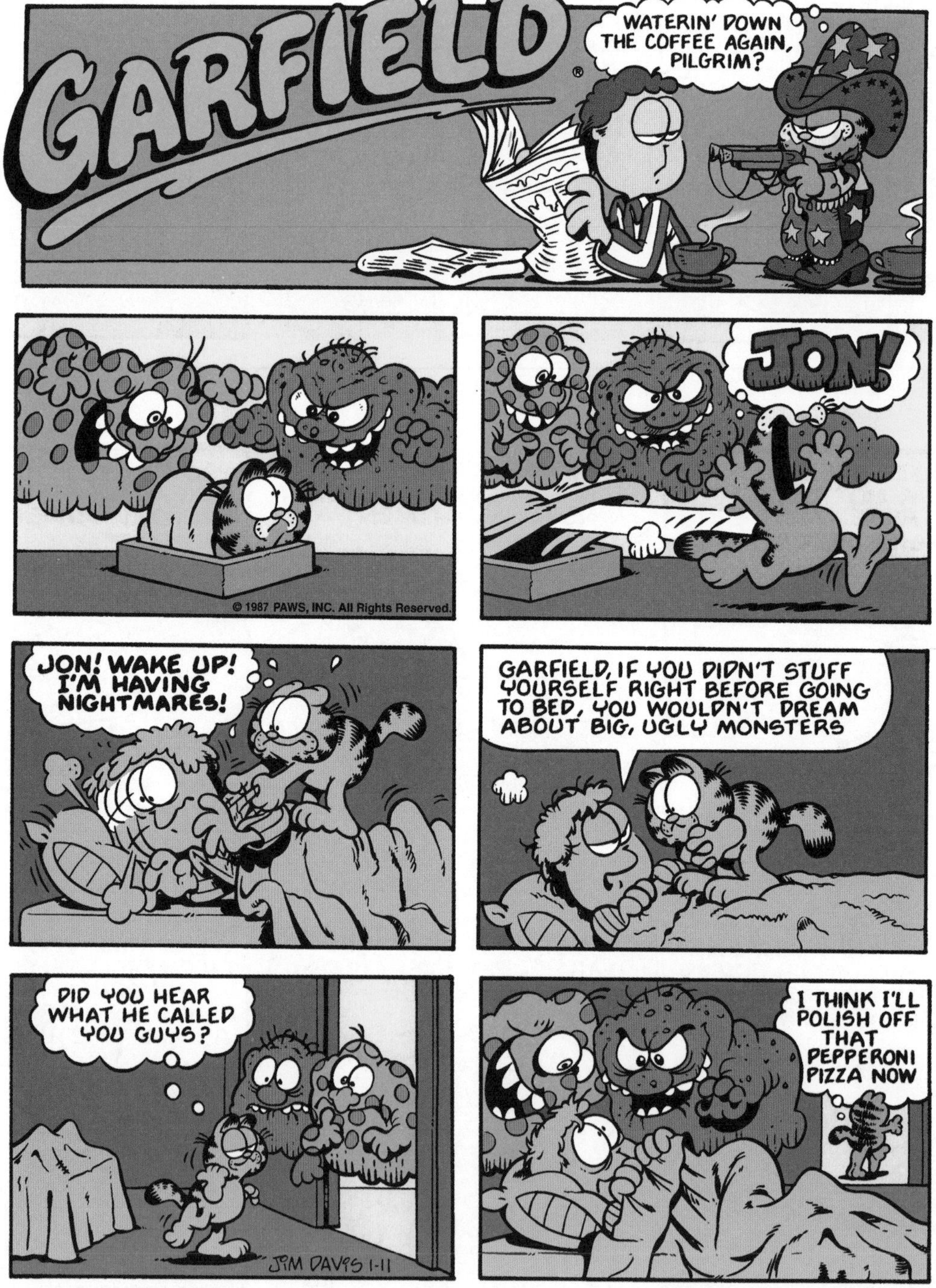
GARFIELD®
WATERIN' DOWN THE COFFEE AGAIN, PILGRIM?
© 1987 PAWS, INC. All Rights Reserved.
JON!
JON! WAKE UP! I'M HAVING NIGHTMARES!
GARFIELD, IF YOU DIDN'T STUFF YOURSELF RIGHT BEFORE GOING TO BED, YOU WOULDN'T DREAM ABOUT BIG, UGLY MONSTERS
DID YOU HEAR WHAT HE CALLED YOU GUYS?
JIM DAVIS 1-11
I THINK I'LL POLISH OFF THAT PEPPERONI PIZZA NOW

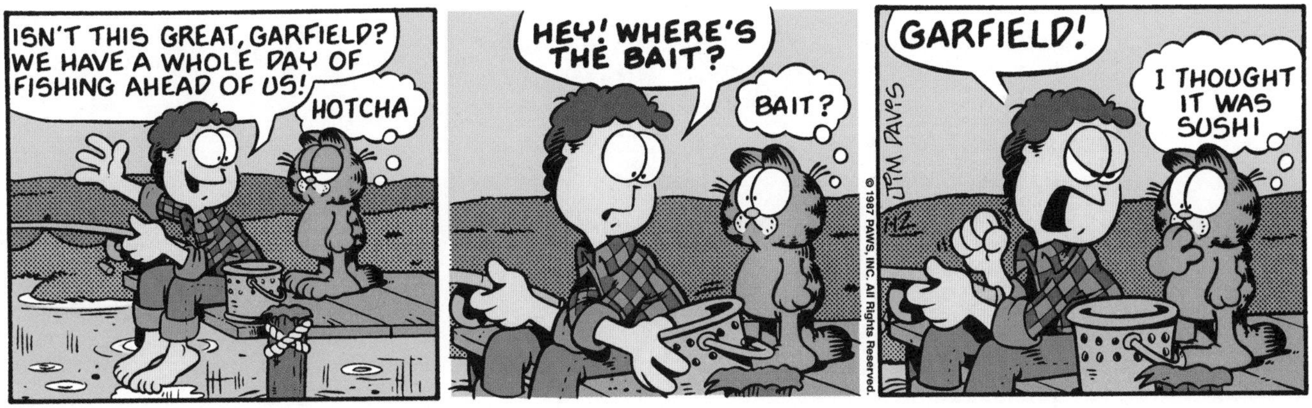
ISN'T THIS GREAT, GARFIELD? WE HAVE A WHOLE DAY OF FISHING AHEAD OF US!
HOTCHA
HEY! WHERE'S THE BAIT?
BAIT?
GARFIELD!
I THOUGHT IT WAS SUSHI
© 1987 PAWS, INC. All Rights Reserved.
JIM DAVIS 1-12

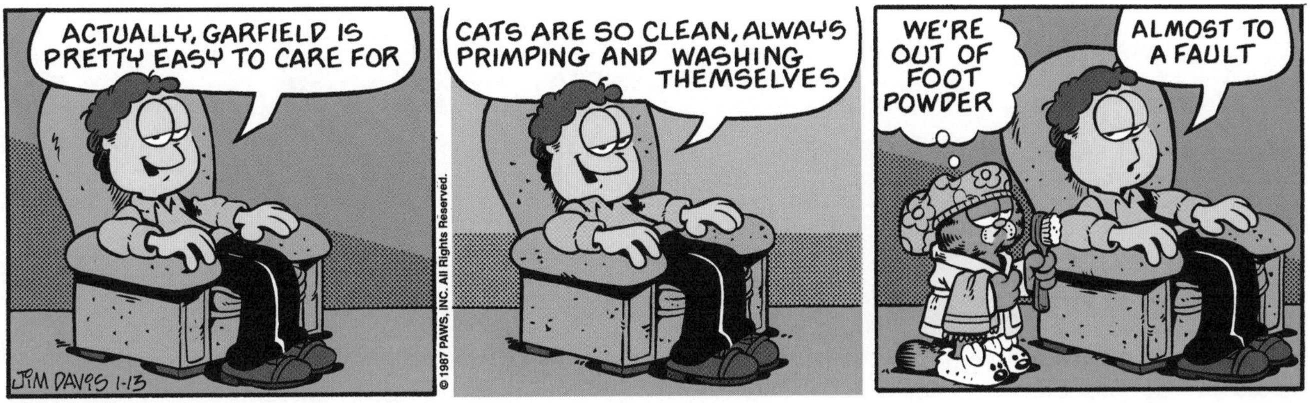
ACTUALLY, GARFIELD IS PRETTY EASY TO CARE FOR
CATS ARE SO CLEAN, ALWAYS PRIMPING AND WASHING THEMSELVES
WE'RE OUT OF FOOT POWDER
ALMOST TO A FAULT
JIM DAVIS 1-13
© 1987 PAWS, INC. All Rights Reserved.

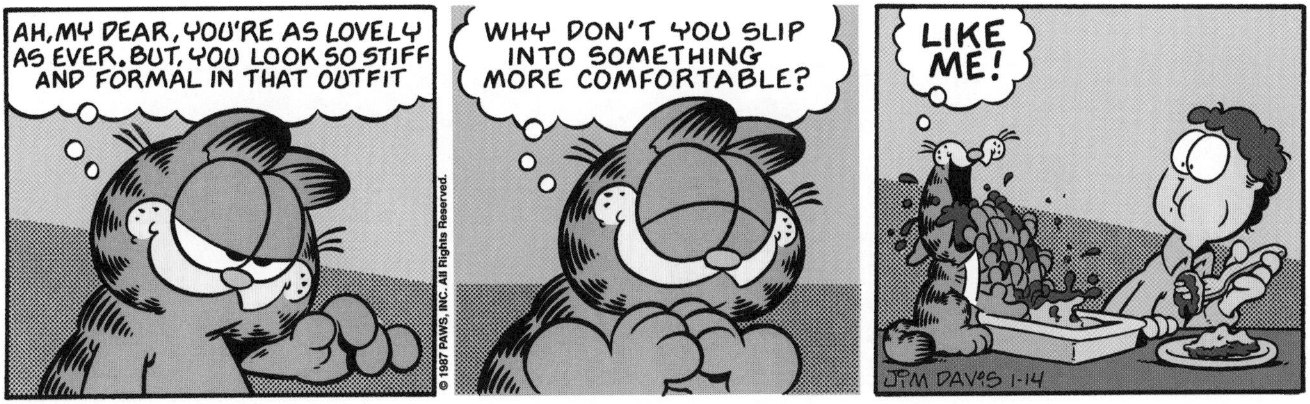
AH, MY DEAR, YOU'RE AS LOVELY AS EVER. BUT, YOU LOOK SO STIFF AND FORMAL IN THAT OUTFIT
WHY DON'T YOU SLIP INTO SOMETHING MORE COMFORTABLE?
LIKE ME!
© 1987 PAWS, INC. All Rights Reserved.
JIM DAVIS 1-14

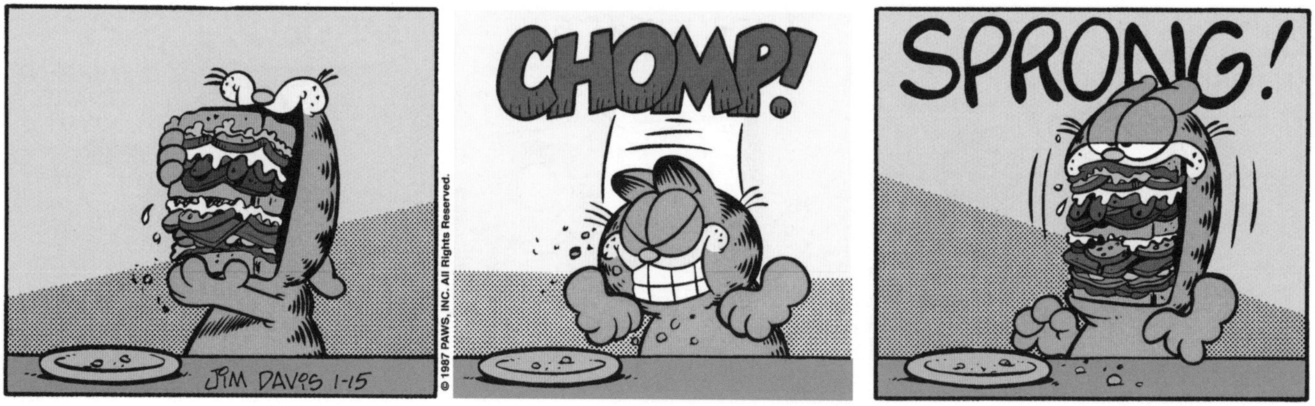
JIM DAVIS 1-15
CHOMP!
© 1987 PAWS, INC. All Rights Reserved.
SPRONG!

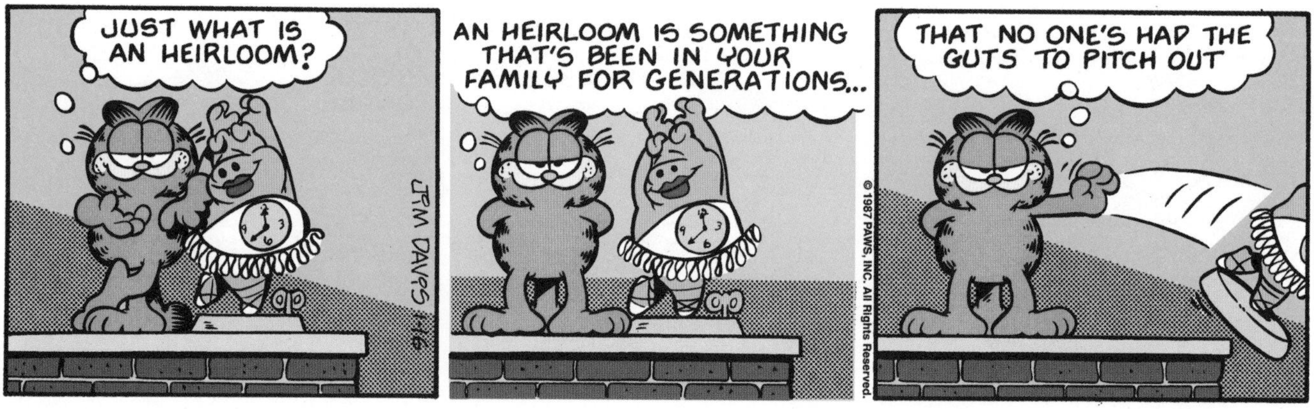
JUST WHAT IS AN HEIRLOOM?
JIM DAVIS 1-16
AN HEIRLOOM IS SOMETHING THAT'S BEEN IN YOUR FAMILY FOR GENERATIONS...
© 1987 PAWS, INC. All Rights Reserved.
THAT NO ONE'S HAD THE GUTS TO PITCH OUT

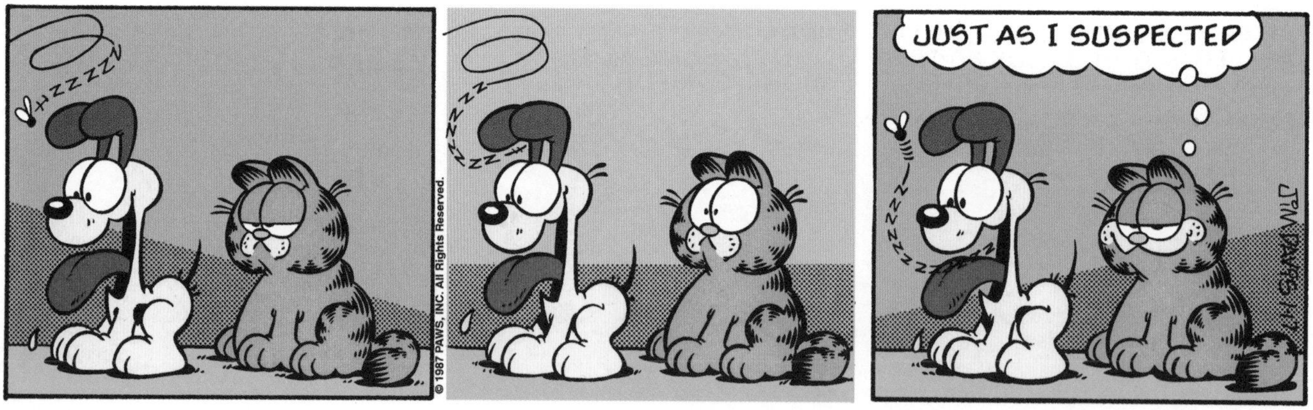
ZZZZZ
© 1987 PAWS, INC. All Rights Reserved.
ZZZ
JUST AS I SUSPECTED
JIM DAVIS 1-17

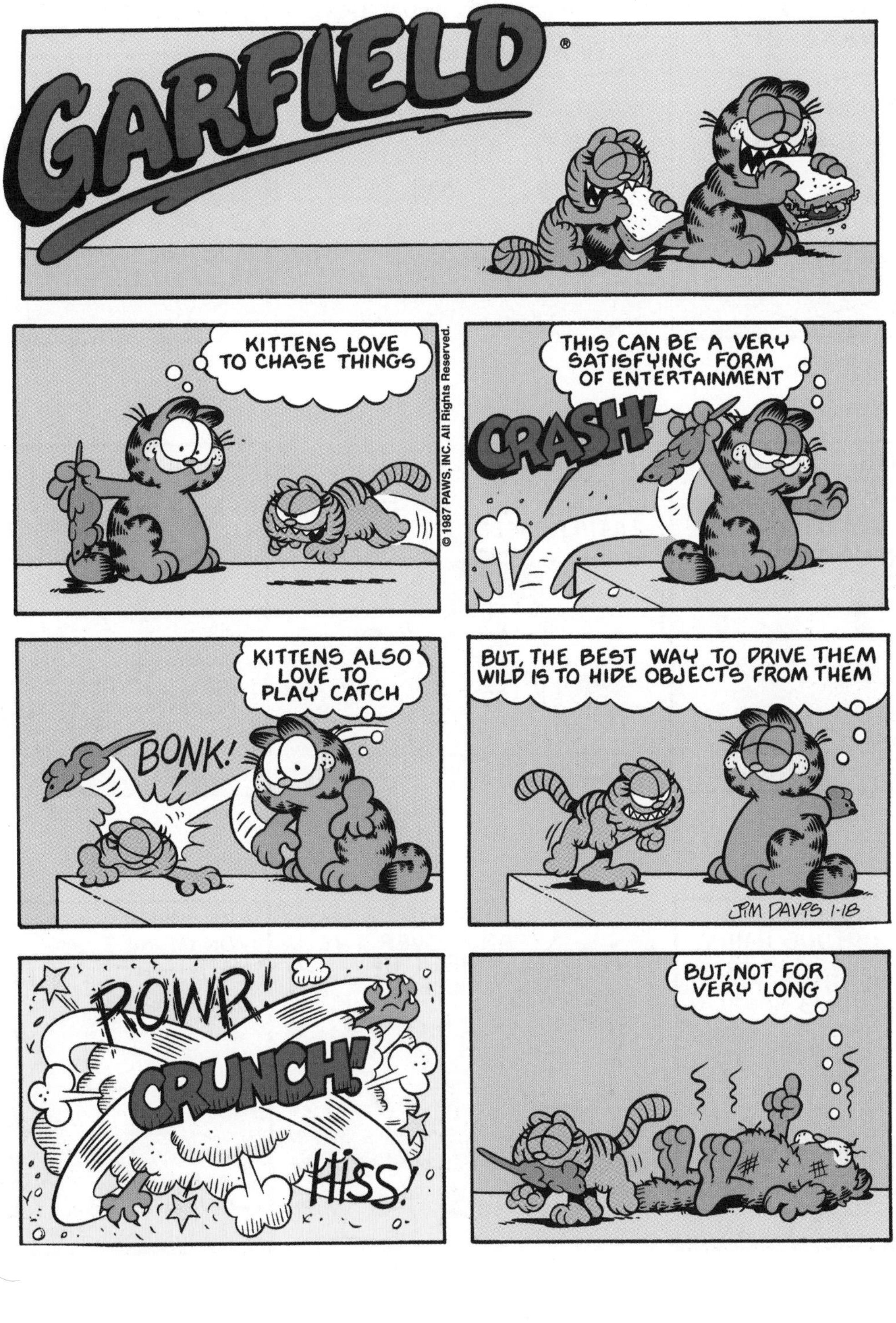
GARFIELD®
© 1987 PAWS, INC. All Rights Reserved.
KITTENS LOVE TO CHASE THINGS
THIS CAN BE A VERY SATISFYING FORM OF ENTERTAINMENT
CRASH!
KITTENS ALSO LOVE TO PLAY CATCH
BONK!
BUT, THE BEST WAY TO DRIVE THEM WILD IS TO HIDE OBJECTS FROM THEM
JIM DAVIS 1-18
ROWR!
CRUNCH!
HISS!
BUT, NOT FOR VERY LONG

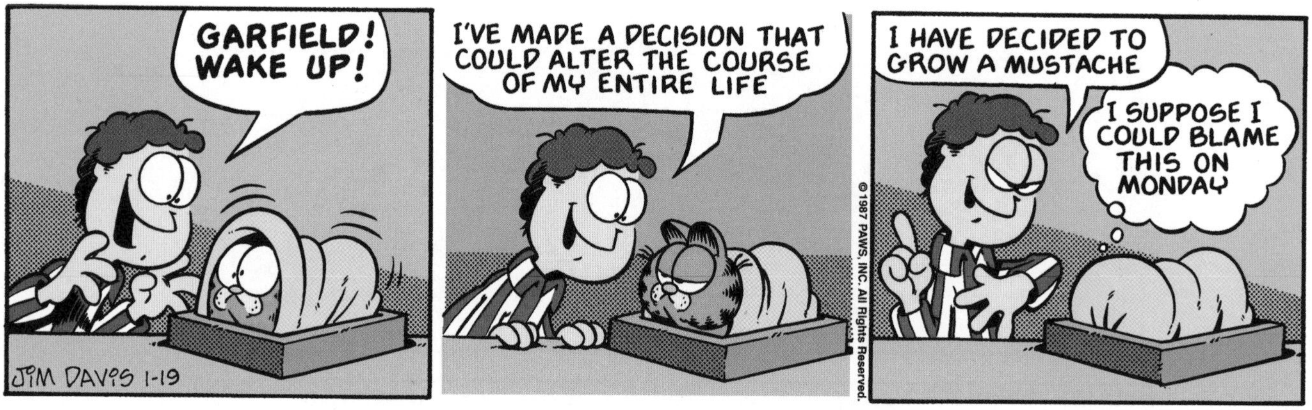
GARFIELD! WAKE UP!
JIM DAVIS 1-19
I'VE MADE A DECISION THAT COULD ALTER THE COURSE OF MY ENTIRE LIFE
© 1987 PAWS, INC. All Rights Reserved.
I HAVE DECIDED TO GROW A MUSTACHE
I SUPPOSE I COULD BLAME THIS ON MONDAY

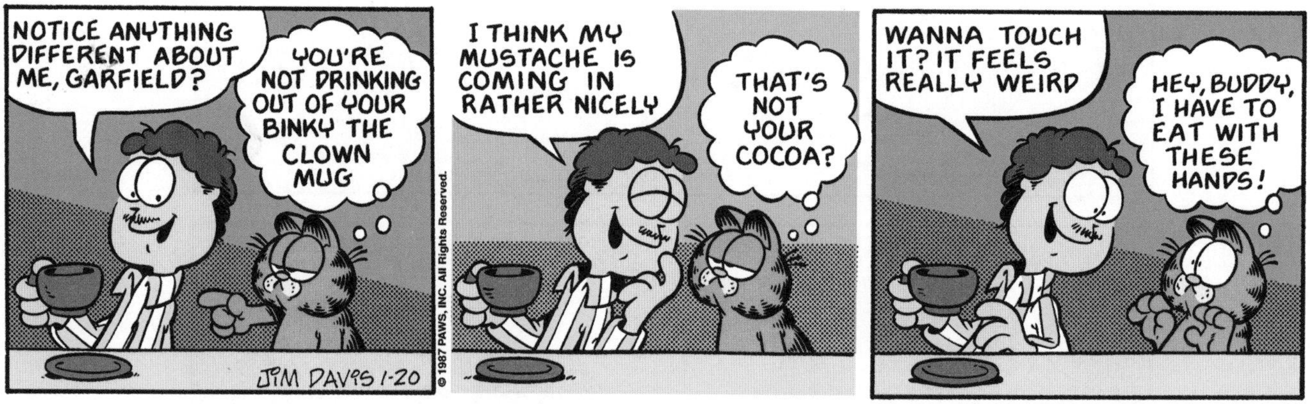
NOTICE ANYTHING DIFFERENT ABOUT ME, GARFIELD?
YOU'RE NOT DRINKING OUT OF YOUR BINKY THE CLOWN MUG
JIM DAVIS 1-20
© 1987 PAWS, INC. All Rights Reserved.
I THINK MY MUSTACHE IS COMING IN RATHER NICELY
THAT'S NOT YOUR COCOA?
WANNA TOUCH IT? IT FEELS REALLY WEIRD
HEY, BUDDY, I HAVE TO EAT WITH THESE HANDS!

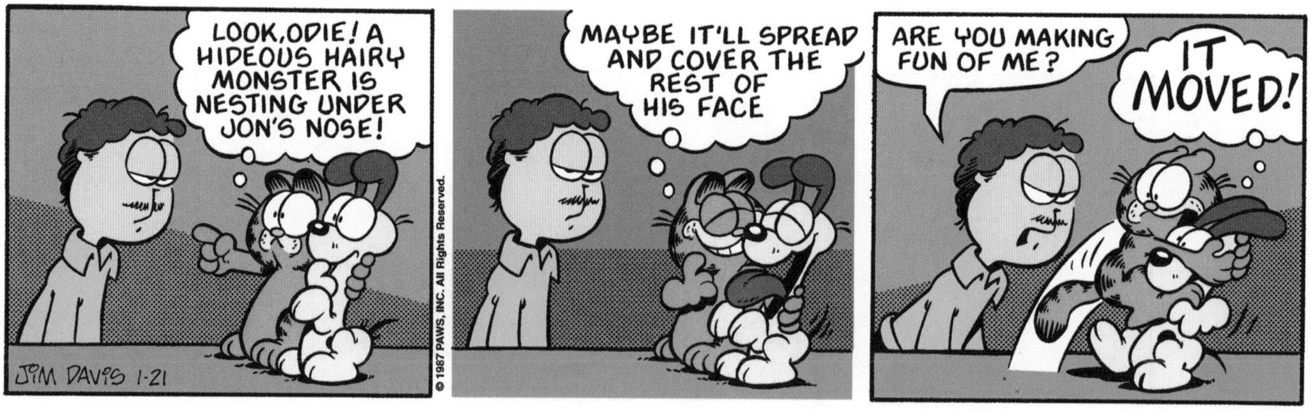
LOOK, ODIE! A HIDEOUS HAIRY MONSTER IS NESTING UNDER JON'S NOSE!
JIM DAVIS 1-21
© 1987 PAWS, INC. All Rights Reserved.
MAYBE IT'LL SPREAD AND COVER THE REST OF HIS FACE
ARE YOU MAKING FUN OF ME?
IT MOVED!

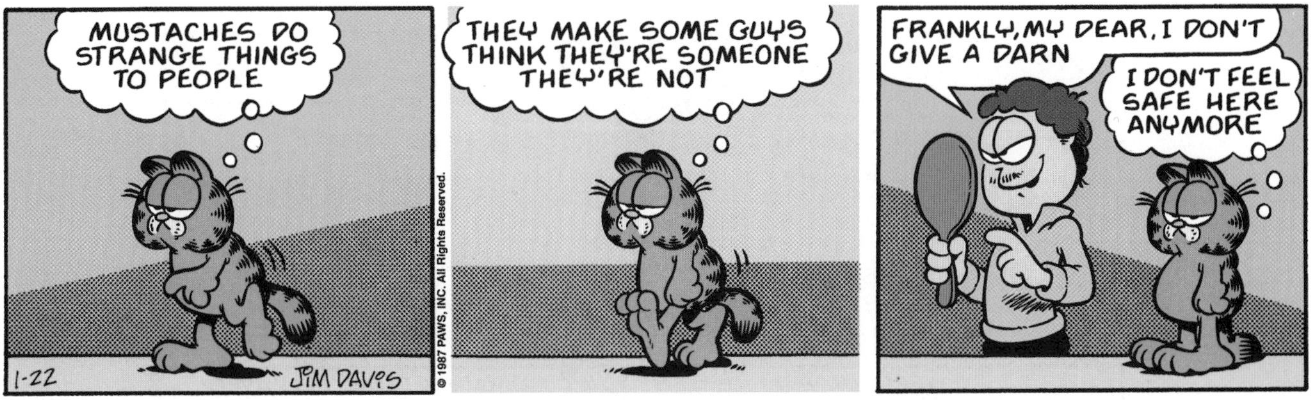
MUSTACHES DO STRANGE THINGS TO PEOPLE
1-22
JIM DAVIS
© 1987 PAWS, INC. All Rights Reserved.
THEY MAKE SOME GUYS THINK THEY'RE SOMEONE THEY'RE NOT
FRANKLY, MY DEAR, I DON'T GIVE A DARN
I DON'T FEEL SAFE HERE ANYMORE

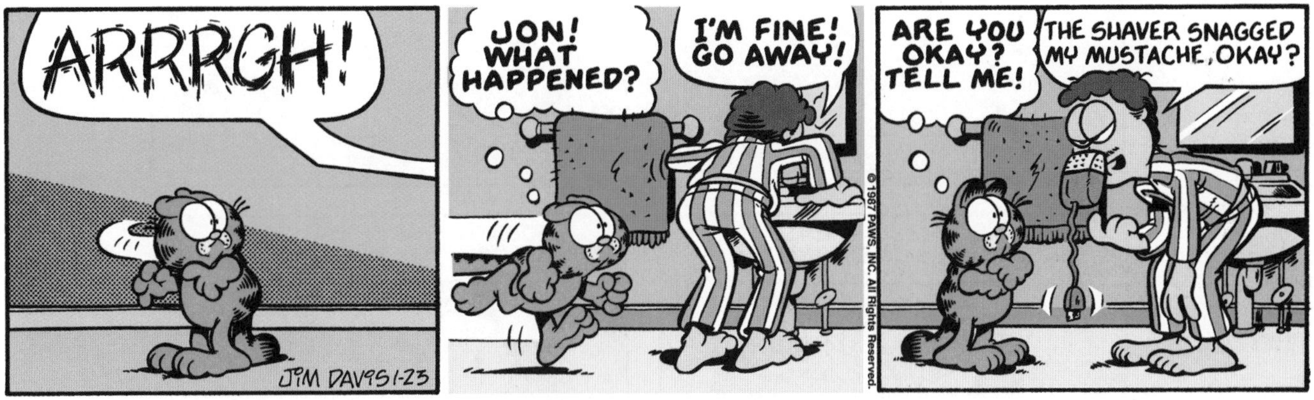
ARRRGH!
JIM DAVIS 1-23
JON! WHAT HAPPENED?
I'M FINE! GO AWAY!
© 1987 PAWS, INC. All Rights Reserved.
ARE YOU OKAY? TELL ME!
THE SHAVER SNAGGED MY MUSTACHE, OKAY?

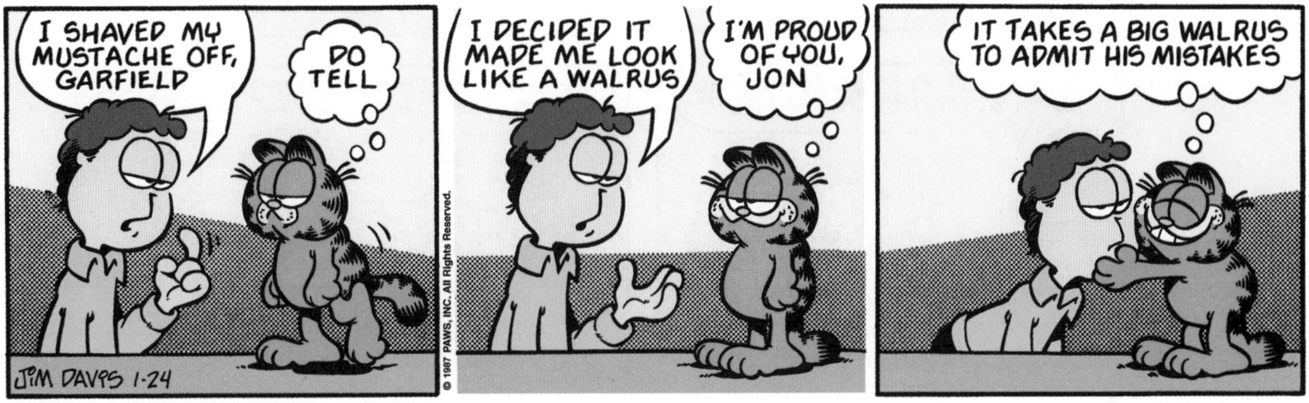
I SHAVED MY MUSTACHE OFF, GARFIELD
DO TELL
JIM DAVIS 1-24
© 1987 PAWS, INC. All Rights Reserved.
I DECIDED IT MADE ME LOOK LIKE A WALRUS
I'M PROUD OF YOU, JON
IT TAKES A BIG WALRUS TO ADMIT HIS MISTAKES

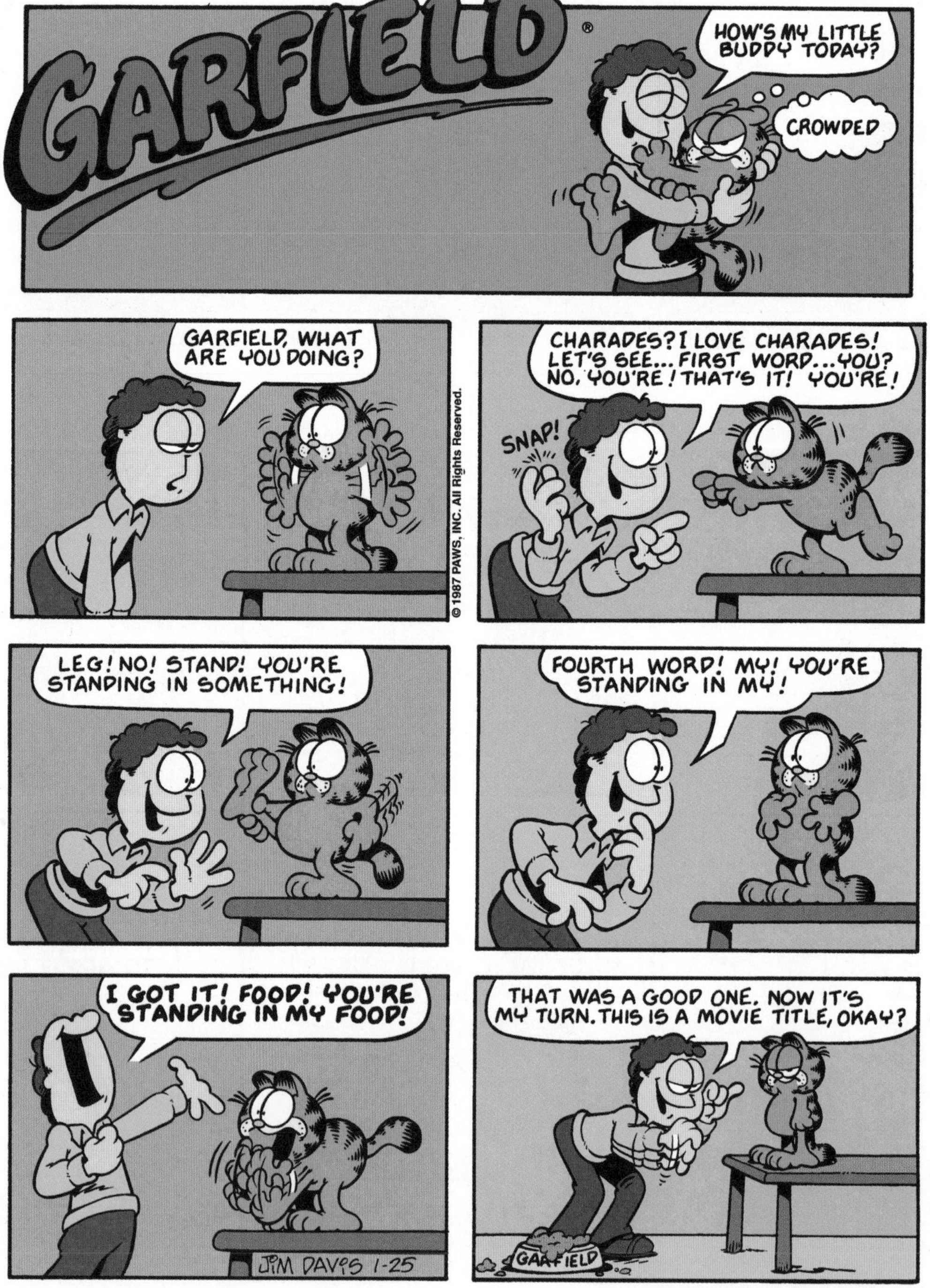
GARFIELD®
HOW'S MY LITTLE BUDDY TODAY?
CROWDED
GARFIELD, WHAT ARE YOU DOING?
© 1987 PAWS, INC. All Rights Reserved.
CHARADES? I LOVE CHARADES! LET'S SEE... FIRST WORD... YOU? NO, YOU'RE! THAT'S IT! YOU'RE!
SNAP!
LEG! NO! STAND! YOU'RE STANDING IN SOMETHING!
FOURTH WORD! MY! YOU'RE STANDING IN MY!
I GOT IT! FOOD! YOU'RE STANDING IN MY FOOD!
JIM DAVIS 1-25
THAT WAS A GOOD ONE. NOW IT'S MY TURN. THIS IS A MOVIE TITLE, OKAY?
GARFIELD

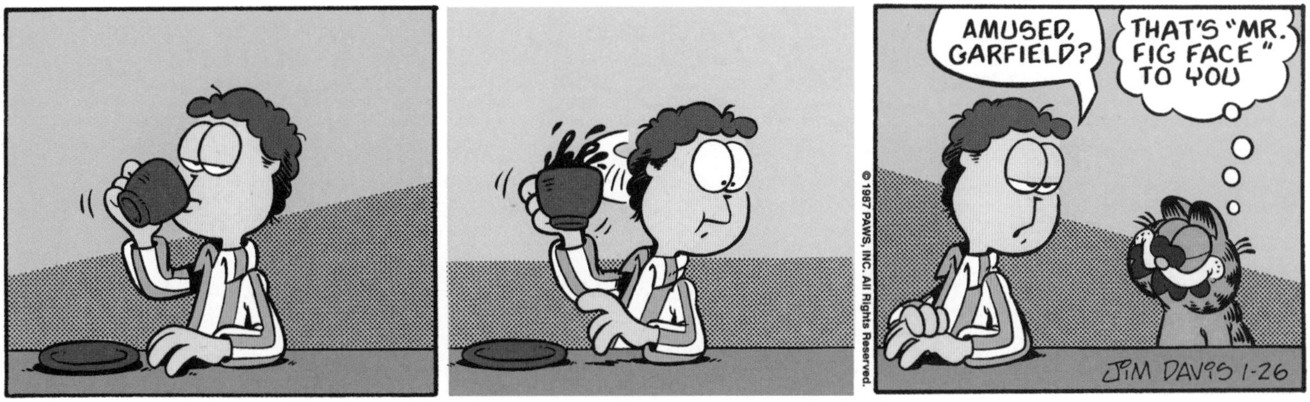
AMUSED, GARFIELD?
THAT'S "MR. FIG FACE" TO YOU
© 1987 PAWS, INC. All Rights Reserved.
JIM DAVIS 1-26

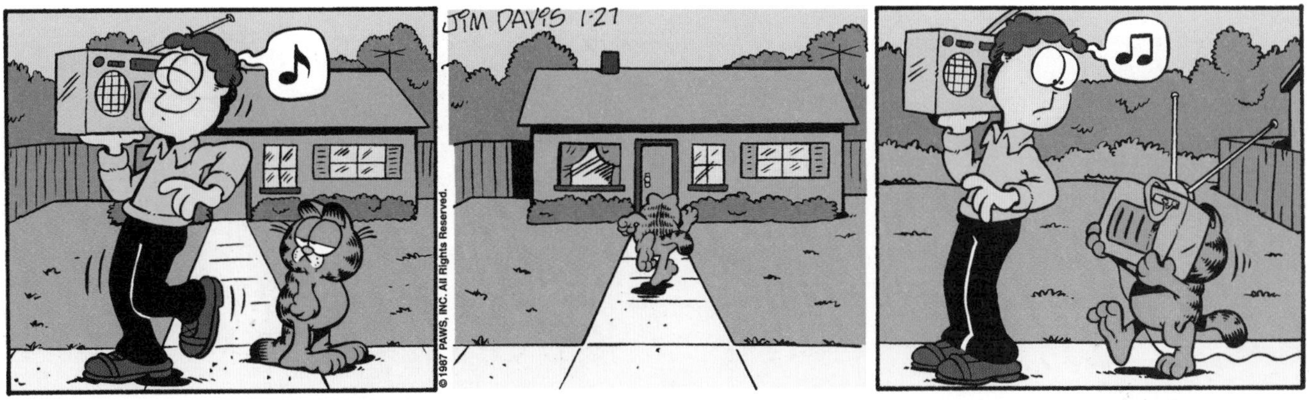
JIM DAVIS 1-27
© 1987 PAWS, INC. All Rights Reserved.

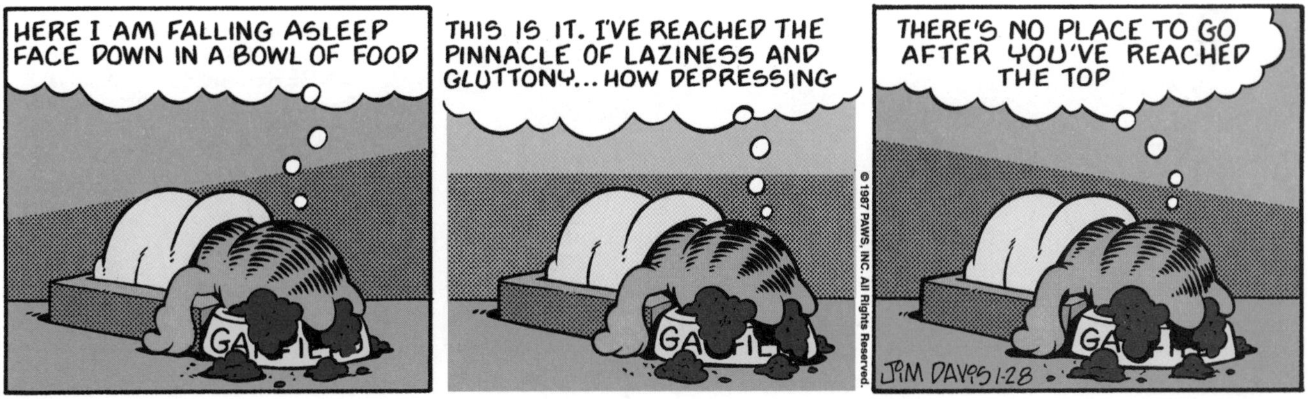
HERE I AM FALLING ASLEEP FACE DOWN IN A BOWL OF FOOD
THIS IS IT. I'VE REACHED THE PINNACLE OF LAZINESS AND GLUTTONY... HOW DEPRESSING
THERE'S NO PLACE TO GO AFTER YOU'VE REACHED THE TOP
© 1987 PAWS, INC. All Rights Reserved.
JIM DAVIS 1-28

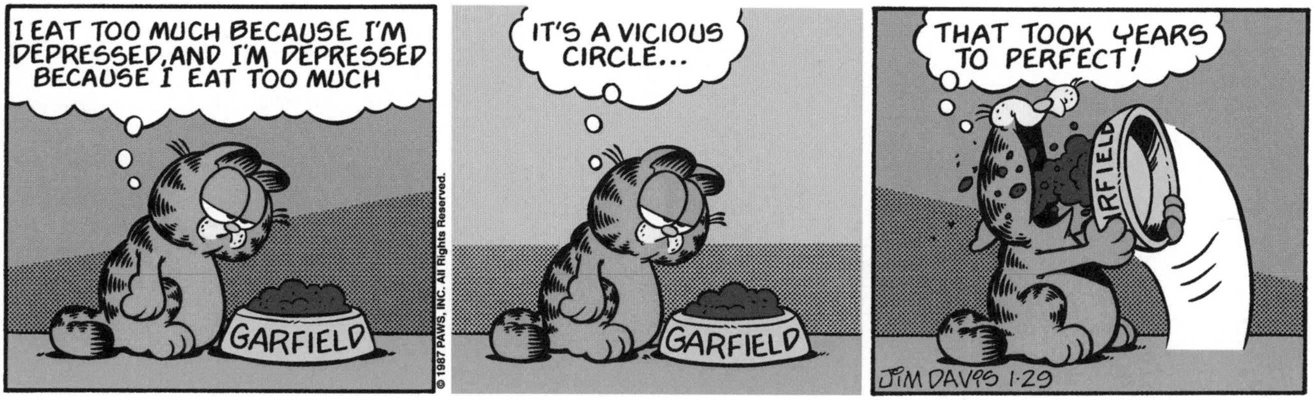
I EAT TOO MUCH BECAUSE I'M DEPRESSED, AND I'M DEPRESSED BECAUSE I EAT TOO MUCH
GARFIELD
© 1987 PAWS, INC. All Rights Reserved.
IT'S A VICIOUS CIRCLE...
GARFIELD
THAT TOOK YEARS TO PERFECT!
RFIELD
JIM DAVIS 1-29

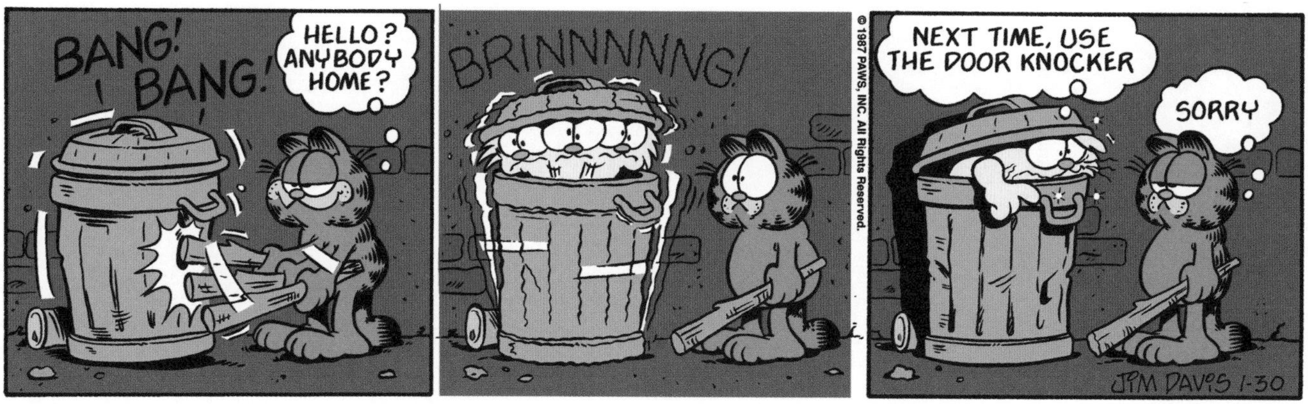
BANG! BANG!
HELLO? ANYBODY HOME?
BRINNNNNNG!
© 1987 PAWS, INC. All Rights Reserved.
NEXT TIME, USE THE DOOR KNOCKER
SORRY
JIM DAVIS 1-30

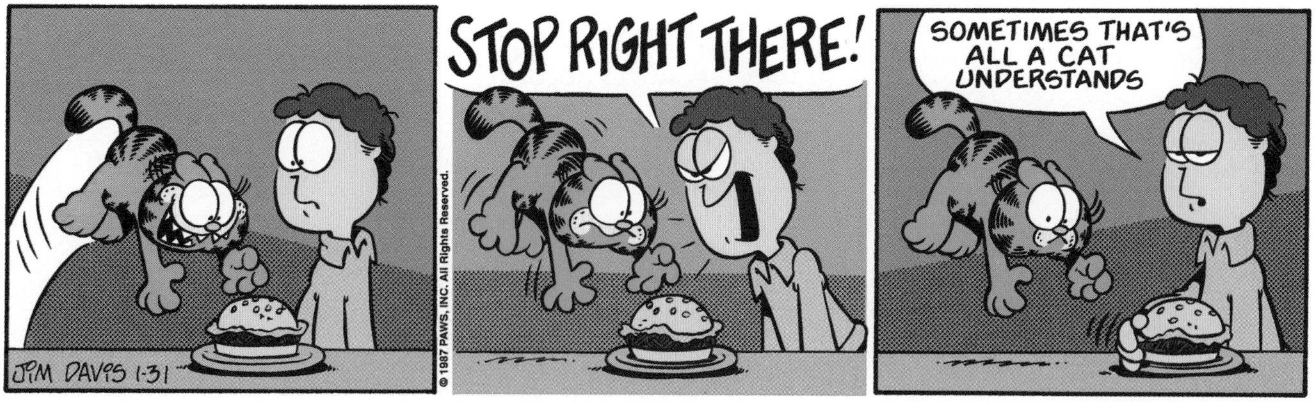
JIM DAVIS 1-31
© 1987 PAWS, INC. All Rights Reserved.
STOP RIGHT THERE!
SOMETIMES THAT'S ALL A CAT UNDERSTANDS

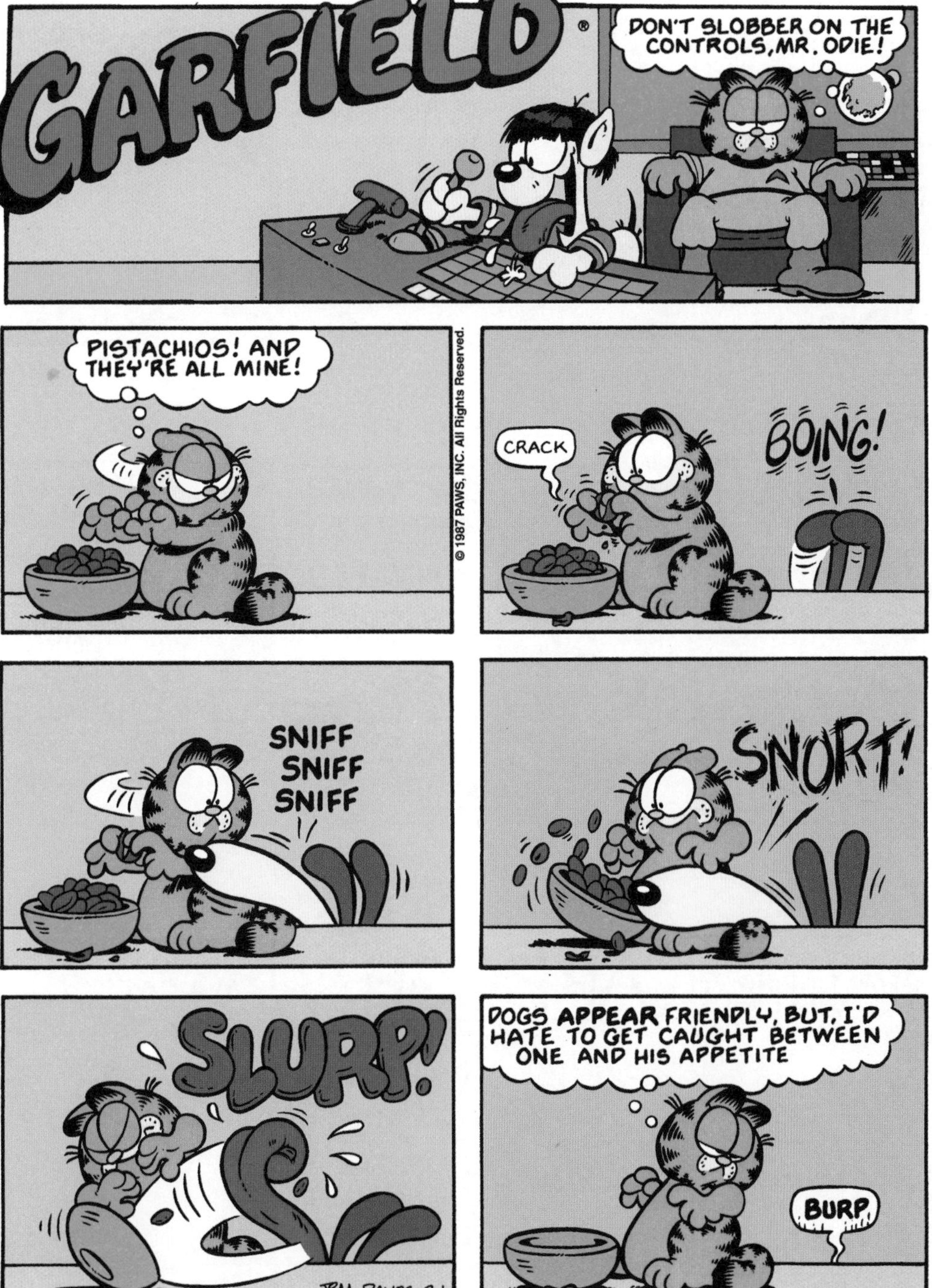
GARFIELD®
DON'T SLOBBER ON THE CONTROLS, MR. ODIE!
PISTACHIOS! AND THEY'RE ALL MINE!
CRACK
BOING!
SNIFF SNIFF SNIFF
SNORT!
SLURP!
JIM DAVIS 2-1
DOGS APPEAR FRIENDLY, BUT, I'D HATE TO GET CAUGHT BETWEEN ONE AND HIS APPETITE
BURP

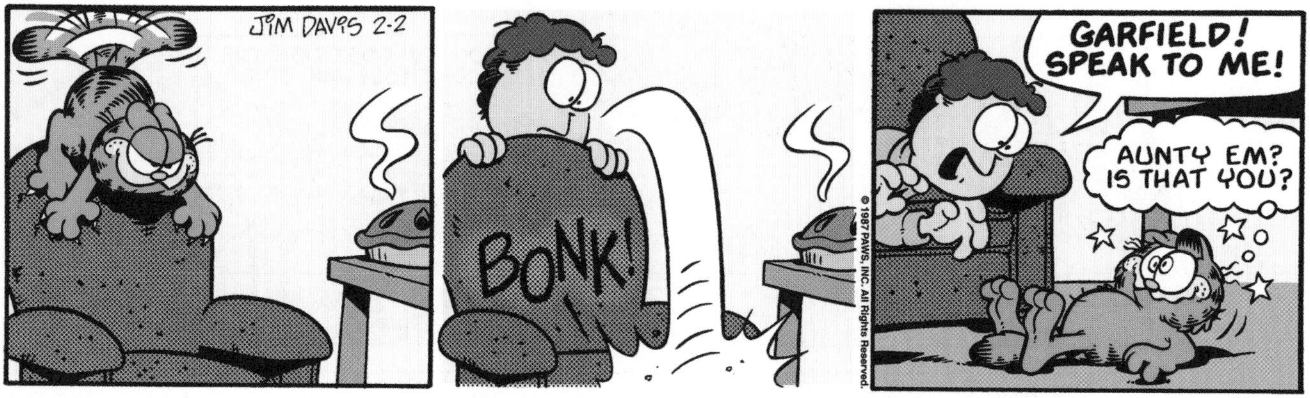
JIM DAVIS 2-2
BONK!
GARFIELD! SPEAK TO ME!
AUNTY EM? IS THAT YOU?
© 1987 PAWS, INC. All Rights Reserved.

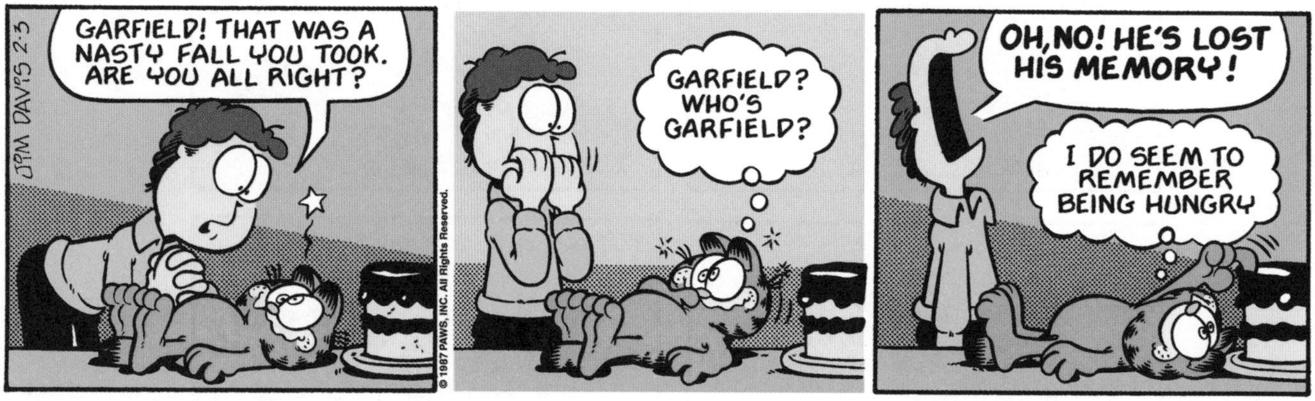
GARFIELD! THAT WAS A NASTY FALL YOU TOOK. ARE YOU ALL RIGHT?
JIM DAVIS 2-3
GARFIELD? WHO'S GARFIELD?
OH, NO! HE'S LOST HIS MEMORY!
I DO SEEM TO REMEMBER BEING HUNGRY
© 1987 PAWS, INC. All Rights Reserved.

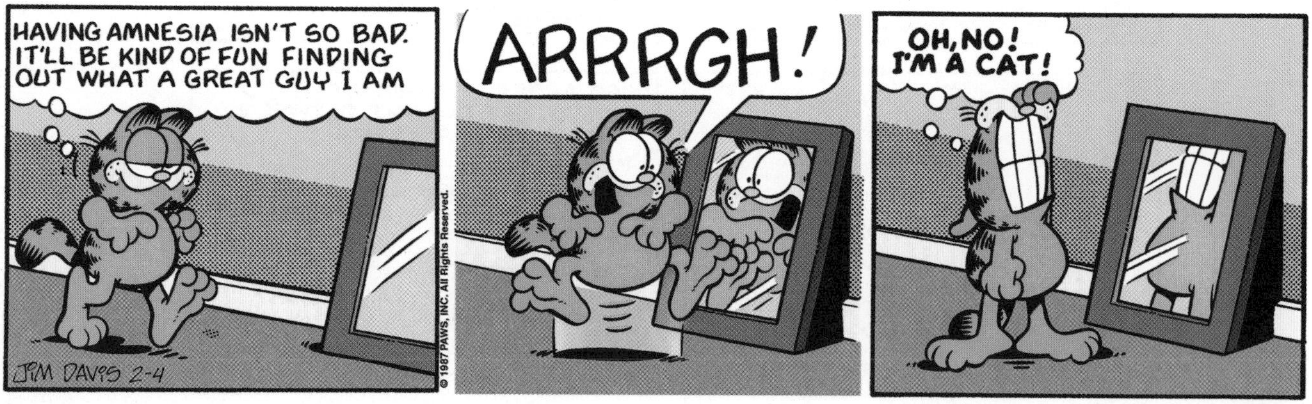
HAVING AMNESIA ISN'T SO BAD. IT'LL BE KIND OF FUN FINDING OUT WHAT A GREAT GUY I AM
JIM DAVIS 2-4
ARRRGH!
OH, NO! I'M A CAT!
© 1987 PAWS, INC. All Rights Reserved.

MAYBE SEEING ODIE WILL JOG YOUR MEMORY
WHAT A SWELL LOOKING DOG. PUT 'ER THERE
© 1987 PAWS, INC. All Rights Reserved.
YIP! YIP! YIP!
I WONDER IF I'M GOING TO LIKE THIS GARFIELD?
JIM DAVIS 2-5

LOOK, GARFIELD. IT'S POOKY! YOUR FAVORITE POSSESSION AND CLOSEST FRIEND. DO YOU REMEMBER POOKY?
JIM DAVIS 2-6
DON'T BE SILLY. I'M A GROWN CAT. WHAT WOULD I NEED WITH A TEDDY BEAR?
© 1987 PAWS, INC. All Rights Reserved.

AMNESIA HAS WIPED MY SLATE CLEAN. I START ESTABLISHING WHO I AM TODAY
JIM DAVIS 2-7
© 1987 PAWS, INC. All Rights Reserved.
I AM (BURP) A GLUTTON

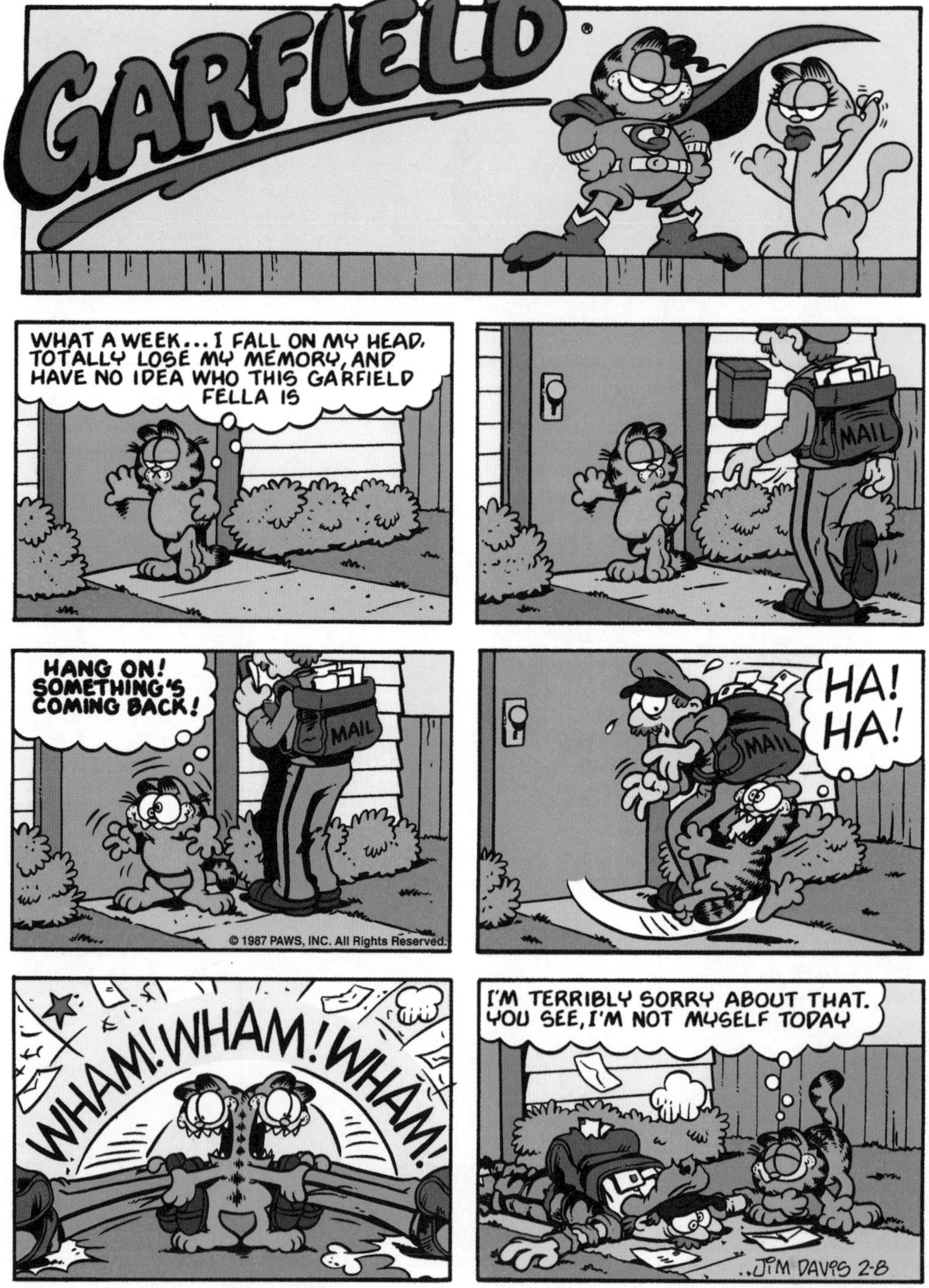
GARFIELD®
WHAT A WEEK... I FALL ON MY HEAD, TOTALLY LOSE MY MEMORY, AND HAVE NO IDEA WHO THIS GARFIELD FELLA IS
MAIL
HANG ON! SOMETHING'S COMING BACK!
MAIL
© 1987 PAWS, INC. All Rights Reserved.
MAIL
HA! HA!
WHAM! WHAM! WHAM!
I'M TERRIBLY SORRY ABOUT THAT. YOU SEE, I'M NOT MYSELF TODAY
JIM DAVIS 2-8

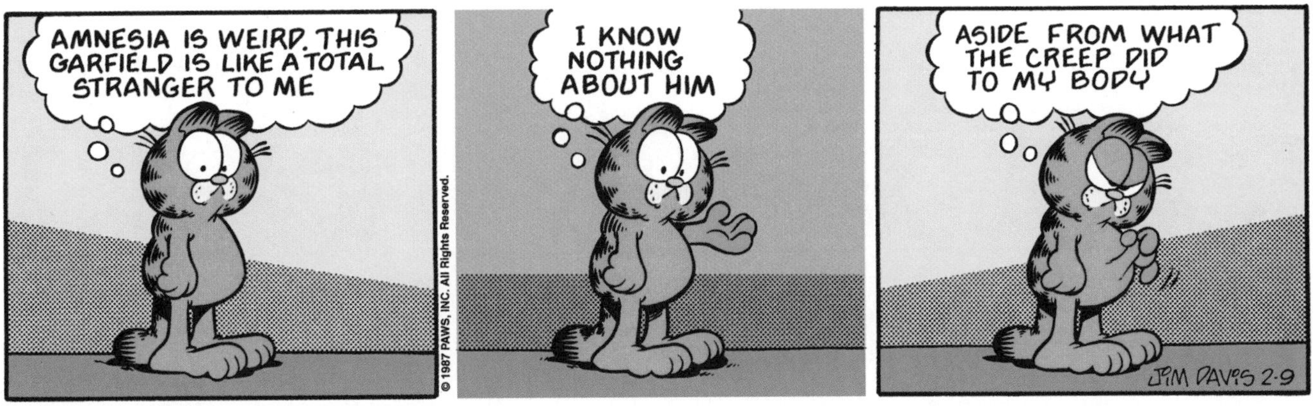
AMNESIA IS WEIRD. THIS GARFIELD IS LIKE A TOTAL STRANGER TO ME
© 1987 PAWS, INC. All Rights Reserved.
I KNOW NOTHING ABOUT HIM
ASIDE FROM WHAT THE CREEP DID TO MY BODY
JIM DAVIS 2-9

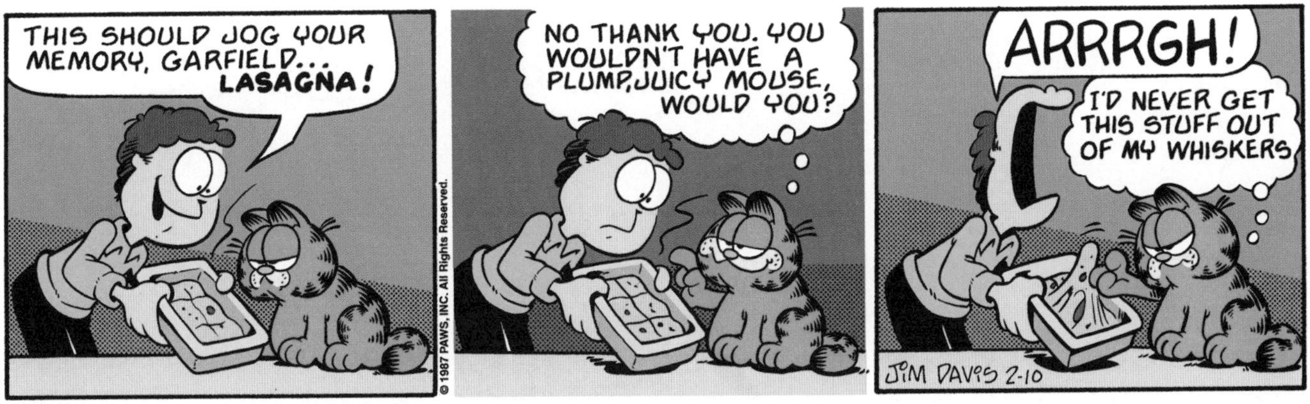
THIS SHOULD JOG YOUR MEMORY, GARFIELD... LASAGNA!
© 1987 PAWS, INC. All Rights Reserved.
NO THANK YOU. YOU WOULDN'T HAVE A PLUMP, JUICY MOUSE, WOULD YOU?
ARRRGH!
I'D NEVER GET THIS STUFF OUT OF MY WHISKERS
JIM DAVIS 2-10

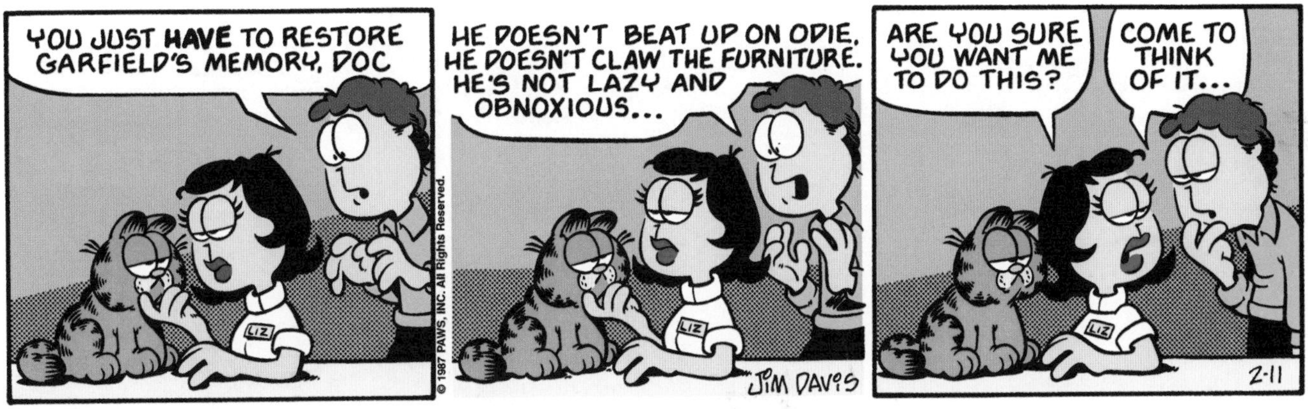
YOU JUST HAVE TO RESTORE GARFIELD'S MEMORY, DOC
LIZ
© 1987 PAWS, INC. All Rights Reserved.
HE DOESN'T BEAT UP ON ODIE. HE DOESN'T CLAW THE FURNITURE. HE'S NOT LAZY AND OBNOXIOUS...
LIZ
JIM DAVIS
ARE YOU SURE YOU WANT ME TO DO THIS?
COME TO THINK OF IT...
LIZ
2-11

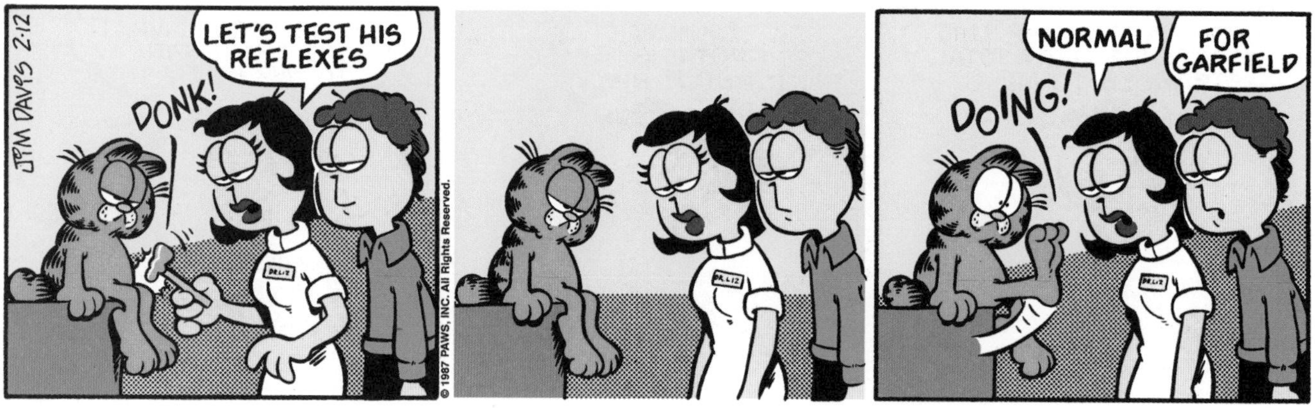
JIM DAVIS 2-12
LET'S TEST HIS REFLEXES
DONK!
DR. LIZ
© 1987 PAWS, INC. All Rights Reserved.
DOING!
NORMAL
FOR GARFIELD

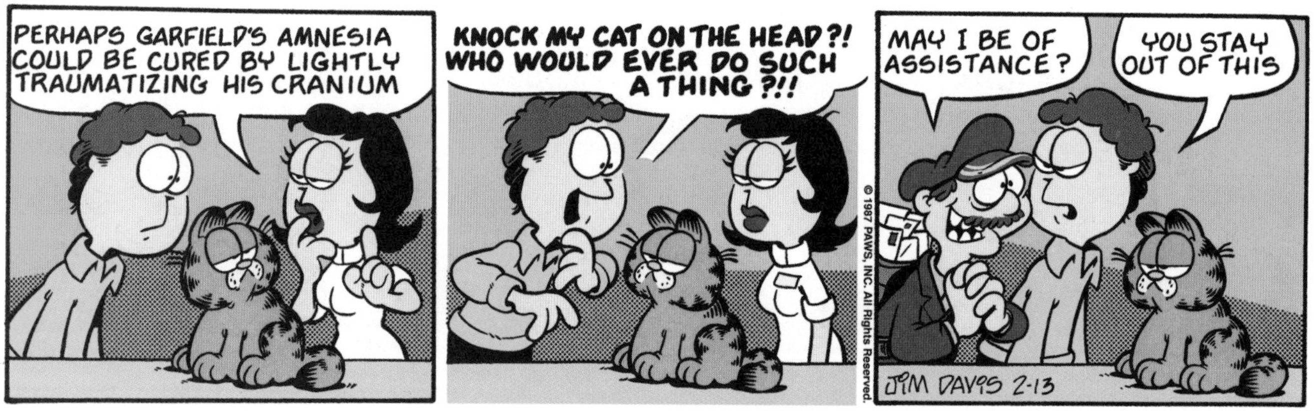
PERHAPS GARFIELD'S AMNESIA COULD BE CURED BY LIGHTLY TRAUMATIZING HIS CRANIUM
KNOCK MY CAT ON THE HEAD?! WHO WOULD EVER DO SUCH A THING?!!
© 1987 PAWS, INC. All Rights Reserved.
MAY I BE OF ASSISTANCE?
YOU STAY OUT OF THIS
JIM DAVIS 2-13

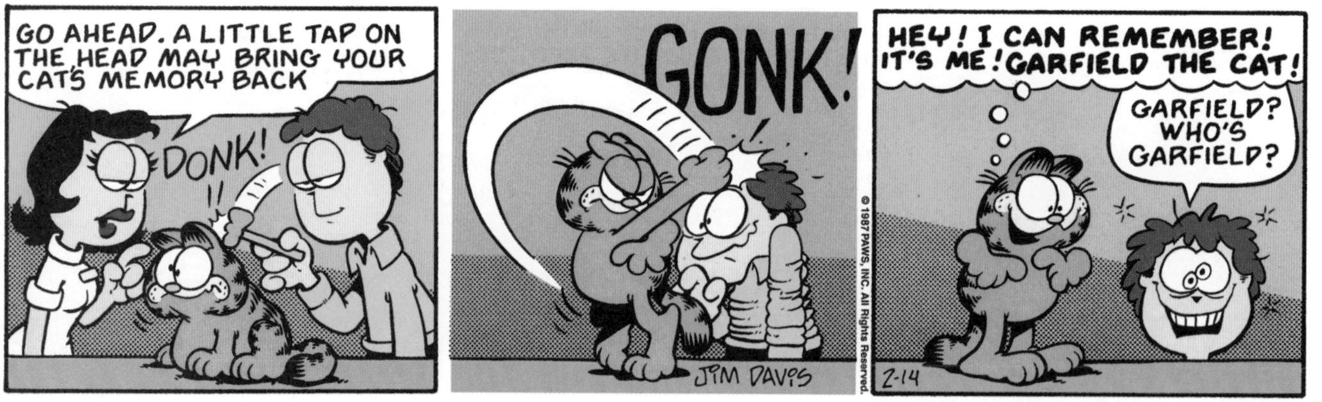
GO AHEAD. A LITTLE TAP ON THE HEAD MAY BRING YOUR CAT'S MEMORY BACK
DONK!
GONK!
JIM DAVIS
© 1987 PAWS, INC. All Rights Reserved.
HEY! I CAN REMEMBER! IT'S ME! GARFIELD THE CAT!
GARFIELD? WHO'S GARFIELD?
2-14

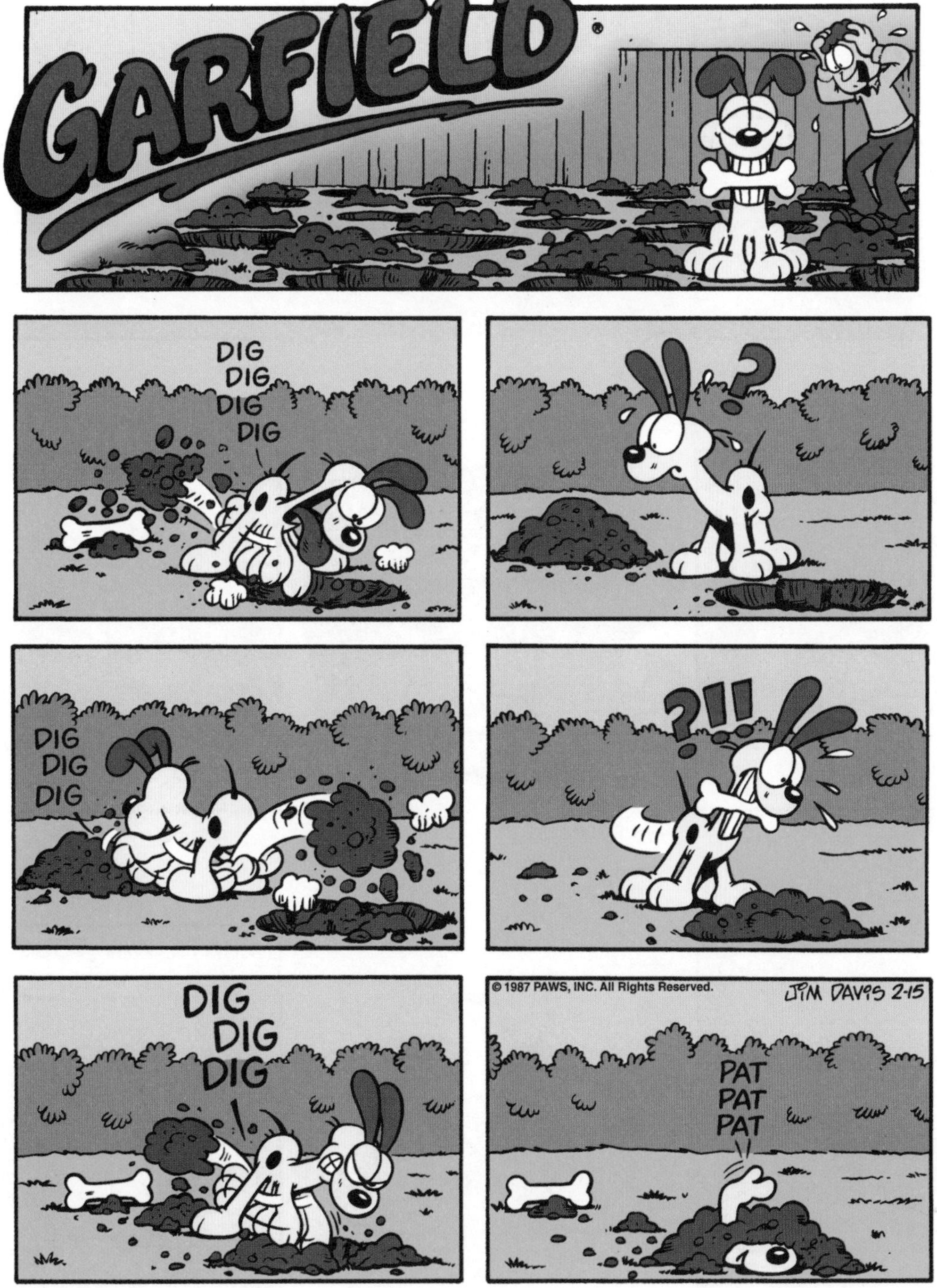
GARFIELD
DIG DIG DIG DIG
?
DIG DIG DIG
?!!
DIG DIG DIG
!
© 1987 PAWS, INC. All Rights Reserved.
JIM DAVIS 2-15
PAT PAT PAT

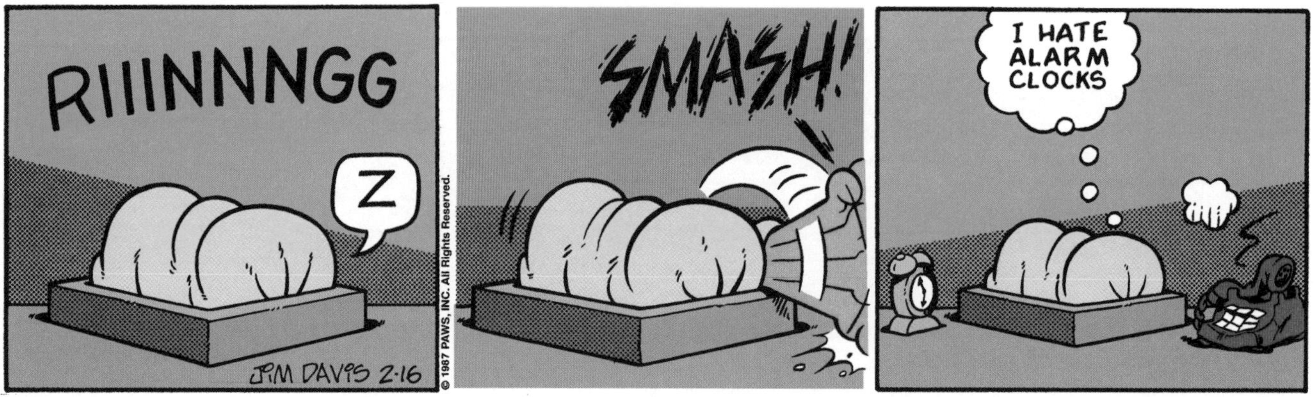
RIIINNNGG
Z
JIM DAVIS 2-16
© 1987 PAWS, INC. All Rights Reserved.
SMASH!
I HATE ALARM CLOCKS

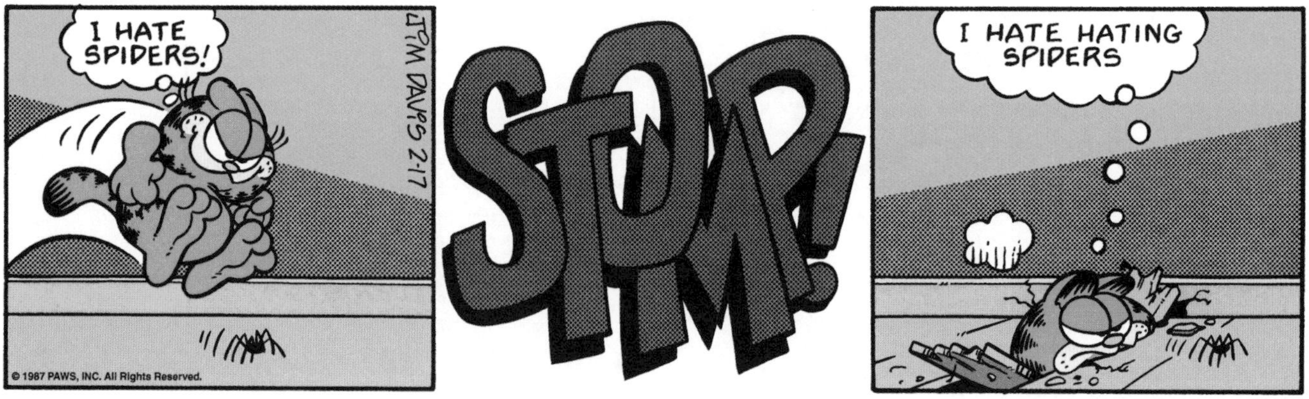
I HATE SPIDERS!
JIM DAVIS 2-17
© 1987 PAWS, INC. All Rights Reserved.
STOMP!
I HATE HATING SPIDERS

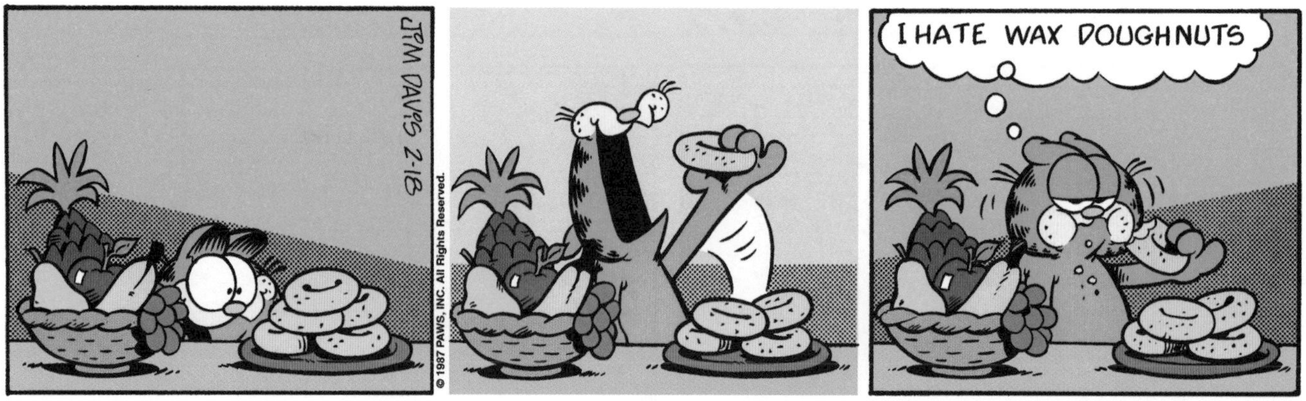
JIM DAVIS 2-18
© 1987 PAWS, INC. All Rights Reserved.
I HATE WAX DOUGHNUTS

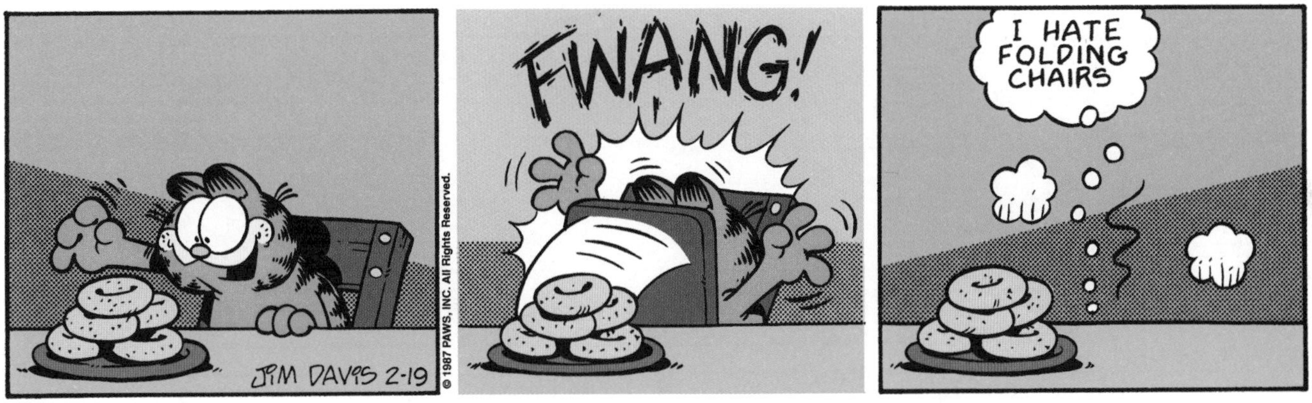
JIM DAVIS 2-19
© 1987 PAWS, INC. All Rights Reserved.
FWANG!
I HATE FOLDING CHAIRS

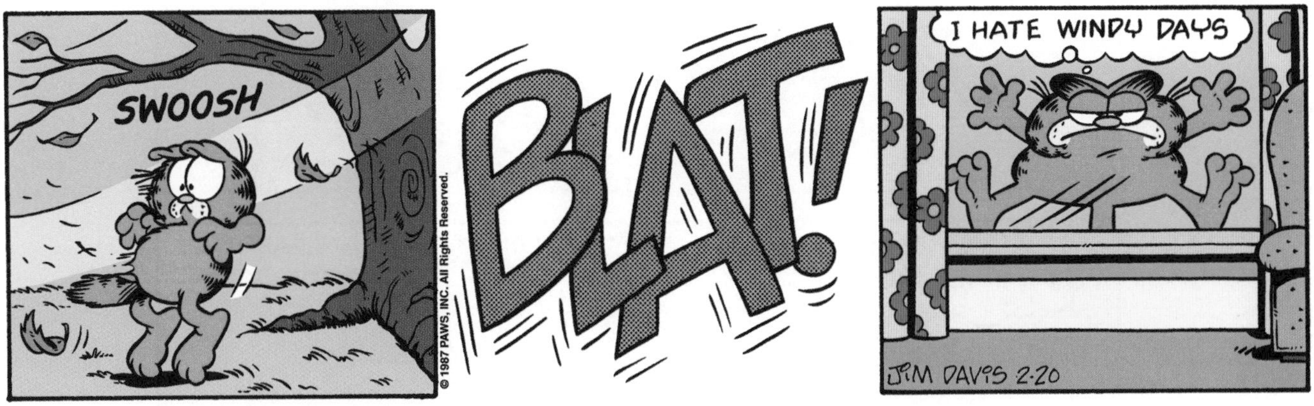
SWOOSH
© 1987 PAWS, INC. All Rights Reserved.
BLAT!
I HATE WINDY DAYS
JIM DAVIS 2-20

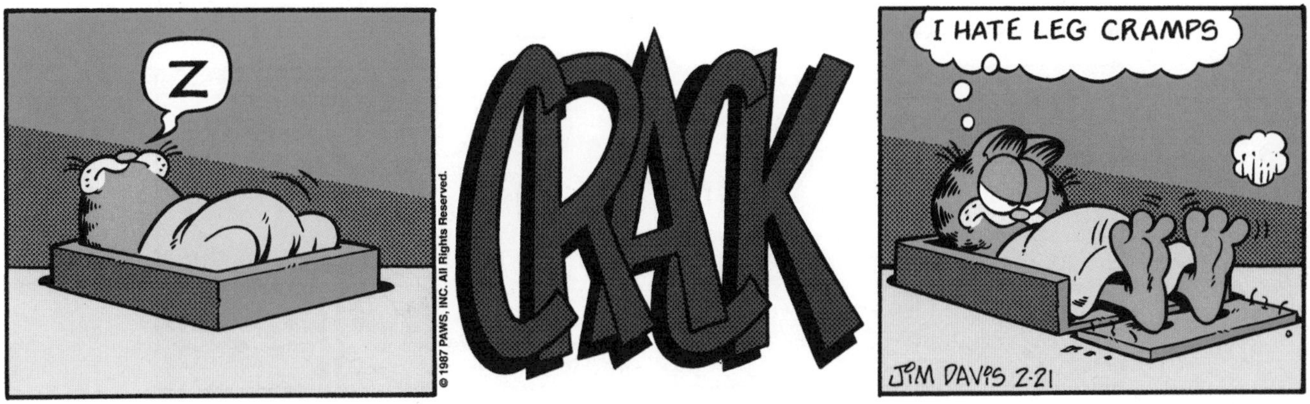
Z
© 1987 PAWS, INC. All Rights Reserved.
CRACK
I HATE LEG CRAMPS
JIM DAVIS 2-21

GARFIELD®
THIS KIND OF TIRED CALLS FOR COFFEE STRAIGHT UP
COFFEE
IT'S ONE OF THOSE MORNINGS
THE KIND OF MORNING WHERE YOU'VE BEEN UP FOR TWO MINUTES AND IT FEELS LIKE TWO DAYS
© 1987 PAWS, INC. All Rights Reserved.
IF I CAN JUST MAKE IT TO MY COFFEE, I'LL BE ALL RIGHT
JIM DAVIS 2·22
IT'S IN SIGHT! COME ON, GARFIELD! YOU CAN MAKE IT!
WHUMP!
SO CLOSE, AND YET SO FAR
Z

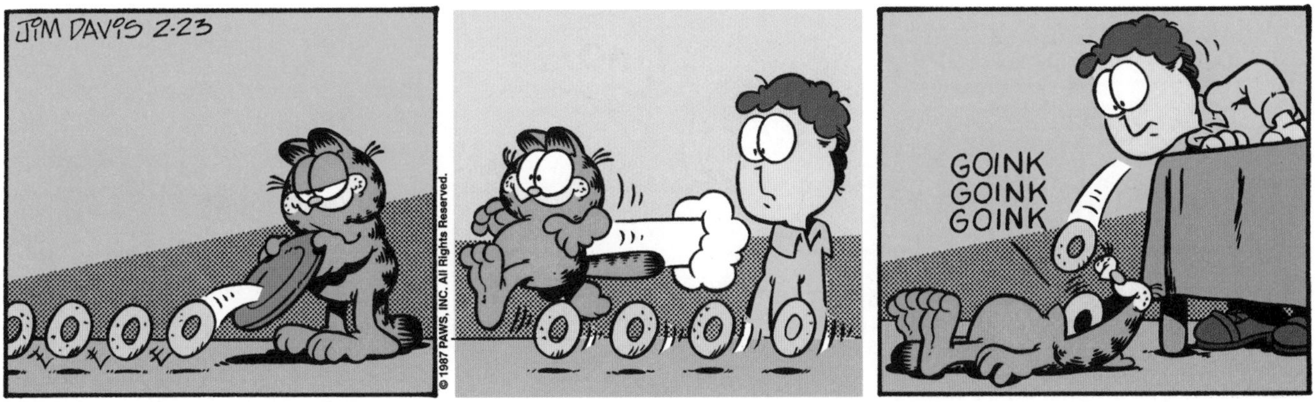
JIM DAVIS 2-23
© 1987 PAWS, INC. All Rights Reserved.
GOINK
GOINK
GOINK

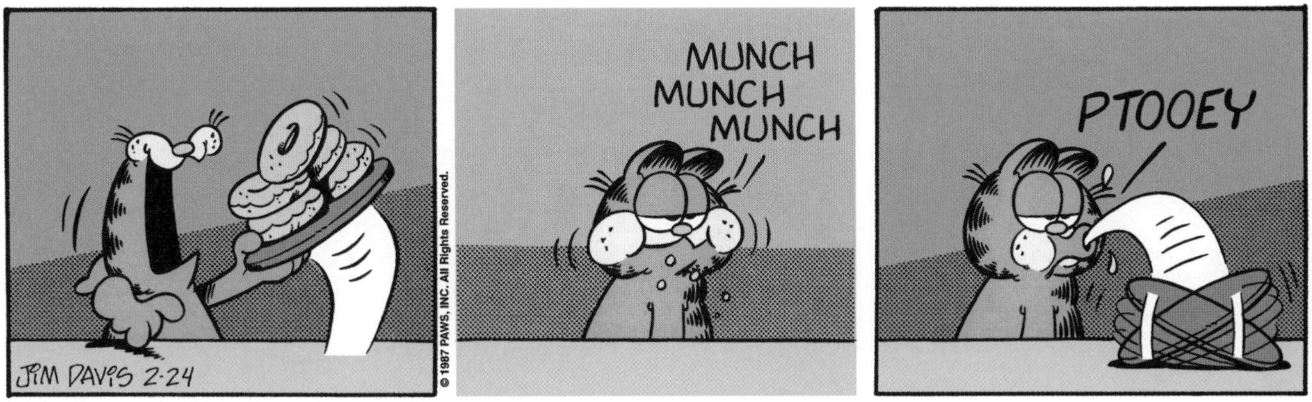
JIM DAVIS 2-24
© 1987 PAWS, INC. All Rights Reserved.
MUNCH
MUNCH
MUNCH
PTOOEY

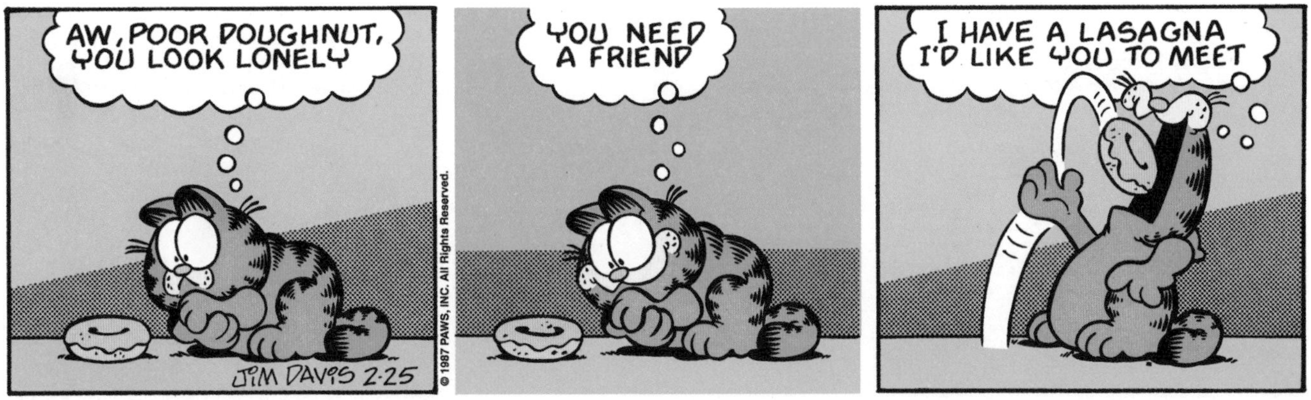
AW, POOR DOUGHNUT, YOU LOOK LONELY
JIM DAVIS 2-25
© 1987 PAWS, INC. All Rights Reserved.
YOU NEED A FRIEND
I HAVE A LASAGNA I'D LIKE YOU TO MEET

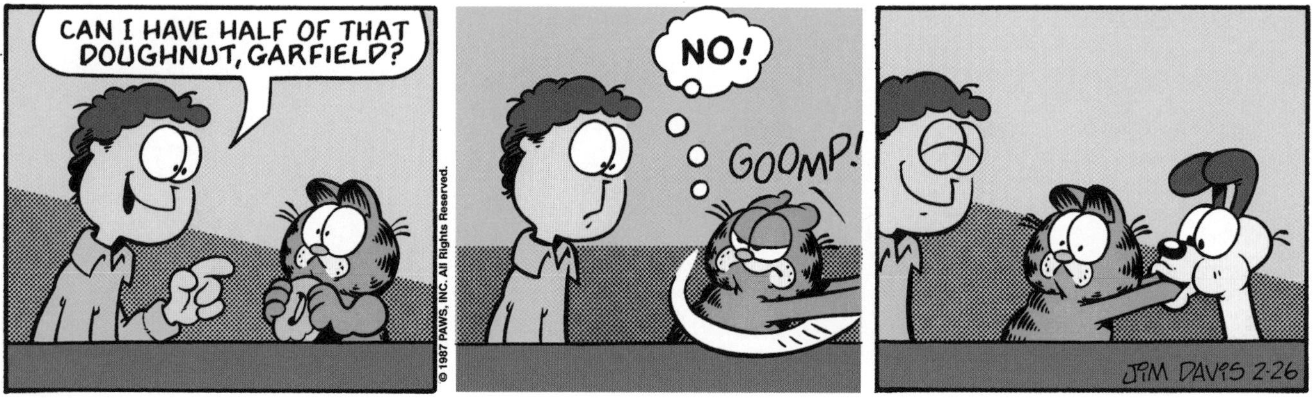
CAN I HAVE HALF OF THAT DOUGHNUT, GARFIELD?
NO!
GOOMP!
JIM DAVIS 2-26

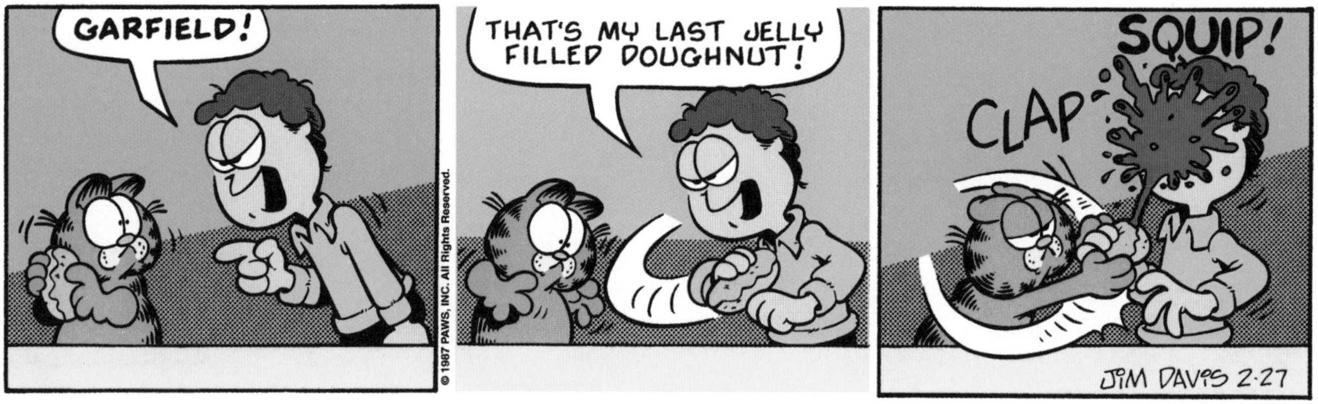
GARFIELD!
THAT'S MY LAST JELLY FILLED DOUGHNUT!
SQUIP!
CLAP
JIM DAVIS 2-27

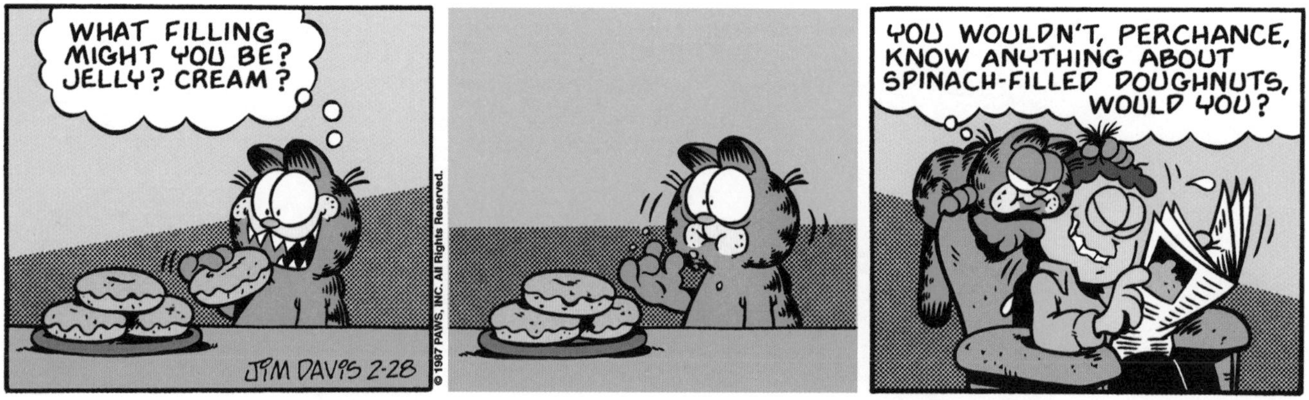
WHAT FILLING MIGHT YOU BE? JELLY? CREAM?
JIM DAVIS 2-28
YOU WOULDN'T, PERCHANCE, KNOW ANYTHING ABOUT SPINACH-FILLED DOUGHNUTS, WOULD YOU?

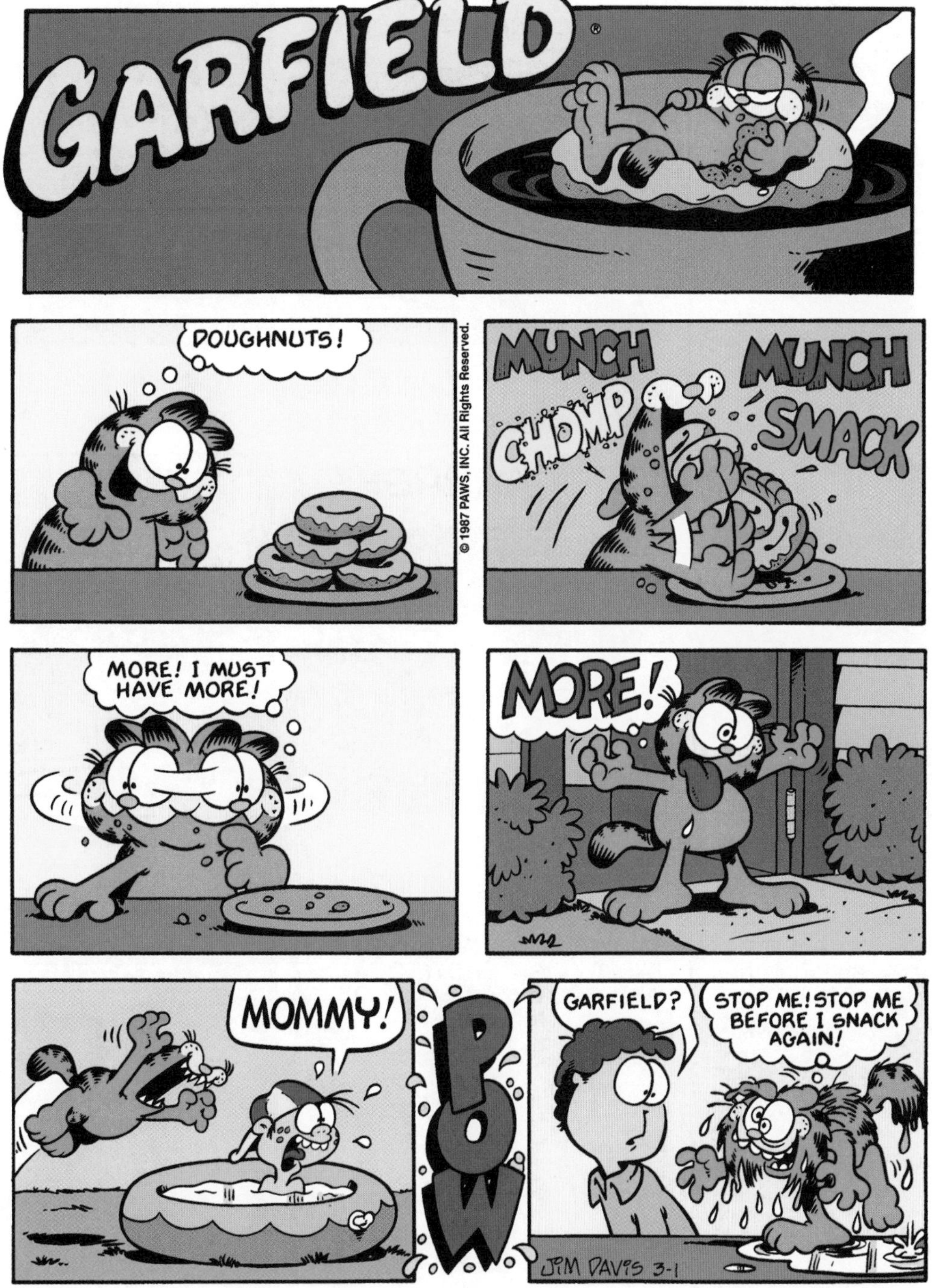
GARFIELD
© 1987 PAWS, INC. All Rights Reserved.
DOUGHNUTS!
MUNCH
CHOMP
MUNCH
SMACK
MORE! I MUST HAVE MORE!
MORE!
MOMMY!
POW
GARFIELD?
STOP ME! STOP ME BEFORE I SNACK AGAIN!
JIM DAVIS 3-1

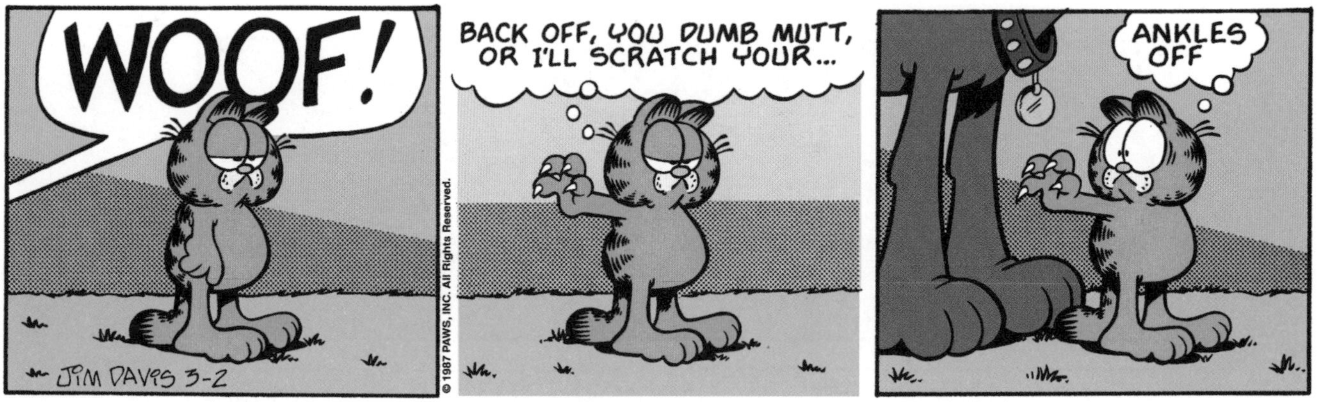
WOOF!
BACK OFF, YOU DUMB MUTT, OR I'LL SCRATCH YOUR...
ANKLES OFF
JIM DAVIS 3-2
© 1987 PAWS, INC. All Rights Reserved.

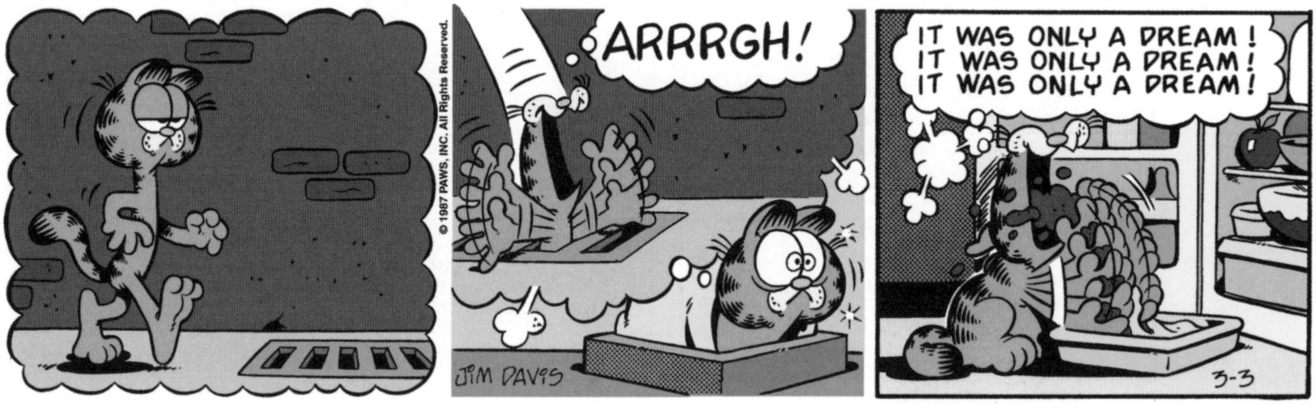
ARRRGH!
IT WAS ONLY A DREAM! IT WAS ONLY A DREAM! IT WAS ONLY A DREAM!
JIM DAVIS 3-3
© 1987 PAWS, INC. All Rights Reserved.

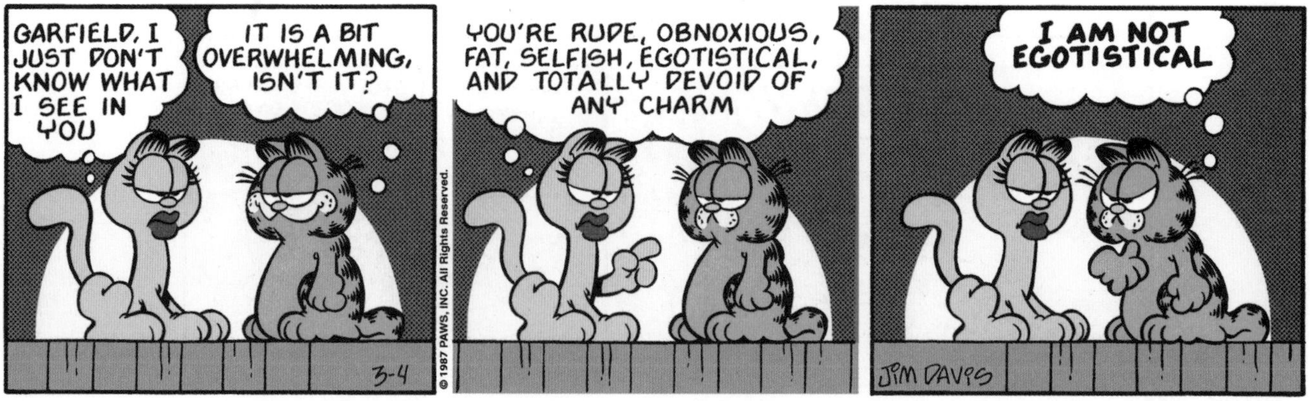
GARFIELD, I JUST DON'T KNOW WHAT I SEE IN YOU
IT IS A BIT OVERWHELMING, ISN'T IT?
YOU'RE RUDE, OBNOXIOUS, FAT, SELFISH, EGOTISTICAL, AND TOTALLY DEVOID OF ANY CHARM
I AM NOT EGOTISTICAL
3-4
JIM DAVIS
© 1987 PAWS, INC. All Rights Reserved.

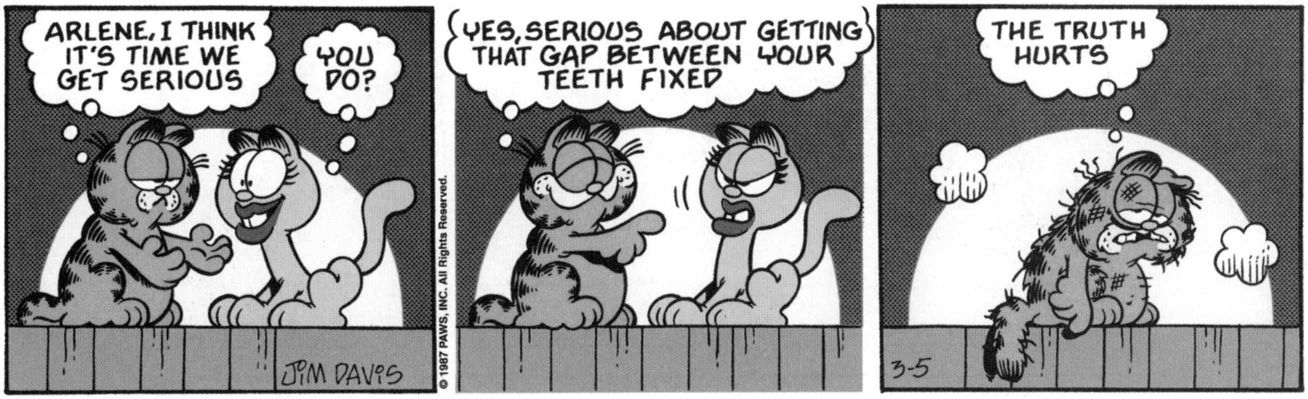
ARLENE, I THINK IT'S TIME WE GET SERIOUS
YOU DO?
JIM DAVIS
© 1987 PAWS, INC. All Rights Reserved.
YES, SERIOUS ABOUT GETTING THAT GAP BETWEEN YOUR TEETH FIXED
THE TRUTH HURTS
3-5

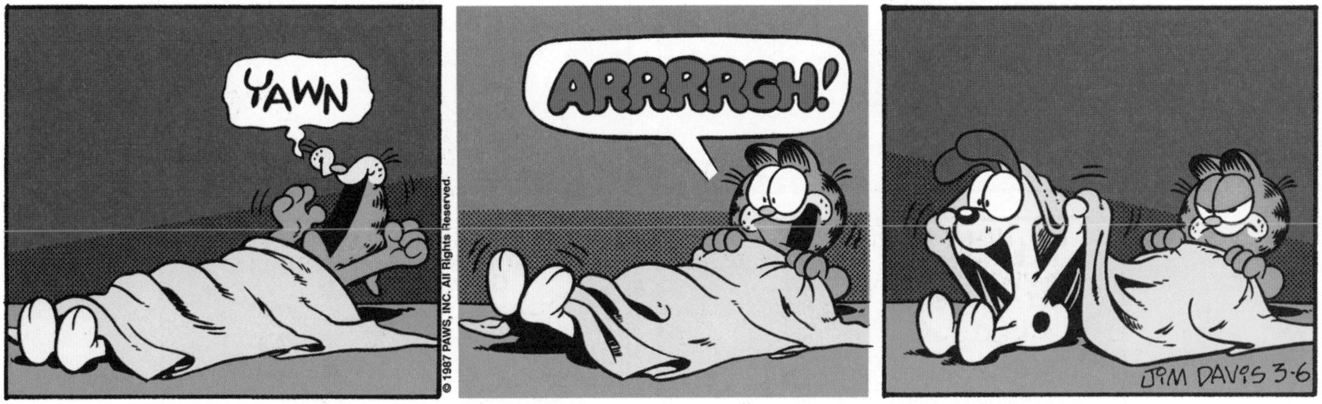
YAWN
© 1987 PAWS, INC. All Rights Reserved.
ARRRRGH!
JIM DAVIS 3-6

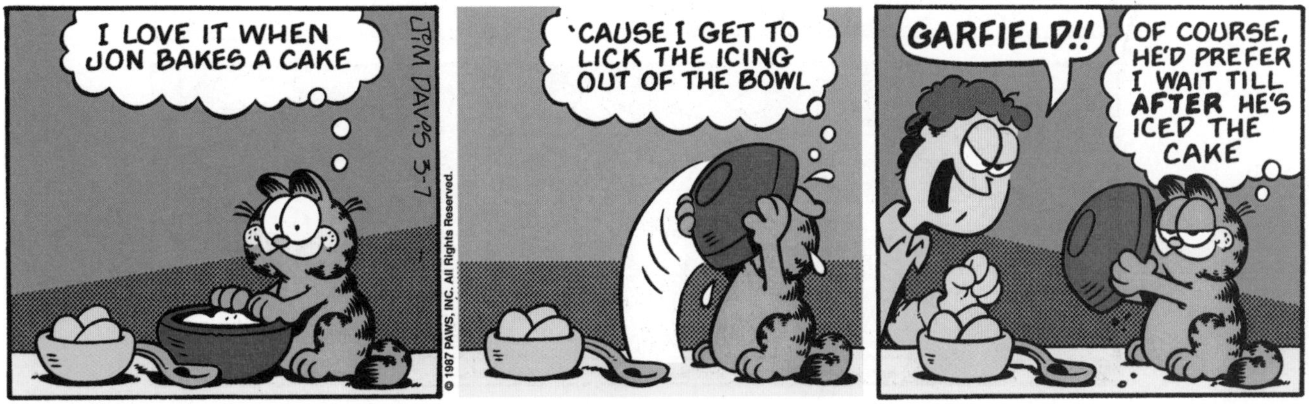
I LOVE IT WHEN JON BAKES A CAKE
JIM DAVIS 3-7
© 1987 PAWS, INC. All Rights Reserved.
'CAUSE I GET TO LICK THE ICING OUT OF THE BOWL
GARFIELD!!
OF COURSE, HE'D PREFER I WAIT TILL AFTER HE'S ICED THE CAKE

GARFIELD®
RATS! THE WASHER'S BROKEN
FFT! BANG! UGH!
COME ON, GARFIELD, WE HAVE TO GO TO THE LAUNDROMAT
NO, JON! PLEASE ANYWHERE BUT THERE
YOU KNOW WHAT THAT PLACE IS LIKE! ESPECIALLY ON WEEKENDS
JIM DAVIS 3-8
LAUNDRY
I'LL GET HIM FOR THIS
Out of Order

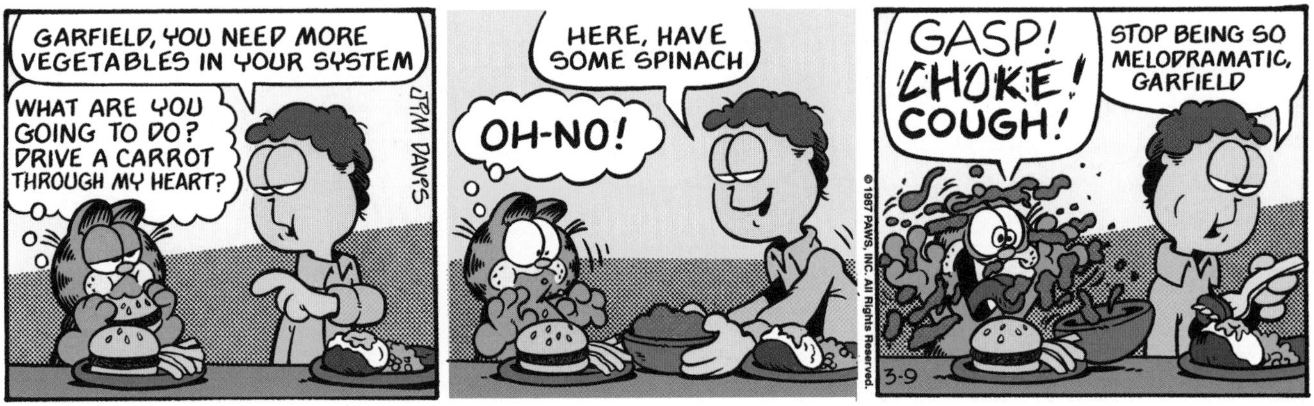
GARFIELD, YOU NEED MORE VEGETABLES IN YOUR SYSTEM
WHAT ARE YOU GOING TO DO? DRIVE A CARROT THROUGH MY HEART?
JIM DAVIS
HERE, HAVE SOME SPINACH
OH-NO!
© 1987 PAWS, INC. All Rights Reserved.
GASP! CHOKE! COUGH!
STOP BEING SO MELODRAMATIC, GARFIELD
3-9

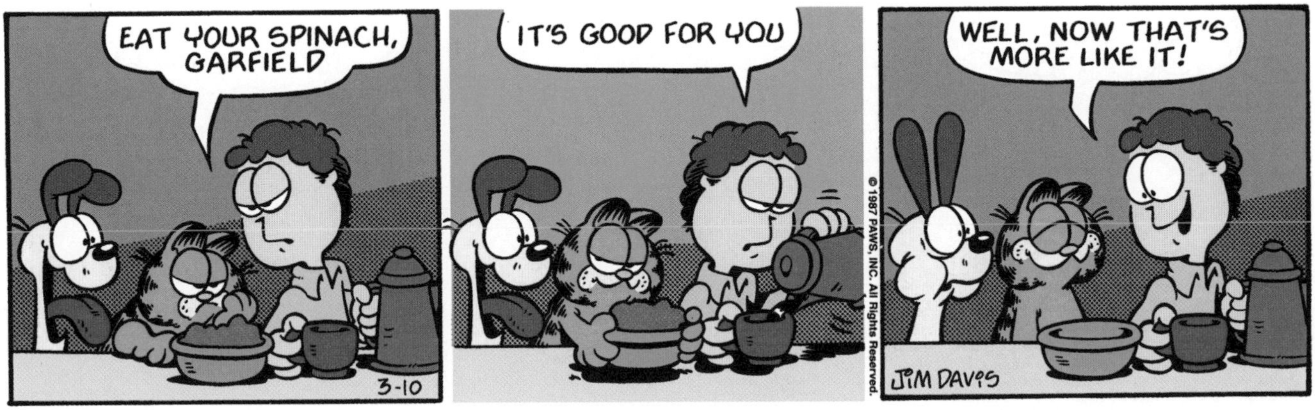
EAT YOUR SPINACH, GARFIELD
3-10
IT'S GOOD FOR YOU
© 1987 PAWS, INC. All Rights Reserved.
WELL, NOW THAT'S MORE LIKE IT!
JIM DAVIS

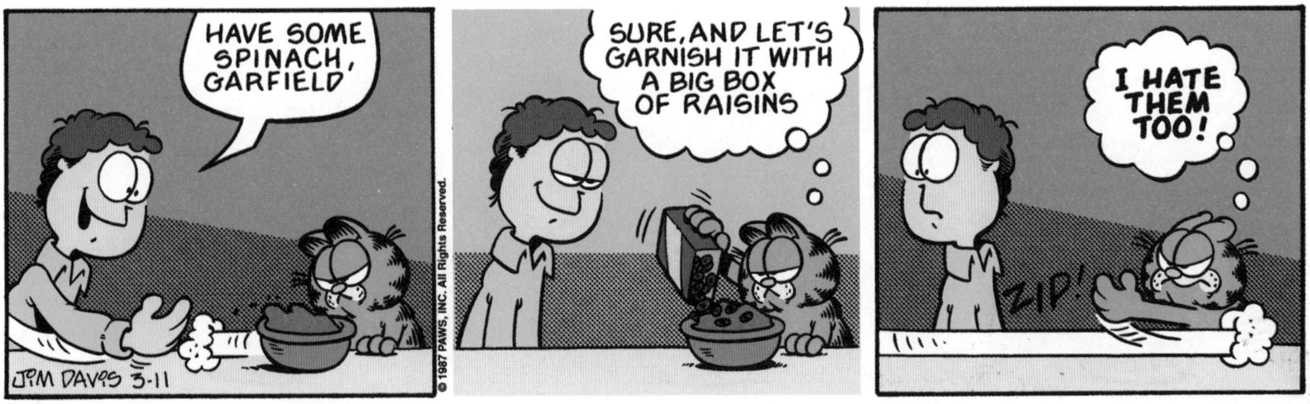
HAVE SOME SPINACH, GARFIELD
JIM DAVIS 3-11
© 1987 PAWS, INC. All Rights Reserved.
SURE, AND LET'S GARNISH IT WITH A BIG BOX OF RAISINS
I HATE THEM TOO!
ZIP!

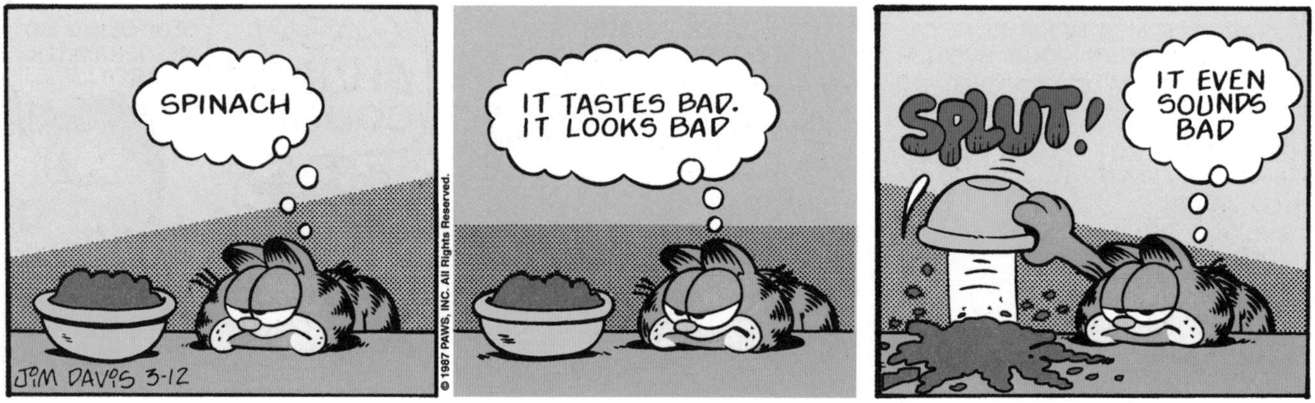
SPINACH
JIM DAVIS 3-12
© 1987 PAWS, INC. All Rights Reserved.
IT TASTES BAD. IT LOOKS BAD
SPLUT!
IT EVEN SOUNDS BAD

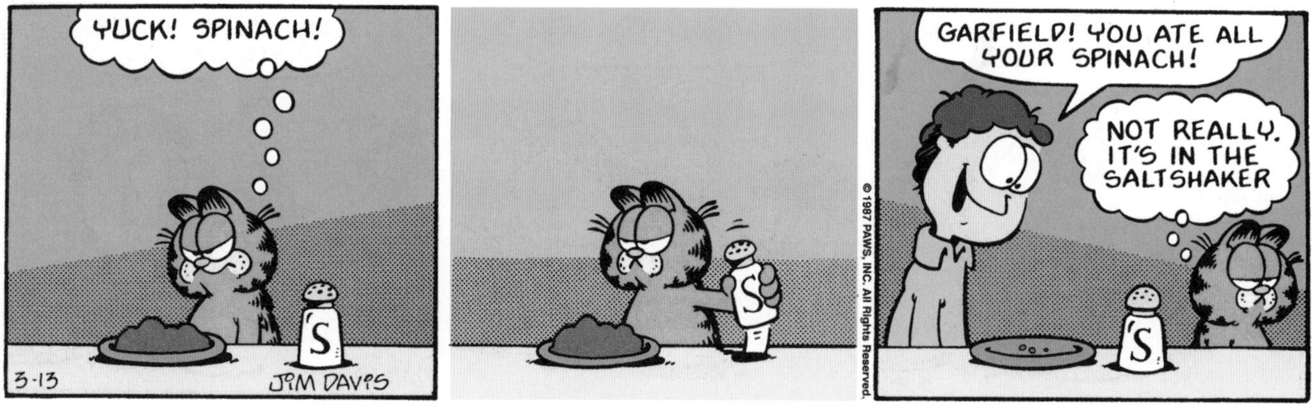
YUCK! SPINACH!
3-13
JIM DAVIS
S
© 1987 PAWS, INC. All Rights Reserved.
GARFIELD! YOU ATE ALL YOUR SPINACH!
NOT REALLY. IT'S IN THE SALTSHAKER

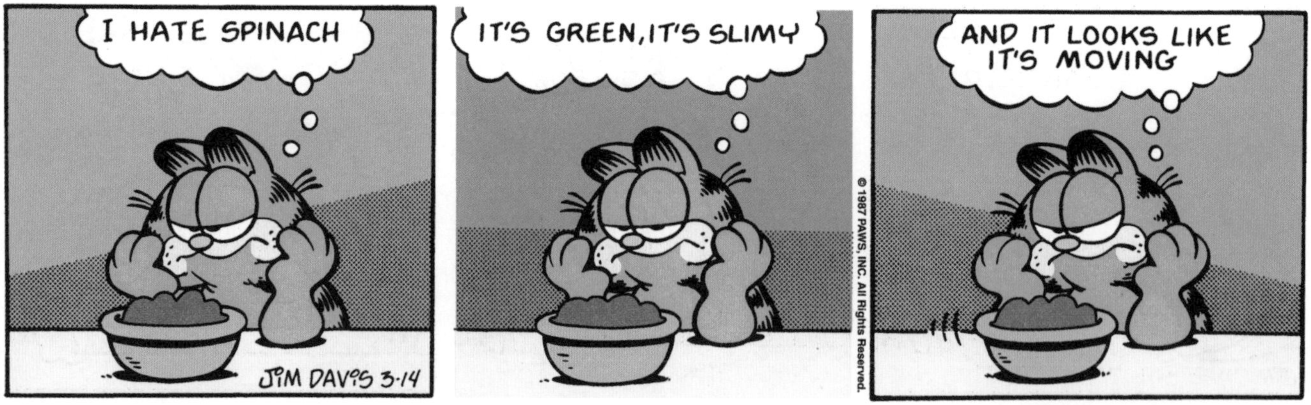
I HATE SPINACH
JIM DAVIS 3-14
IT'S GREEN, IT'S SLIMY
© 1987 PAWS, INC. All Rights Reserved.
AND IT LOOKS LIKE IT'S MOVING

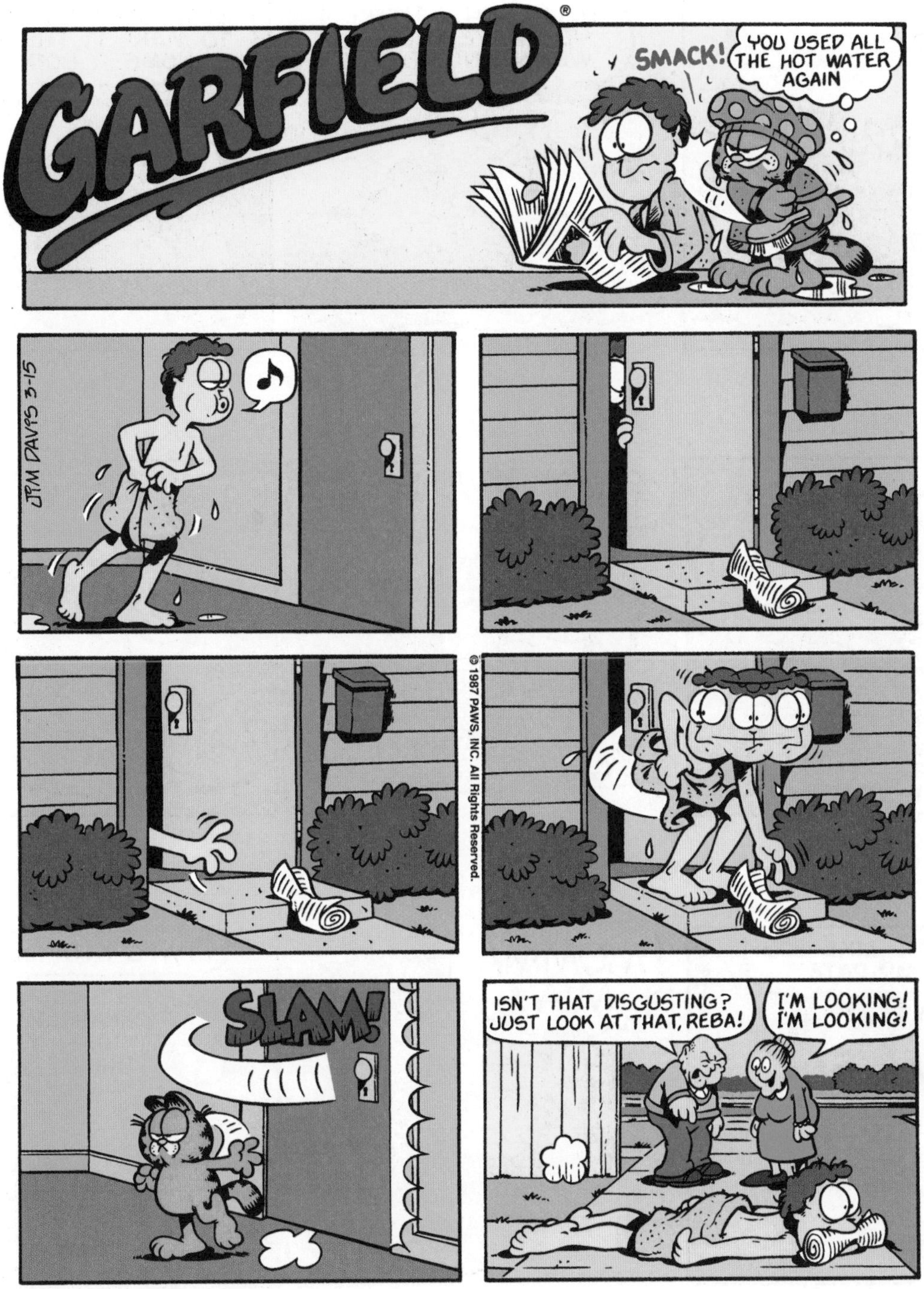
GARFIELD®
SMACK!
YOU USED ALL THE HOT WATER AGAIN
JIM DAVIS 3-15
© 1987 PAWS, INC. All Rights Reserved.
SLAM!
ISN'T THAT DISGUSTING? JUST LOOK AT THAT, REBA!
I'M LOOKING! I'M LOOKING!

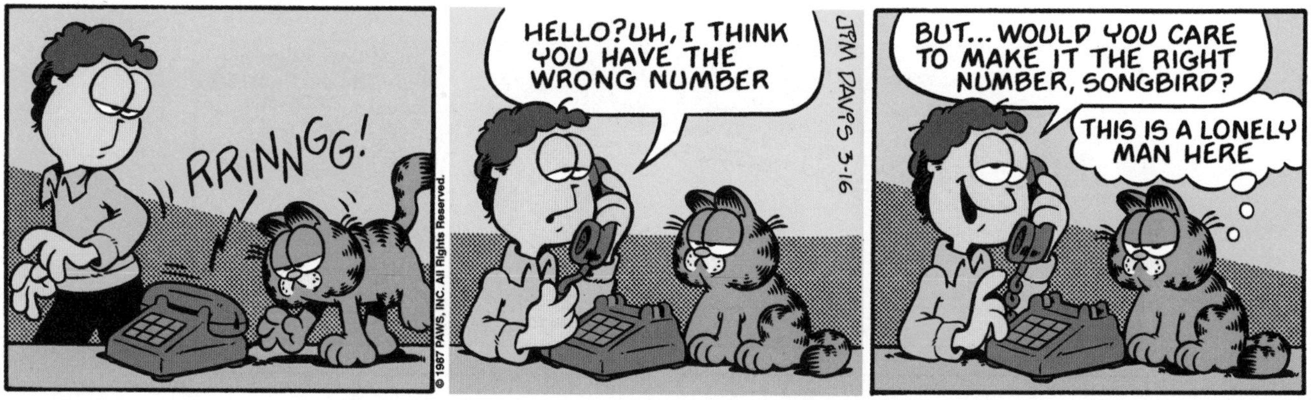
RRINNGG!
HELLO? UH, I THINK YOU HAVE THE WRONG NUMBER
JIM DAVIS 3-16
BUT... WOULD YOU CARE TO MAKE IT THE RIGHT NUMBER, SONGBIRD?
THIS IS A LONELY MAN HERE
© 1987 PAWS, INC. All Rights Reserved.

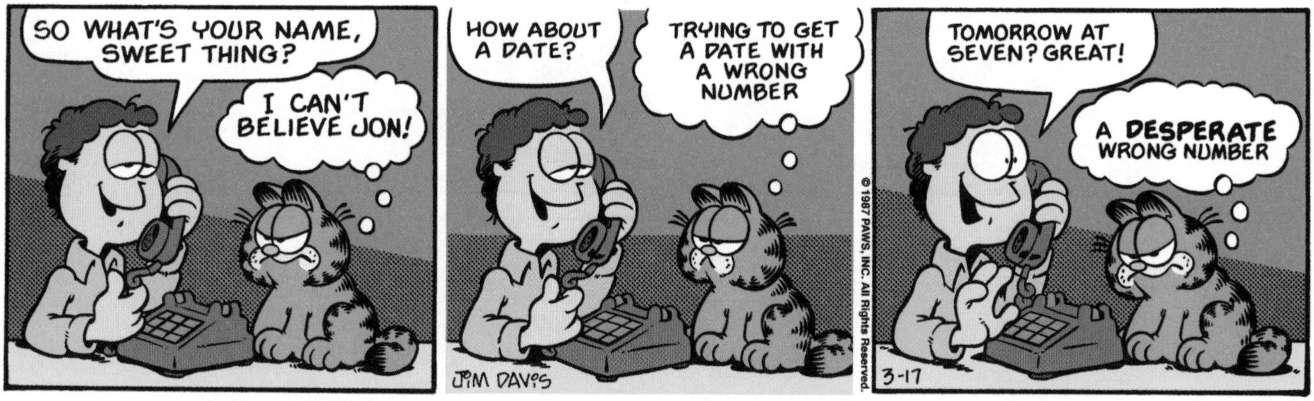
SO WHAT'S YOUR NAME, SWEET THING?
I CAN'T BELIEVE JON!
HOW ABOUT A DATE?
TRYING TO GET A DATE WITH A WRONG NUMBER
JIM DAVIS
TOMORROW AT SEVEN? GREAT!
A DESPERATE WRONG NUMBER
3-17
© 1987 PAWS, INC. All Rights Reserved.

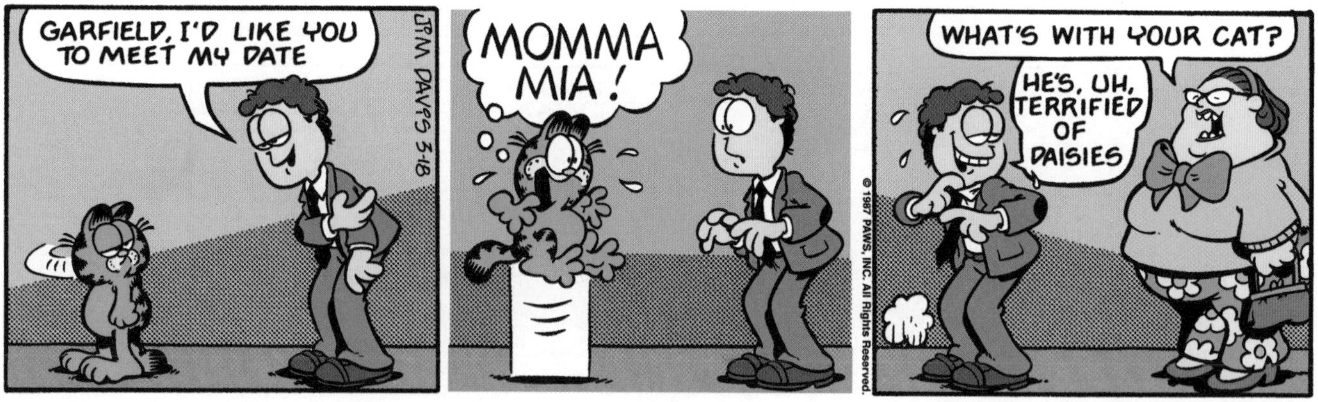
GARFIELD, I'D LIKE YOU TO MEET MY DATE
JIM DAVIS 3-18
MOMMA MIA!
WHAT'S WITH YOUR CAT?
HE'S, UH, TERRIFIED OF DAISIES
© 1987 PAWS, INC. All Rights Reserved.

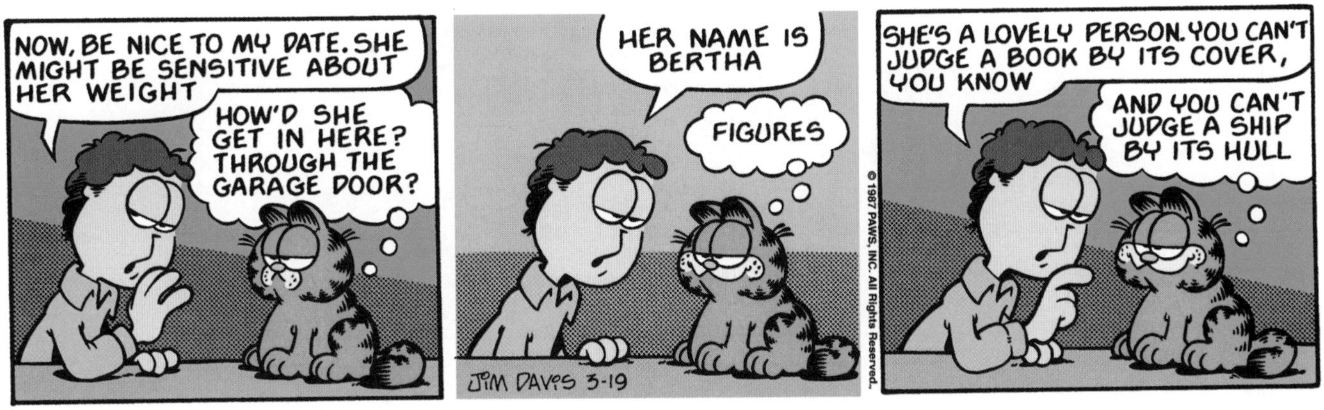
NOW, BE NICE TO MY DATE. SHE MIGHT BE SENSITIVE ABOUT HER WEIGHT
HOW'D SHE GET IN HERE? THROUGH THE GARAGE DOOR?
HER NAME IS BERTHA
FIGURES
JIM DAVIS 3-19
© 1987 PAWS, INC. All Rights Reserved.
SHE'S A LOVELY PERSON. YOU CAN'T JUDGE A BOOK BY ITS COVER, YOU KNOW
AND YOU CAN'T JUDGE A SHIP BY ITS HULL

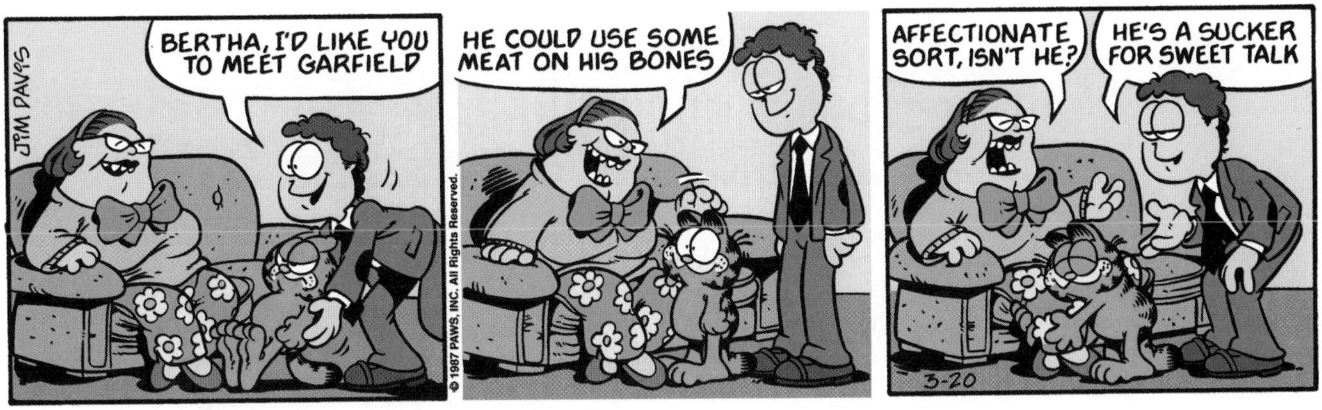
JIM DAVIS
BERTHA, I'D LIKE YOU TO MEET GARFIELD
© 1987 PAWS, INC. All Rights Reserved.
HE COULD USE SOME MEAT ON HIS BONES
AFFECTIONATE SORT, ISN'T HE?
HE'S A SUCKER FOR SWEET TALK
3-20

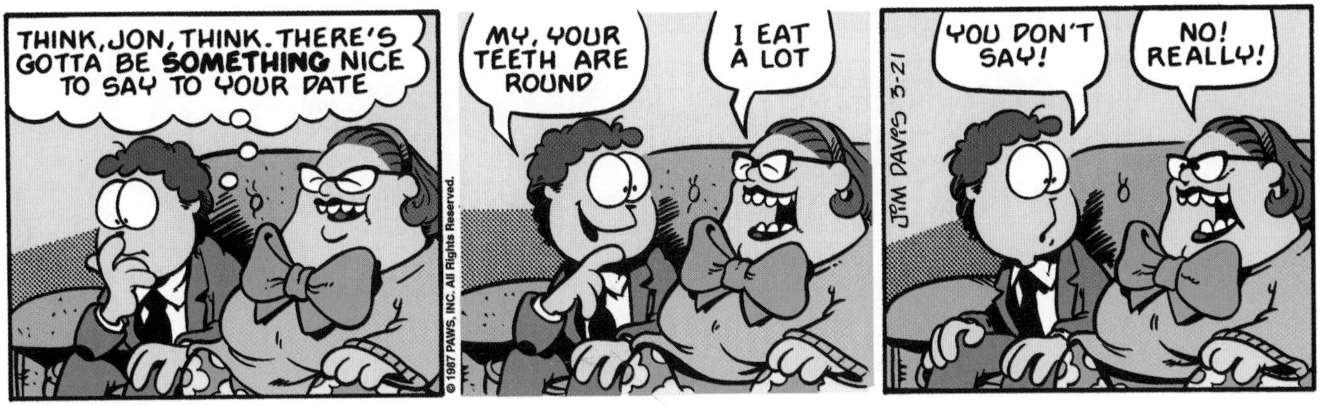
THINK, JON, THINK. THERE'S GOTTA BE SOMETHING NICE TO SAY TO YOUR DATE
© 1987 PAWS, INC. All Rights Reserved.
MY, YOUR TEETH ARE ROUND
I EAT A LOT
JIM DAVIS 3-21
YOU DON'T SAY!
NO! REALLY!

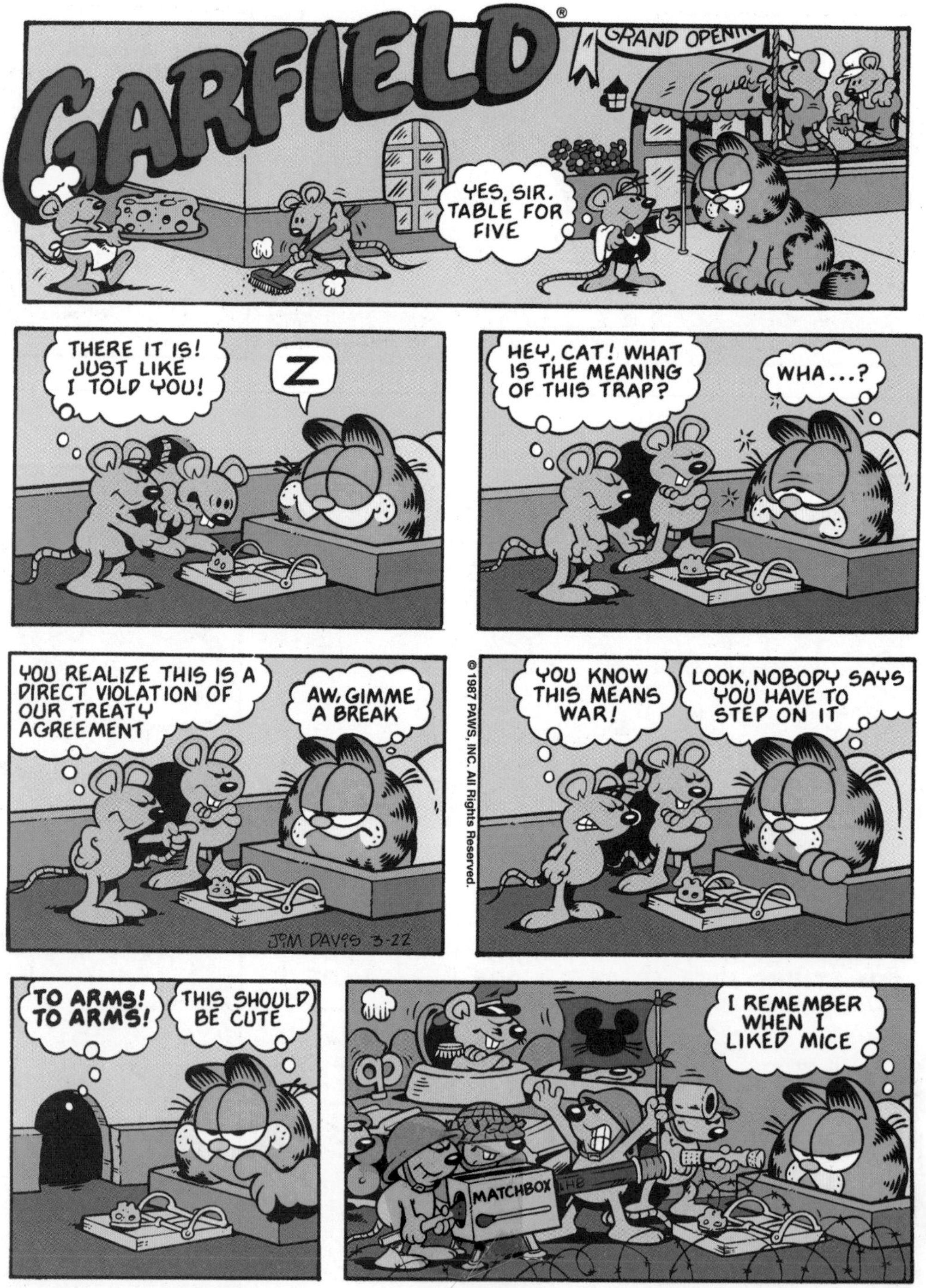
GARFIELD®
GRAND OPENI
Squei
YES, SIR. TABLE FOR FIVE
THERE IT IS! JUST LIKE I TOLD YOU!
Z
HEY, CAT! WHAT IS THE MEANING OF THIS TRAP?
WHA...?
YOU REALIZE THIS IS A DIRECT VIOLATION OF OUR TREATY AGREEMENT
AW, GIMME A BREAK
JIM DAVIS 3-22
© 1987 PAWS, INC. All Rights Reserved.
YOU KNOW THIS MEANS WAR!
LOOK, NOBODY SAYS YOU HAVE TO STEP ON IT
TO ARMS! TO ARMS!
THIS SHOULD BE CUTE
I REMEMBER WHEN I LIKED MICE
MATCHBOX

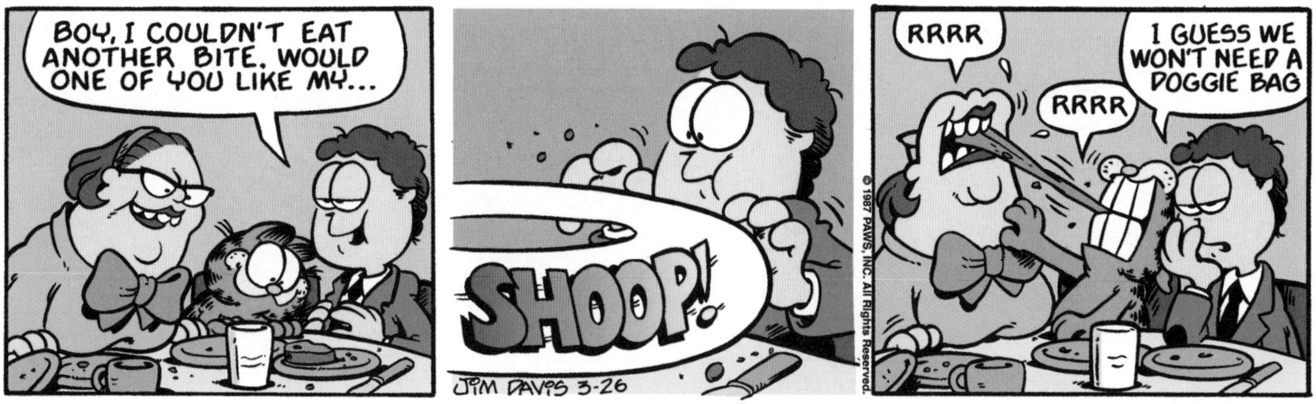
BOY, I COULDN'T EAT ANOTHER BITE. WOULD ONE OF YOU LIKE MY...
SHOOP!
JIM DAVIS 3-26
© 1987 PAWS, INC. All Rights Reserved.
RRRR
RRRR
I GUESS WE WON'T NEED A DOGGIE BAG

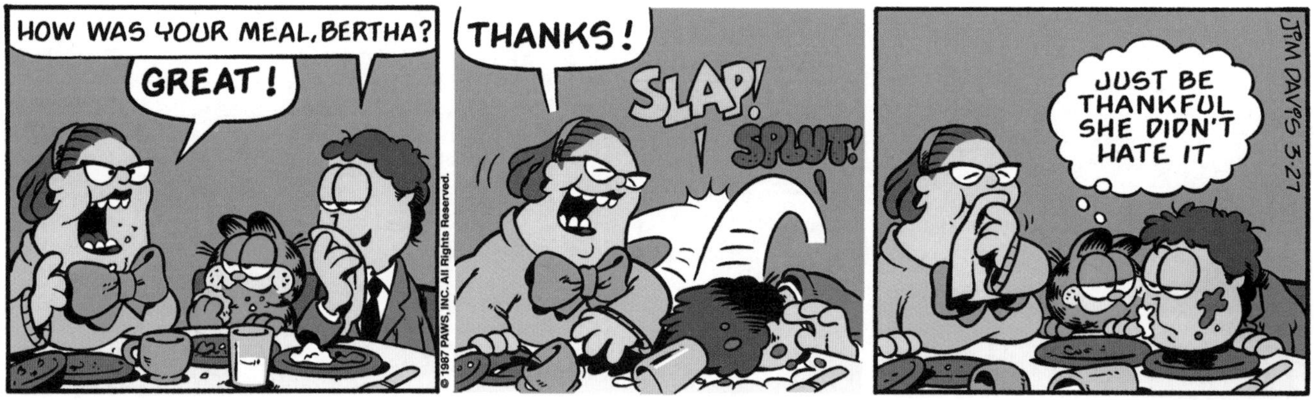
HOW WAS YOUR MEAL, BERTHA?
GREAT!
© 1987 PAWS, INC. All Rights Reserved.
THANKS!
SLAP!
SPLUT!
JUST BE THANKFUL SHE DIDN'T HATE IT
JIM DAVIS 3-27

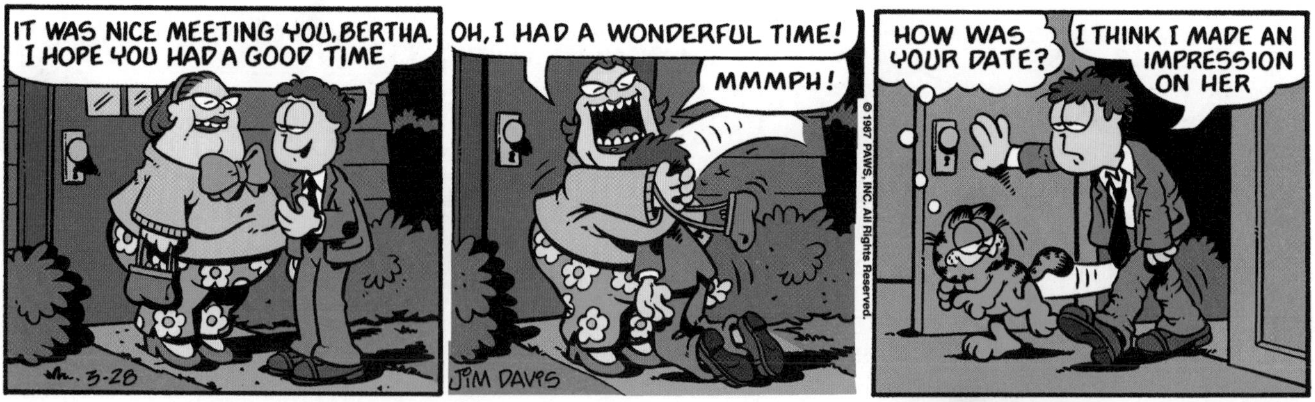
IT WAS NICE MEETING YOU, BERTHA. I HOPE YOU HAD A GOOD TIME
3-28
OH, I HAD A WONDERFUL TIME!
MMMPH!
JIM DAVIS
© 1987 PAWS, INC. All Rights Reserved.
HOW WAS YOUR DATE?
I THINK I MADE AN IMPRESSION ON HER

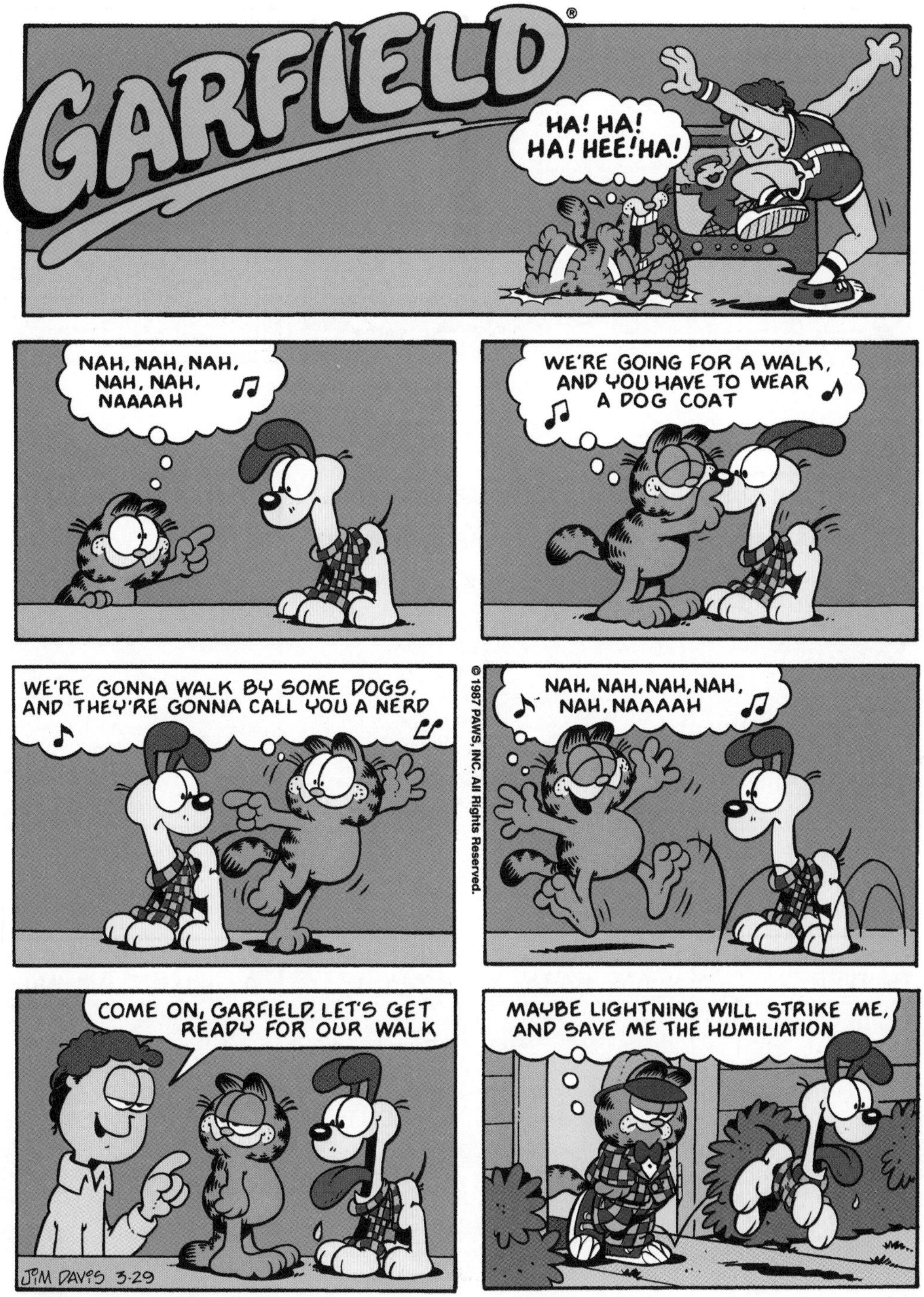
GARFIELD®
HA! HA! HA! HEE! HA!
NAH, NAH, NAH, NAH, NAH, NAAAAH
WE'RE GOING FOR A WALK, AND YOU HAVE TO WEAR A DOG COAT
WE'RE GONNA WALK BY SOME DOGS, AND THEY'RE GONNA CALL YOU A NERD
NAH, NAH, NAH, NAH, NAH, NAAAAH
COME ON, GARFIELD. LET'S GET READY FOR OUR WALK
JIM DAVIS 3-29
MAYBE LIGHTNING WILL STRIKE ME, AND SAVE ME THE HUMILIATION

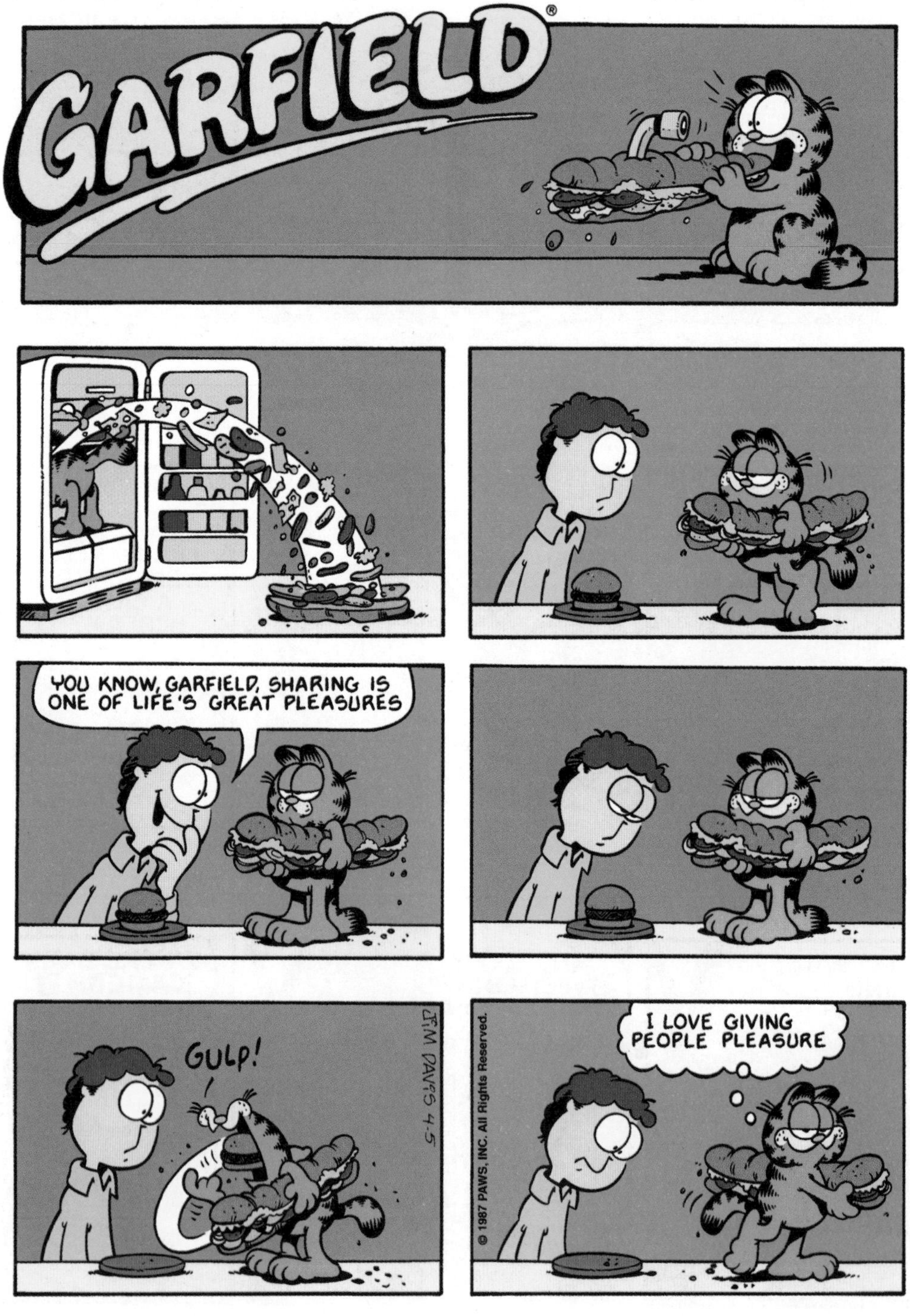
GARFIELD®
YOU KNOW, GARFIELD, SHARING IS ONE OF LIFE'S GREAT PLEASURES
GULP!
JIM DAVIS 4-5
© 1987 PAWS, INC. All Rights Reserved.
I LOVE GIVING PEOPLE PLEASURE

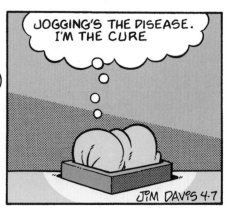

THE LONE GOURMET STRIKES AGAIN

YAWN

YOU GO OUT AND PLAY, POOKY

WHAT THE...?

ZZIP!

HEY, WAIT A MINUTE! I'M NAILED INTO BED!

WHA?!!

JIM DAVIS 4-12

I SUPPOSE THIS WAS FOR PUTTING THE LIZARD IN YOUR SHOE?

NOW WE'RE EVEN

© 1987 PAWS, INC. All Rights Reserved.

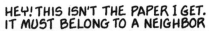

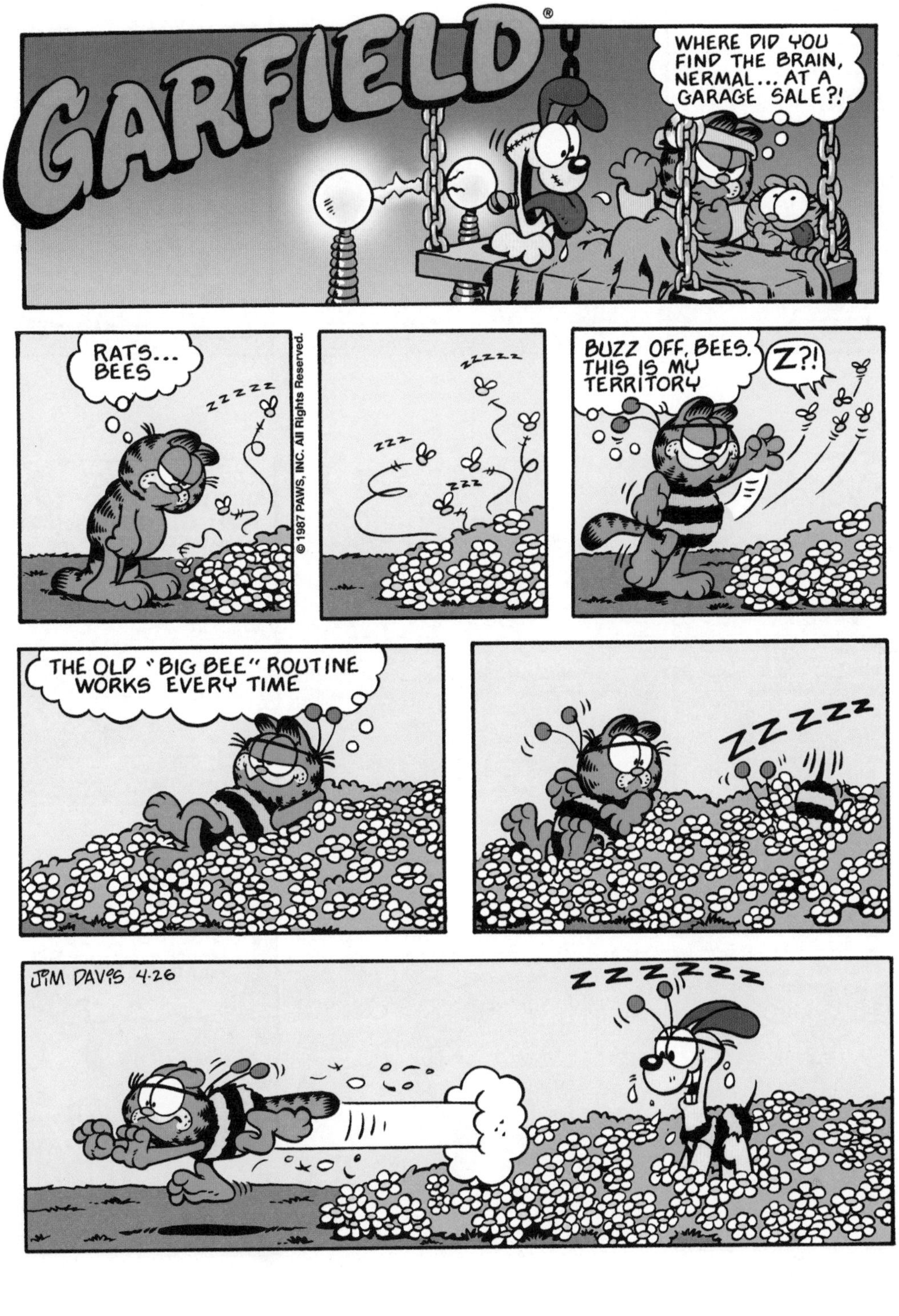
GARFIELD®
WHERE DID YOU FIND THE BRAIN, NERMAL... AT A GARAGE SALE?!
RATS... BEES
ZZZZZ
© 1987 PAWS, INC. All Rights Reserved.
ZZZZZ
ZZZ
ZZZ
BUZZ OFF, BEES. THIS IS MY TERRITORY
Z?!
THE OLD "BIG BEE" ROUTINE WORKS EVERY TIME
ZZZZZ
JIM DAVIS 4-26
ZZZZZZZ

© 1987 PAWS, INC. All Rights Reserved.

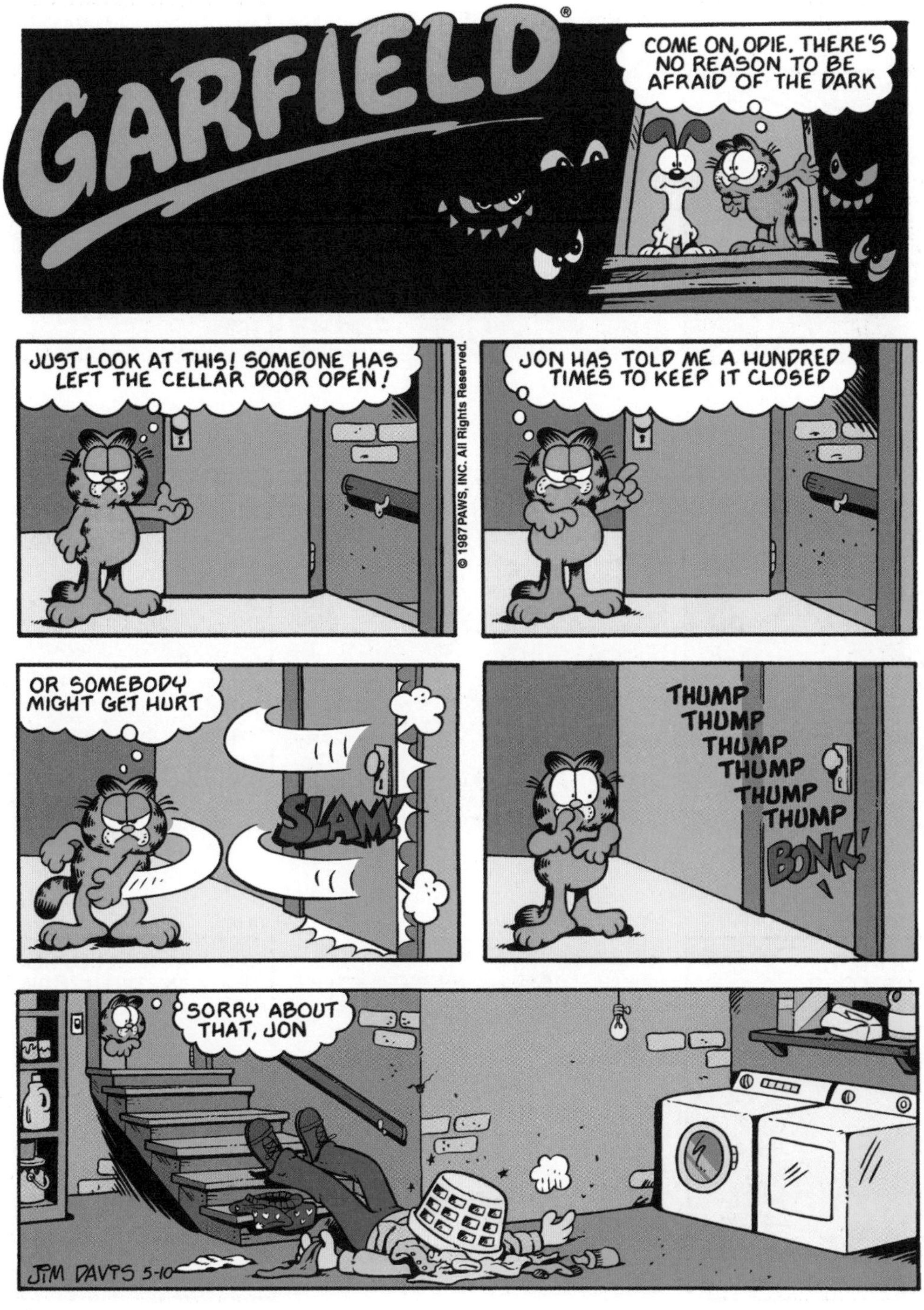
GARFIELD®
COME ON, ODIE. THERE'S NO REASON TO BE AFRAID OF THE DARK
JUST LOOK AT THIS! SOMEONE HAS LEFT THE CELLAR DOOR OPEN!
© 1987 PAWS, INC. All Rights Reserved.
JON HAS TOLD ME A HUNDRED TIMES TO KEEP IT CLOSED
OR SOMEBODY MIGHT GET HURT
SLAM!
THUMP
THUMP
THUMP
THUMP
THUMP
THUMP
BONK!
SORRY ABOUT THAT, JON
JIM DAVIS 5-10

© 1987 PAWS, INC. All Rights Reserved.